LINES TO

6/2005 - Remarks in INK NOTED

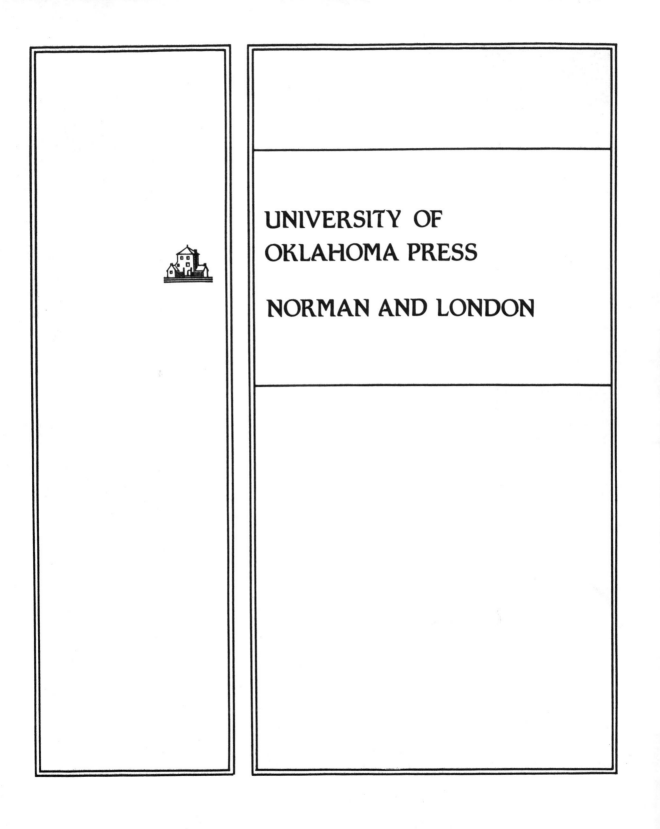

UNIVERSITY OF
OKLAHOMA PRESS

NORMAN AND LONDON

EVAN HADINGHAM

LINES TO THE MOUNTAIN GODS

Nazca and the Mysteries of Peru

By Evan Hadingham

The Fighting Triplanes (New York, 1969)
Ancient Carvings in Britain (London, 1974)
Circles and Standing Stones: An Illustrated Exploration of Magalith Mysteries of Early Britain (New York, 1975)
Secrets of the Ice Age: A Reappraisal of Prehistoric Man (New York, 1981)
Early Man and the Cosmos: Explorations in Astroarchaeology (New York, 1984; Norman, 1985)
Lines to the Mountain Gods: Nazca and the Mysteries of Peru (New York, 1987; Norman, 1988)

This book is for
Anna Gabrielle,
with love and hopes for an
adventurous future

Library of Congress Catalog Card Number: 87-40562

ISBN: 0-8061-2130-0

P82687

Contents

Author's Note To The Paperback Edition

Since this book first went to press nearly two years ago, several researchers have written to suggest revisions or provide updated information. The following notes summarize this new material.

Astronomy and the Nazca Lines

In Chapter 7 and elsewhere, I describe the recent survey work and interpretations of the Nazca lines by Colgate University researchers Anthony Aveni and Gary Urton. Their continuing examination of survey data has tended to confirm most of the conclusions presented tentatively on pages 133 and 134.

In his final analysis of the ray center alignments, Aveni has noted "a slight excess" of lines around azimuth 105 degrees from true north. This direction corresponds to the area of the horizon where the sun rises in late October, the time when water is most abundant in Nazca's underground aqueducts. Such evidence hints at the possibility of a connection between certain lines and a solar calendar for agriculture or ritual, a theory first advanced by Paul Kosok and Maria Reiche forty years ago.

Nevertheless, as explained in Chapters 6 and 7, Aveni and Urton have also shown that only a small proportion of the lines can be related to astronomy. For an authoritative presentation of the evidence, see the forthcoming volume edited by Aveni, *The Nazca Lines,* to be published by the American Philosophical Society.

New Evidence on the Culture and Society of Ancient Nazca.

Since the first edition appeared, Helaine Silverman of the University of Illinois has continued to excavate the major Nazca ceremonial site at Cahuachi and to map settlement patterns in the neighboring valleys. This has led her to comment on some of the ideas about Nazca society presented in Chapter 8, particularly on pages 157 and 158.

Silverman's survey shows Cahuachi to be more than twice as extensive and far more complex than depicted in Strong's original plan. To help interpret the ruins, Silverman has studied present-day pilgrimage and ceremonial activities at a Catholic sanctuary at Yauca in the Ica Valley. During their temporary visits to the modern shrine, the pilgrims leave patterns of refuse strikingly similar to the remains unearthed at Cahuachi. These include makeshift hearths, abandoned temporary structures of reed and cane, broken earth floors, and discarded pieces of fine and crude pottery.

The comparison leads Silverman to conclude that during its heyday Cahuachi was the central shrine of the Nazca people, visited regularly in accordance with a ritual calendar. She speculates that it would become crowded on the occasion of each ceremony, then empty out again as pilgrims returned to their fields, leaving only priests and retainers in permanent residence. If her views are correct, Cahuachi was never a city in the ordinary sense.

Further evidence may soon be available to test Silverman's theory. An Italian archaeological team led by Guiseppe Orefici (of the Centro Italiano Studi e Ricerche Archeologiche Precolumbiane, Brescia) has been excavating at the site for several years, so far without publishing any of its finds.

Meanwhile, Silverman has also continued to probe the question of Nazca's influence over its neighbors. She believes her evidence now revives the possibility of the "military empire" theory discussed on pages 155 and 157. Her views are based on the abrupt appearance of Nazca pottery in outlying areas, accompanied by dramatic rebuilding changes at sites like Tambo Viejo. These have led her to reconsider the idea that Cahuachi's leaders may have used military force to take over neighboring valleys. If so, then Nazca's conquests clearly did not result in an elaborate bureaucratic administration, as happened later under the Incas. Cahuachi probably owed its power as much to religious ceremonies and control over prestige goods as to military force.

All the dates for Nazca culture quoted in the text are highly uncertain because of the wide variation in Nazca radiocarbon dates currently available. However, the text on page 158 implies that the decline of Cahuachi (which Silverman now estimates at around 300 A.D.) was followed swiftly by the shift to the Late Nazca art style with its restless, militaristic motifs. In fact, Silverman and others believe this change occurred well after the decline of Cahuachi, probably around 400 to 500 A.D.

New Survey of the Nazca Aqueducts

This 400–500 A.D. period seems to represent a turning point in Nazca culture. It marks not only the appearance of Late Nazca art but also the first of the underground aqueducts, according to an important new unpublished study by Katharina J. Schreiber of the University of California. Her fieldwork suggests that Nazca farmers developed their hydraulic expertise slowly, drawing on centuries of familiarity with the local geology. It now seems most unlikely that the aqueducts were introduced suddenly by a foreign stone-building power, a theory discussed on pages 191 and 192. (In fact, Nazcans *did* build in stone if it was conveniently available. Schreiber has identified stone-built Nazca sites of all periods in the valleys).

Nazca society must surely have changed as the aqueduct system gradually evolved, but what the changes were is still far from clear. And the question of just how deeply Nazca was influenced or controlled by later highland "empires" such as Huari remains controversial.

Meanwhile, Schreiber has corrected faulty observations of the aqueducts by previous researchers on which I based my account on pages 189 through 192. For example, 35 aqueducts exist today and it is uncertain that there were as many as 40 as stated on page 189. The longest is about 1,500 meters—barely one mile—not 2 to 3 miles, and it is unlikely that any of them interconnect, despite local rumors to that effect.

Most aqueducts start next to or under the normally dry river bed (not close to the hillsides), and they usually run parallel to the course of the river. Some take the form of open trenches up to 10 meters deep that empty into a reservoir at their lower end. More frequently, an aqueduct starts as an open trench but soon turns into a tunnel. Schreiber's evidence suggests that tunneling was the preferred construction method, rather than filling in an open trench, as implied on page 191.

Beliefs and Ceremonies of the High Andes

In Chapter 14, I discuss ethnographic and folklore sources which all suggest a link between the desert markings and beliefs about water, fertility, and sacred mountains. While this link was first discussed by British filmmaker and explorer Tony Morrison, it was American anthropologist Johan Reinhard who developed the idea further and drew attention to much of the supporting evidence cited in my own account on pages 244 through 260. To learn more about Reinhard's important ideas, the reader should consult his booklet *The Nazca Lines: A New Perspective on Their Origins and Meaning* (published by Editorial Los Pinos, Casilla 5147, Lima 18, Peru).

—EVAN HADINGHAM
Cambridge, Massachusetts, October, 1987

Acknowledgments

Everyone interested in Nazca owes a debt to Maria Reiche, and to her sister Renate Reiche-Grosse, for their years of dedication to the study and preservation of the desert lines. They offered me invaluable advice on many of the issues that I raised as I wrote this book.

My wife, Janet Hadingham, and my editor at Random House, Derek Johns, provided constant support and editorial help at every stage.

My research and travels in Peru were greatly encouraged by Peter Spry-Leverton, producer of the Central Television series *Mysteries of Peru*. In addition, Gary Urton and Johan Reinhard generously shared the results of their separate investigations among traditional communities in the Andes. Particular thanks are also due to Anthony Aveni for the opportunity to refer to recent survey work.

While it would be difficult to name everyone else who helped inspire and guide my Andean studies, the following individuals presented important contributions and criticisms: Catherine Allen, Robert A. Benfer, Fernando Cabieses, R. Clark Mallam, Persis Clarkson, Geoffrey W. Conrad, Jim Crawford, Marlene Dobkin De Rios, Christopher B. Donnan, Robert A. Feldman, John Hyslop, Gerald S. Hawkins, William L. Johnson, Josue Lancho, Mark Matthewman, Tony Morrison, Michael E. Moseley, Patricia Netherly, Gary Olson, Charles R. Ortloff, Anne Paul, Allison Paulsen, Phyllis Pitluga, Jeffrey Quilter, Dietrich Schulz, Douglas Sharon, William R. Shawcross and Helaine Silverman.

Finally, my thanks go to the staff of the Tozzer Library, Peabody Museum, Harvard University, where I researched this book.

—Evan Hadingham
Cambridge, Massachusetts, 1987

LINES TO THE MOUNTAIN GODS

*Sea mist shrouds the cliffs at Paracas on
Peru's southern coast.*

INTRODUCTION

IF YOU HEAD SOUTH from Peru's capital city, Lima, your route takes you through a wilderness of high sand dunes fronting the Pacific. During the winter months, a perpetual mist hovers over these giant ridges of sterile sand running down to the ocean. This oppressive landscape continues for hour after hour, relieved only by a series of river valleys made fertile by irrigation. Eventually the road begins to swing inland; the dunes give way to rocky passes through the foothills of the Andes, while the river valleys become progressively steeper and narrower. In one of these valleys, the road leads between cotton fields fed by canals from the Ingenio River, then veers sharply up toward an elevated plateau.

In contrast to the green valley below, you are now surrounded by a dull expanse of red-brown pebbles. This plateau is the Nazca "pampa," a stony desert seemingly devoid of vegetation or animal life. Its featureless surface stretches away to the south in a series of gently sloping pavements, framed along the eastern side by the rugged outskirts of the Andes. The road heads directly across the pampa for another twenty miles or so before eventually descending to the next green valley, surrounding the town of Nazca.

At first glance, there is nothing in the pampa's bleak landscape to arouse interest. If there were no signs announcing

"Lines of Nazca" and warning travelers to keep off, you would never suspect their existence. Here and there a few breaks in the pavement suggest the possibility of markings, but that is all.

From an aircraft, on the other hand, this same surface presents an extraordinary spectacle. Like a gigantic abandoned sketch pad, the pampa is crowded with a profusion of man-made designs. Colossal triangles and rectangles stretch for hundreds of meters with startling precision. Between these shapes, dense networks of lines fan out at all angles. Some of the lines run for mile after mile, aimed with the straightness of a projectile path toward the distant mountains.

Elsewhere, geometric designs such as spirals and zigzags can be seen, together with realistic outlines of animals and plants. Many of these naturalistic figures are surprisingly well proportioned when viewed from the air. If you were to visit them on the ground, however, their immense size would make it difficult to recognize their identity without plotting their outlines on paper.

What could have inspired drawing exercises on the inhospitable pampa, where temperatures regularly reach the nineties? And why did the Nazca artists, some two thousand years ago, apparently ignore the earthbound perspective of an ordinary

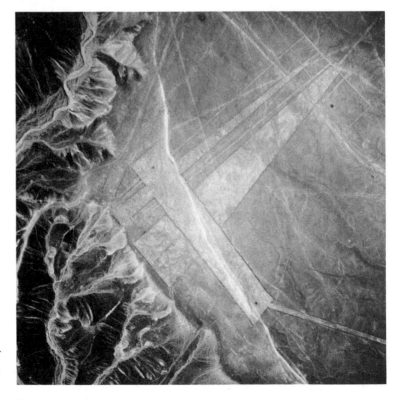

Strange geometric shapes on the surface of a stony plateau high above the Palpa Valley in southern Peru, seen from the air.

viewer? Since the ground drawings seem to have been neither particularly intelligible nor impressive once they were made, the devotion of so much skill and energy to them poses a baffling mystery.

The problem has aroused all sorts of speculation, including suggestions that the ancient Nazcans soared over the pampa in primitive gliders or hot-air balloons, or built their giant trapezoids as landing strips for extraterrestrial visitors. Many popular writers assume that the original designers *must* have flown somehow in order to appreciate their work as we do today. However, as discussed in Chapter 2, no solid evidence exists to support such a notion, while such writers usually ignore alternative possibilities.

What other purposes could the lines have served besides aerial viewing? One of the most widely circulated theories is that they were set out to point toward critical risings and settings of the sun, moon and stars—in other words, that they functioned as an astronomical calendar. The chief advocate of this view is a German-born ex-teacher of mathematics, Maria Reiche, who believes that such a calendar would have assisted ancient Nazca farmers in timing critical operations of their agricultural cycle.

In pursuit of this idea, as well as in an effort to survey and protect the markings, Reiche has devoted over forty years of her life, much of it spent in total isolation on the pampa and without any regular financial support. Her remarkable life is one of the most colorful aspects of the Nazca story, yet her calendar theory is almost certainly mistaken. As discussed in Chapter 5, the theory represents another example of how tempting it is to impose a narrow technical explanation on the complexities of the desert markings.

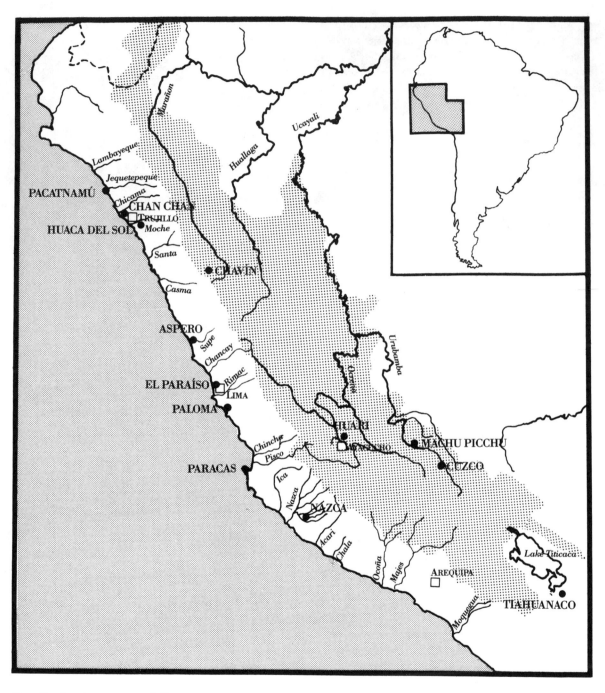

Map of major place names and sites
described in this book.

This is not to deny the likelihood that the Nazcans possessed astronomical knowledge or a calendar system. In fact, recent research among the villages of the high Andes reveals that intricate sky lore from the period of the Incas has persisted for over four centuries to the present day. Nevertheless, it now seems clear that astronomical theories can account for only a small proportion of the lines present on the pampa. Furthermore, we probably won't ever be able to identify exactly which lines these are.

The difficulties encountered by any straightforward "practical" explanation of the lines suggest that we must look beyond the technical and scientific interests of our own age to understand them. To begin with, we know that line building was not a single isolated burst of activity, since similar (though less spectacular) lines have been reported from Chile all the way up to Ecuador. Even at Nazca, the practice of desert drawing is thought to have spanned at least one thousand years. Some of the purposes served by the drawings undoubtedly changed over that period. Nevertheless, it seems clear that the builders were fundamentally conservative and mindful of tradition in their outlook, and that their motivations were also shared widely outside Nazca.

Rather than seeking a single key to the mystery, we can begin to make sense of the markings only if we try to understand the Andean world as a whole, particularly the traditional beliefs and outlook that have enabled its inhabitants to cope with one of the most unpredictable environments on earth. Despite an appalling succession of earthquakes, floods and droughts, their record is one of remarkable success. We now know, for instance, that pre-Conquest farmers in Peru's northern coastal desert cultivated at least 40 percent more land than is worked at the present day. This was made possible not by elaborate technology, but by a thorough grasp of irrigation principles. In fact, their working knowledge of canal engineering was so highly developed that it was unsurpassed in the modern world until the end of the Victorian era.

Coupled with this efficient exploitation of the desert was a complex belief system, with roots that can be traced back well before 1000 B.C. Among its many aspects, this tradition involved a belief in severed, mummified human heads as sources of spiritual power. Many such heads have actually been dug up from sites on the south coast. The heads also figure so prominently in the painted and woven images of Nazca art that they must have been an essential ingredient in the beliefs of the line builders.

Another important aspect of the religious tradition was the taking of powerful plant hallucinogens. This was a sacred activ-

tied in w/ crystal skull process?

Centuries-old religious rites linger on in many parts of the Andes. Here, among the Aymara of Bolivia, a traditional healer supervises offerings of incense at a mountaintop shrine.

ity, intended to bring the participant into contact with supernatural powers. It is remarkable that remnants of this traditional use of hallucinogens still flourish even today among folk healers on Peru's north coast. In the midst of their trances, the modern healers often call upon supernatural animals as helpers; it may not be coincidence that several of these animals correspond to the species figured on the surface of the pampa.

The persistence of this and many other aspects of Andean religion is extraordinary, considering the havoc wrought by floods, earthquakes and the effects of the Spanish Conquest. In the face of abrupt disasters and constant oppression, this conservative core of belief has continued to mold the actions and outlook of the Andean peoples. It surely must have been a vital part of the motives behind the Nazca lines.

Perhaps the most exciting evidence of all links the ancient lines to ceremonies still performed at the ends of straight-line pathways. As described in Chapter 14, these pathways cross remote regions of the bleak high-altitude Bolivian plain, or alti-plano. Similar to other ceremonies conducted throughout the Andes, the pathway rituals are often dedicated to the worship of mountain deities. These deities have shifting and multiple personalities, for their powers are identified with ever-changing natural forces, particularly weather phenomena and fertility.

Incidentally, one of the most interesting aspects of this complex body of belief is that it seems to express more than mere

Time chart of some of the ancient Peruvian cultures described in this book.

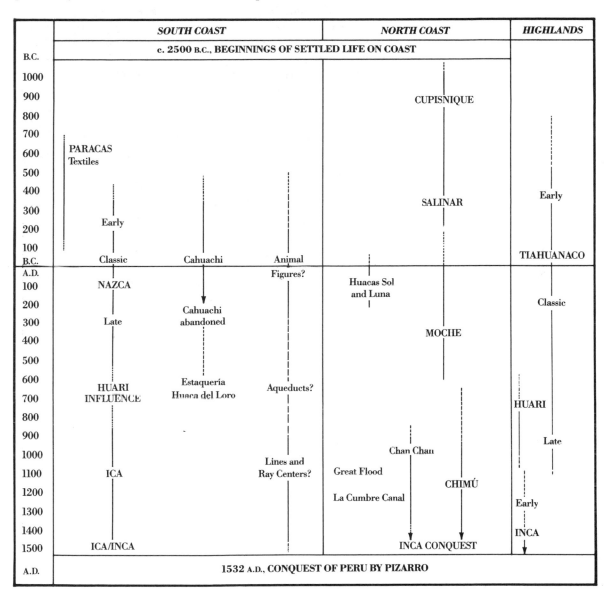

	SOUTH COAST			NORTH COAST		HIGHLANDS
B.C.	c. 2500 B.C., BEGINNINGS OF SETTLED LIFE ON COAST					
1000						
900				CUPISNIQUE		
800						
700						
600	PARACAS Textiles					
500						
400						Early
300				SALINAR		
200	Early					
100 B.C.	Classic	Cahuachi	Animal			TIAHUANACO
A.D.			Figures?			
100	NAZCA			Huacas Sol and Luna		
200		Cahuachi				Classic
300	Late	abandoned			MOCHE	
400						
500						
600	HUARI INFLUENCE	Estaquería Huaca del Loro	Aqueducts?			HUARI
700						
800						
900						Late
1000			Lines and Ray Centers?	Chan Chan		
1100	ICA			Great Flood		
1200					CHIMÚ	Early
1300				La Cumbre Canal		
1400						INCA
1500	ICA/INCA			INCA CONQUEST		
A.D.	1532 A.D., CONQUEST OF PERU BY PIZARRO					

irrational superstition. Many of the myths and rites appear to symbolize careful observation of the landscape and of the night sky. They reflect actual cycles of rainfall and regeneration that have been accurately perceived by the Andean peoples.

In any case, a striking parallel can be drawn between the practices of modern and ancient line builders, which suggests that the meaning of the lines is not lost to prehistory, but is linked to a many-sided tradition still very much alive today. In this book, I hope to show that this suggestion represents more than just another single solution to the mystery. Instead, I believe the evidence indicates that the lines are the product of an entire world view that extends far beyond the time and place of the Nazca culture. If this interpretation is correct, then the lines represent more than an obscure episode of the Peruvian past; they illuminate the special achievement of all Andean peoples.

This achievement was the result of an attitude toward spiritual and material resources very different from that of our own civilization. For century after century before the arrival of the Spanish, it sustained thriving communities and empires in a coastal desert where rainfall is virtually absent. Considering the present state of the Peruvian economy, who is to say whether the technology of the modern state will be any more successful in coping with the unusual stresses of the Andean environment?

From this point of view, the Nazca lines are not only a spectacle in themselves but a token of the adaptability and resourcefulness of the people who forged pre-Columbian civilization.

CONQUEST AND CATASTROPHE

CHAPTER 1

El Niño:
Peru's Cycle of Disaster

EACH YEAR LESS THAN ONE-TENTH OF AN INCH OF RAIN falls on most
places along Peru's coastal desert. The inhabitants of Piura,
a city in the extreme north, experience a nightly "rain," but it
is in the form of sand particles, not moisture. This is how the
phenomenon was described by the Peruvian novelist Mario Vargas Llosa in his celebrated novel *The Green House:*

> As it crosses the dune region, the wind that comes down off
> the Andes heats up and stiffens: reinforced with sand, it fol-
> lows the course of the river, and when it gets to the city it can
> be seen floating between the earth and the sky like a dazzling
> layer of armor. It empties out its insides there: every day of
> the year, at dusk, a dry rain, fine as sawdust, ceasing only at
> dawn, falls on the squares, the roofs, the towers, the belfries,
> the balconies, and the trees, and it paves the streets of Piura
> with whiteness. Outsiders are mistaken when they say, *"The
> houses in this town are ready to collapse."* That nocturnal
> creaking does not come from the buildings, which are ancient
> but strong; it comes from the invisible, uncountable minute
> projectiles of sand as they hit the doors and windows.

One night in January 1983, Piura's residents were awakened
by an unaccustomed sound: the patter of real raindrops against
their roofs and shutters. Next day and every day following that,
the showers returned, sometimes turning to heavy downpours.

A typical view of the northern coastal desert near the Cupisnique Valley.

On one occasion, over six inches of rain fell in a single day. When a respite finally came three months later, the inhabitants of Piura celebrated: no rain had fallen for two days in a row.

By then they were entirely cut off from the outside world: the only major road link along the Peruvian coast, the Panamerican Highway, had been washed out in numerous places as torrents raced down normally bone-dry washes and ravines. Entire bridges had been swept away, including a new one over the Chira River. Most of the local irrigated crops had been leveled by the rainstorms, so that with the breakdown of communications came shortages of food, fuel and water. As temperatures climbed to a sticky 85 degrees, patches of the desert were transformed into unhealthy swamps. There were outbreaks of typhoid and salmonella in many of the isolated villages.

Meanwhile, in the mountains, landslides severed Peru's major oil pipeline across the Andes and swept away the railroads servicing the vast copper and silver mines of La Oroya. One conservative estimate put the overall damage to the gross national product for the year at more than 10 percent. Already weakened by a massive foreign debt, this new economic blow threatened Peru's precarious hold on democracy. It is still not clear even today whether the country's electoral system, introduced in 1980 after twelve years of military rule, will survive the crisis.

Grave as the consequences were for Peru, it was not the only

Above, *an improvised bridge across the swollen Moche River during the massive El Niño of 1925. The 1983 event caused almost equally severe damage throughout coastal Peru. Left, a street in the northern village of Chulucana in May 1983.*

country to suffer a catastrophic shift in weather patterns during the early months of 1983. In Australia, for instance, the worst drought of the century forced farmers to destroy thousands of sheep and cattle, while seventy-five people died in fires that raged through the outback. In Botswana, the failure of the rains drove over half the nation's population into emergency relief camps. Other parts of southern Africa endured record levels of malnutrition and disease as crop production fell and livestock perished.

Meanwhile, on the other side of the world, torrential rains caused half a billion dollars' worth of damage to roads, property and crops in California and along the Colorado River. Six successive cyclones swept through the Pacific islands of Polynesia, leaving twenty-five thousand people homeless in Tahiti alone. The worldwide toll of destruction was appalling: more than one thousand people lost their lives as a direct result of the climatic shift; the global figure for damage was roughly estimated at nearly nine billion dollars.

The catastrophes of 1983 were all linked to a phenomenon known by its Peruvian nickname, *El Niño*, "The Child." The name comes from the Spanish term for the Christ Child, since a switch to abnormal weather conditions along the Peruvian coast is often noted around Christmastime. The cold, northward-flowing Humboldt Current, laden with plankton and other nutrients stirred up from the ocean floor, temporarily subsides. In its place a narrow tongue of warm water moves in from the equator and sweeps southward along the coast. The temperature of the sea begins to rise, wiping out the shoals of plankton and the fish that feed on them. If the El Niño current is unusually strong, it creates humid air masses that move inland, dropping rain on normally parched areas of the coastal desert. With only sparse vegetation to soak up the showers, severe flash floods inevitably follow.

An El Niño event is triggered by a highly complex weather mechanism still not properly understood by meteorologists. In an ordinary year, the trade winds blow westward across the Pacific toward a low pressure system centered over southeast Asia —the same system that brings the annual monsoon rains to India and Indonesia. An El Niño begins when this normally stable weather pattern shifts away from Asia toward the Americas, causing the trade winds to slacken. As the winds falter, the usual flow of ocean currents is disrupted, so that the tropical ocean surges eastward. When this intruding bank of warm water reaches the American continent, it is deflected southward, squeezing out the cold Humboldt Current.

Since this delicate balance of winds and currents spans more than a quarter of the earth's surface, a severe El Niño has a worldwide impact. Furthermore, once the El Niño current begins its southward flow, it displaces the jet stream from its normal course across the southern hemisphere. (In 1983 it was over 800 miles south of its normal position.) This in turn affects the flow of the northern hemisphere's jet stream. Between them, these two major air currents are thought to have an enormous influence on the balance of the earth's climate. Their disturbance may explain why such severe droughts were experienced in Africa as well as in Australia.

On the coast of Peru, weak El Niño phenomena seem to recur regularly about every six years. Although the temperature of the ocean rises, there is usually little increase in the flow of rivers or in the amount of rainfall inland. Every fifteen or sixteen years a strong El Niño arrives, although rainstorms are still a rarity and the rivers usually remain at manageable levels.

Unfortunately, truly catastrophic events such as those of 1983 are more difficult to predict. The last severe El Niño struck in 1925, when the trade winds completely reversed direction. Crocodiles and other tropical fauna from the river estuaries of Ecuador were captured by the warm current and swept down to the northern coastline of Peru, where they were stranded on desert beaches. Farther inland, floods destroyed the entire network of modern irrigation canals and submerged the major city of Trujillo under nine inches of rain in just three days. The death toll of marine organisms was so great that a putrid discharge of gas from the ocean floor blackened the hulls of ships and the sides of houses along the shore.

Though its immediate impact was not quite so dramatic, another El Niño in 1972 had grave long-term consequences for both the natural ecology and the subsistence of human populations along the Peruvian coast. For generations the mainstay of the national economy was not its legendary hoards of gold and silver but guano, a natural fertilizer culled from the droppings of birds on coastal rock outcrops. At the height of the guano trade a century ago, as many as three hundred transatlantic cargo ships were to be seen berthed along the Chincha estuary alone.

Then in the 1950s Peruvian fishermen turned to a more profitable link in the same food chain—the vast shoals of anchovies on which the seafowl depended. By 1970 an armada of small boats was hauling in some 14 million tons of anchovies a year. This was enough to outstrip all the catches of North and Central America combined, propelling Peru into first place among the world's fishing nations. But this abundance did not last for long.

Peruvian fishermen unload anchovies during the mid-1960s. Most of the industry was wiped out by overfishing and the effect of the 1972 El Niño.

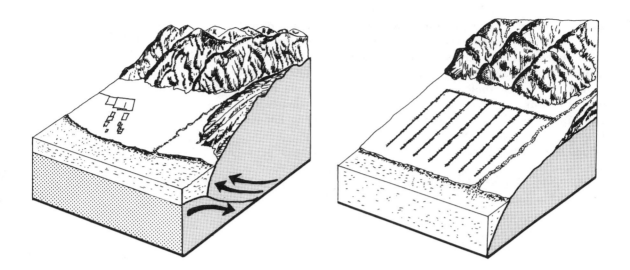

The strong El Niño of 1972 dealt a crippling blow to the anchovy population, already weakened by overfishing. Today they are virtually an endangered species. As for the guano birds, which had naturally suffered from so much human competition, tens of thousands perished along the Pacific shoreline. The impact on human populations has also been heavy: at present, most fish-meal plants still stand idle, and harbor fronts are lined with rusting hulls.

To add to their insecurities, Peruvians must live with the constant threat of severe earthquakes. The worst tremor in recent memory claimed the lives of seventy thousand Peruvians in 1970. The victims included the entire twenty-thousand-strong population of the highland town of Yungay. They were buried by a single 250-mile-an-hour avalanche of partly frozen mud and rock loosened by the tremor. When the first relief workers arrived by helicopter, they were confronted by a wasteland strewn with ice and boulders. No traces of the town were visible at all, except for the tops of four tall palm trees that had marked the corners of the central plaza.

Earth movements exert other, less traumatic pressures on human subsistence. Though the origins of the Andean chain can be traced back to at least 200 million years ago, in geological perspective it is still relatively young; there is constant seismic activity along the coast as well as in the mountains. In fact the origin of all this activity lies off the coast, where a section of the earth's crust known to geologists as the Nazca Plate pushes like a long, shallow wedge underneath the continental landmass. The resulting uplift—averaging at most a few millimeters each

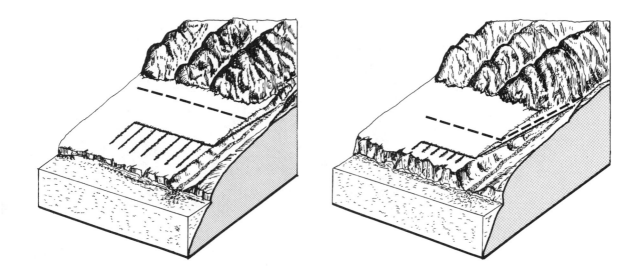

year—sounds negligible, yet this is the force that has built the towering peaks of the Andes.

To document the uplift, geologists and archaeologists have worked together to trace remnants of prehistoric beaches, marooned many meters above the present-day shoreline. Within these beach deposits, they occasionally encounter ancient pottery fragments. The succession of ancient pottery styles in Peru is now sufficiently well known that archaeologists can assign a rough date to the fragments, and hence to the beach deposit itself.

Such evidence has led researchers to conclude that parts of the Peruvian coast have risen, sporadically, by at least 20 feet or more over the past two thousand years. Only the strongest of these episodes of uplift would normally have been perceptible to the ordinary farming population, yet their way of life was profoundly affected by the changes.

In such an arid environment, agriculture is totally dependent on irrigation. As the landmass rises, so the rivers that emerge from the foothills of the Andes begin to cut deeper into their channels. Since many canal systems have their intakes at these upriver points where the flow is strongest, the process of downcutting eventually leaves the canals high and dry.

To restore water to the system, it is necessary to construct new intakes farther downstream. But the flow of water here is diminished by comparison, so the builders must lower their expectations and plan for a less extensive network of canals. Thus, over the centuries, the irrigation systems shrink in size and retreat steadily toward the coast.

Geological activity has contributed to a huge reduction in the area of land cultivated in coastal Peru since ancient times. Tectonic movements off the coast, above, cause a steady uplift inland. As the landscape gradually rises, left to right, rivers cut deeper into their beds. Canal intakes must then be moved progressively farther downstream, where less water power is available. The result is an ever-shrinking canal network.

CONQUEST AND CATASTROPHE • 17

This view of the Moche Valley in northern Peru shows the abrupt contrasts between irrigated fields, the flat desert, and the steep flanks of the Andes. Early Peruvians took advantage of this topography by situating their canal intakes at points where fast-flowing rivers emerged from the Andes.

Indeed, the present-day landscape is only a pale reflection of the agricultural potential exploited in prehistoric times. Difficult though it is to believe, an estimated 40 percent more land was cultivated on the north coast a thousand or more years ago than at the present day.

Some of the loss can undoubtedly be attributed to the disruptions of the Spanish Conquest; previously, native Peruvian leaders had managed the few available water resources with great skill. But the most serious factor at work was undoubtedly the deteriorating environment. In fact, the loss of agricultural land still continues today, driven by the unseen, inexorable forces of uplift.

"Tears Made Torrents": The Triumph of Pizarro

A S IF VIOLENT FLOODS, earthquakes and the steady depletion of agricultural land were not enough to contend with, the course of documented human history in Peru has been marked by almost constant strife and turbulence. Even before Francisco Pizarro and his handful of Spanish soldiers gained a foothold, the Inca empire was in the throes of a bitter civil war between two royal heirs, Huascar and Atahualpa. They were sons of the revered ruler Huayna-Capac, who had succeeded in holding together the immense conquests of his predecessors in relative tranquility. His dominions spanned most of the Andean mountain chain, from southern Colombia all the way to central Chile, a distance greater than the width of the continental United States. This immense realm, rivaling the size of imperial Rome, was the product of a mere hundred years of vigorous military campaigns. By the beginning of the sixteenth century, the Incas were confident they had absorbed most of the civilized world.

Then came an ominous turn of events: Huayna-Capac, struggling against forest tribes in the extreme north during the 1520s, succumbed to a widespread epidemic. This was almost certainly smallpox, introduced by early Spanish settlers in the Caribbean. Native populations there, who had no immunity, were ravaged by the disease. The epidemic must have swept rapidly down through Colombia, outstripping the cautious early explorations of Pizarro and other Spanish adventurers along the Pacific coast. Besides Huayna-Capac himself, most of his court and many thousands of his subjects perished. It was a portent of years of suffering to come.

By 1532, when Pizarro began his bold march inland from the north coast of Peru, signs of the struggle between the legitimate heir, Huascar, and the usurper, Atahualpa, were apparent everywhere. The Spanish passed through major Inca towns that lay in ruins, devastated by the civil strife. In the wake of Atahualpa's triumph over his brother, many individuals loyal to Huascar had been executed; one of Pizarro's scouting expeditions to the hills found their bodies hanging from the trees.

Pizarro hoped to exploit the enmity and confusion of the civil war to overcome the desperate odds he faced. With only 168 soldiers at his command, he could easily have been overwhelmed at many points along the Inca road he followed toward the highlands. However, Atahualpa, flushed with the success of his victory over Huascar, was lulled into a false sense of security about the threat posed by the bearded invaders. His envoys assured him that the Spaniards were disorganized and unfit for battle. They also reported that the Spanish horses, which had initially seemed so alarming, were in fact tied up at night; this may have led the emperor to think that the horses were little cause for concern, since they were apparently useless after dusk.

In any case, the Inca evidently thought he could destroy the

Atahualpa confronts the Spanish forces at Cajamarca. A woodcut dating to about 1600 from the chronicle of Felipe Guaman Poma de Ayala, an Inca of noble descent.

small force at his leisure, so he continued to dally at the hot springs outside Cajamarca. By allowing the Spanish to enter and install themselves in the town, he badly misjudged the ruthlessness and ambition of Pizarro.

That night, Friday, November 15, 1532, the Spaniards laid plans for their ambush. Many soldiers, weary from the long march, trembled at the sight of the Inca army's campfires. These were so numerous, wrote one of Pizarro's men, that they resembled a brilliant star-studded sky.

However, when Atahualpa eventually responded to Pizarro's invitation to visit him "as a friend and brother" the following afternoon, he arrived in town in the midst of an unarmed ceremonial procession. Several thousand retainers clad in splendid robes danced and sang their way to the fatal plaza, bearing their emperor in a litter lined with parrot feathers and studded with silver and gold plates.

On seeing so few Spaniards in the plaza, Atahualpa at first concluded that the Spaniards were awestruck by his retinue. Then Bishop Vincente de Valverde came forward to demand that the Inca recognize the Christian faith and the authority of Emperor Charles V. Though Atahualpa leafed through the bishop's prayer book with curiosity, he soon became indignant and tossed the book to the ground. This was the provocation the Spanish were looking for; the rejection of the bishop gave the signal for the soldiers to charge from the surrounding colonnade and begin the slaughter.

Pizarro himself boldly strode up to the imperial litter and tried unsuccessfully to pull Atahualpa down. Eventually, seven or eight horsemen managed to tip the litter on its side and take the Inca prisoner. Meanwhile, all around him, Atahualpa's attendants and noblemen were savagely put to the sword. Panic-stricken, hundreds fled from the square, pushing over one of the six-foot-thick walls of the plaza in their terror. It is said that six or seven thousand Indians perished in the hour or two that remained before sunset. The only injury to the Spanish was a cut on Pizarro's wrist; it happened as he fended off a sword thrust that one of his comrades imprudently aimed at Atahualpa.

In the days that followed, the Inca army stood by paralyzed while its divine leader bargained for his freedom. Shrewdly adapting himself to the language and habits of his captors, he soon noted their overriding interest in precious stones and metals. Thus he came to propose his famous ransom: he promised to fill an entire room with gold and an entire house twice over with silver within just two months.

While the Inca stood by his side of the bargain, enabling the

Spaniards to amass a treasure worth tens of millions of dollars at present market values, Pizarro had no intention of letting Atahualpa go. Instead, he finally gave in to pressure from his officers and ordered a hasty execution without even the pretense of a trial. Atahualpa was strangled in the Cajamarca plaza on July 26, 1533.

This act brought the Inca dynasty to an end and also dealt a fearful blow to the spirit of the Andean peoples. In their eyes, the Inca was no mere mortal but represented a direct link to the sun and other deities that secured their existence. It is scarcely surprising, then, that Atahualpa's death was mourned as a great natural cataclysm. This is how one native lament of the sixteenth century described it:

> The earth refused to devour the Inca's body,
> Rocks trembled,
> Tears made torrents, the Sun was obscured,
> The Moon made ill.

The execution of Atahualpa, according to the native chronicler Poma. In reality, Atahualpa was strangled at Pizarro's orders.

Genocide and Enslavement

THE DECEIT AND BRUTALITY that began the Conquest set the tone for the colonization that was to follow. The natives were treated like slaves, although in the eyes of the Spanish Crown all Indians were free subjects, entitled to payment for any services they rendered. During the sixteenth century, one royal decree after another reiterated this principle, much to the outrage of Spanish nobles, priests and merchants in Peru. They had grown dependent on tribute and labor exacted from the native population, so much so that Spanish settlers in Cuzco organized a full-scale armed revolt in protest against the royal decrees in 1553.

Though this uprising was crushed nine months later, it indicates how the Spanish had come to regard the enslavement of the Indians as their legitimate right. Since none of the native cultures of Peru had ever functioned around a currency or wage

VERDVGO.PCAST I

Oppression of the Indians, as depicted by Poma.

CAPITVLO DE LOS PASAGEROS
ESPAÑOLES DELTA
vo y criollos mestizos y mula
tos y criollas mestizas y espa
ñoles cristianos
de castilla

Indians carrying burdens for the Spanish: an illustration by Poma.

system, the indifference of the Indians to money made them particularly vulnerable to Spanish exploitation.

Moreover, the tradition of labor service that had flourished under the Incas made it easy for the Spanish to salve their consciences: were they not simply continuing a native custom? In reality, the old system of work quotas had been strictly regulated by Inca bureaucrats; periods of service were usually predictable and short-term. Under the Spanish, however, there was nothing to restrain the greed of their officials, or *encomenderos*, who administered the collection of tribute. Even the local native-born chiefs, or caciques, whose powers had been strictly limited under the Inca chain of command, now joined in the unfettered exploitation of the Indians.

There were, of course, decent and conscientious individuals among the Spanish who communicated their dismay at the conditions faced by the Indians in reports addressed to the Crown. Today many of these reports, such as the 1562 *Memorial* of Bartolomé de Vega, make chilling reading. Vega, who was not given to exaggeration, recorded how one native community had to transport their annual tribute over two hundred miles to Cuzco.

> They sometimes have to carry five hundred *fanegas* [800 bushels or nearly 1,000 cubic feet] of maize. Fifteen hundred Indians transport it, with three carrying one *fanega* . . . and they carry all the things required by the assessment: wheat, maize, cloth, bars of silver, etc. Indian men are loaded with it, and so are the women, the pregnant ones with their . . . swollen bellies and those who have given birth with their babies on top of the loads.

Vega adds that some deliveries of tribute often took two months for the outward and return journey.

Even worse treks were forced upon Indians recruited to serve as porters on expeditions of conquest or exploration. Thousands perished in the course of hopeless quests for the fabulous kingdom of El Dorado that was rumored to lie somewhere in the Amazon jungle; on such journeys they were frequently chained together with iron collars. During the civil wars that raged between rival Spanish factions soon after the Conquest, Indians were forced to transport artillery across the Andes—in one case, from Cuzco all the way to Lima (at least 400 miles).

But the most dreaded of all the tasks exacted by the Spanish was service in the silver and mercury mines. Once again, the Crown specifically decreed that no man was to be pressed into involuntary labor in the mines. As soon as the productivity of the deposits became apparent, however, royal scruples were quickly swept aside.

Indian workers were dispatched in the hundreds from every part of Peru to work the ores at Potosí and Huancavelica, in the high-altitude altiplano. They toiled all day in humid tunnels underground, wearing only thin cotton trousers and shirts. At night they emerged into the freezing air of the Andes; weakened by malnutrition, countless numbers of them died of pneumonia.

By the end of the sixteenth century, the central shaft at Potosí had been driven to a depth of nearly 800 feet. The Indians clambered down three ladders made of leather, which constantly rotted and broke. Once at the bottom, they spent the entire day working by candlelight, subsisting off roasted maize. Every ascent up the ladder, while loaded with sacks of ore, was fraught with danger. Once at the top, a worker could expect to be abused for failing to fulfill his assigned quota for the week, which was often as much as 12,500 pounds. Conditions at Huancavelica were no better, for here every exposed seam released toxic arsenic and mercury vapors.

Eventually, service in the mines was recognized as tantamount to a sentence of death. One province that contributed heavily to the labor force was said to have lost two thirds of its population between 1628 and 1754.

The demands of the Spanish weighed heavily on the spirits of those Indians who survived. An official dispatched from the Spanish court, Hernando de Santillán, wrote affectingly of their bare existence:

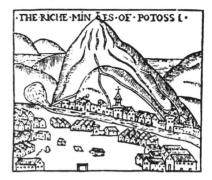

Much of the early literature about the conquest of Peru is concerned with the vast Spanish silver mining operations at Potosí, where hundreds of Indians died from forced labor. Title page from Augustin de Zarate's book published in 1581.

> They live the most wretched and miserable lives of any people on earth. As long as they are healthy they are fully occupied only in working for tribute. Even when they are sick they have no respite, and few survive their first illness, however slight, because of the appalling existence they lead. They sleep on the ground . . . and their diet is maize, chili and vegetables: they never eat meat or anything of substance except some fish if they live on the coast. . . . They sleep at night in the clothes they wear by day and scarcely succeed in clothing their children, most of whom are naked. . . . They are deeply depressed by their misery and servitude . . . and have come to believe that they must continue to work for Spaniards for as long as they or their sons or descendants live, with nothing to enjoy themselves. Because of this they despair; for they ask only for their daily bread and cannot have even that.

The impact of the Conquest was so demoralizing that there was a steep decline in the birthrate. The disruption of family life

The people of the Andes have endured oppressive poverty ever since the coming of the Spanish. According to a 1985 report, the population of 149,000 who live in the highland city of Puno are served by a single hospital, and there is one doctor for every 12,700 inhabitants. Infant mortality runs at over 12 percent, and 82 percent are illiterate. 92 percent live without running water or electricity.

was further aggravated by constant civil warfare and the forcible movement of populations. Even the landscape itself became less productive as the elaborate canal networks and planting terraces maintained by the Incas crumbled into disuse.

Perhaps the greatest threat of all came from disease, which swept through the coastal valleys in a terrible wave during the 1530s and 1540s. On the central coast, the population of the prosperous Chincha Valley had once stood at forty thousand, but forty years after the Conquest it had shrunk to a mere five hundred. The chronicler Cieza de León singled out the Nazca and Ica valleys on the south coast as having been particularly hard hit.

Many Indians who fled to the highlands managed to lessen the risks of infection, yet the overall magnitude of the tragedy was so great it can scarcely be estimated today. Some researchers put the population loss at one half or even three quarters; the historian John Hemming tentatively suggests that the total of the victims may well have exceeded five million.

Faced with desolation everywhere along the coast, some Spanish observers believed that the Andean peoples were doomed to die out altogether. Even the most optimistic among them could hardly pretend that the Conquest had improved the lot of the native Peruvians. They had been decimated by disease, warfare and virtual slavery, and their prospects looked poor indeed compared to those of their ancestors during the previous century of Inca rule. This was openly admitted by one commentator, Fernando de Armellones, as he addressed the Council of the Indies in 1555: "We cannot conceal the great paradox that a barbarian, Huayna-Capac, kept such excellent order that the entire country was calm and all were nourished, whereas today we see only infinite deserted villages on all the roads of the kingdom."

CHAPTER 2

THE ANDEAN MIRAGE

Adam and Eve in Bolivia

FACED BY THIS IMMENSE TRAGEDY, some Spanish writers preferred to turn away from the grim atmosphere of the times
to imagine an earlier Peru, where virtue and innocence prevailed. An idealized image of the past appears in some of the
very earliest writings on the Andes.

Less than a century after the Conquest, a Spanish friar, Bal-
tasar de Salas, decided to explore the shores of Lake Titicaca,
the world's highest lake, located on the Bolivian altiplano. He
took with him two Indians as his guides, a doctor who claimed
to be of royal descent and a "princess" who was said to be over
a hundred years old and who could still "read" the quipus, the
knotted string records of the Incas. As they set out across the
lake, the Indians doubtless told Salas about the legends associated with two small islands still identified today by their old
names, the Island of the Sun and the Island of the Moon. According to Inca tradition, these were the places where the first
human couple, Manco Capac and Mama Ocllo, had been placed
on earth by their father, the Sun.

Enchanted by the dramatic scenery, Salas became convinced
that this story was no myth, but an authentic recollection of the
creation of Adam and Eve recorded in the Old Testament. What
better setting for the Garden of Eden could there be than here
at the foot of snowcapped Illampu? This mountain always ap-

*For Europeans, the conquest of Peru
generated fantasies of lost cities and
unlimited wealth. In this 1550 map by
Pierre Desceliers, genuine place names
appear among images of cannibal armies,
troops of female warriors, or "Amazons,"
and the mythical "white king" of the
Andes.*

peared to be suspended above the horizon of the lake, closer to heaven than to earth. In Salas's mind, there could be no doubt that the chilly expanses of the altiplano had once been the verdant site of Paradise itself.

Salas was not the only cleric who managed to blend Inca and Christian theology into his fanciful writings. León Pinelo, the author of the book *Paradise in the New World*, agreed with Salas's interpretation, but transplanted his Garden of Eden to the jungles of the Amazon. There he identified the four rivers of Paradise mentioned in the Bible with the Amazon, Orinoco, Magdalena and Río de la Plata.

In the minds of many sixteenth-century explorers, these same rivers represented more than just a spiritual delusion. Somewhere along them a "mountain of silver" was waiting to be discovered, where a white king ruled over a land of stone huts and "long-haired deer." Rumors like these were common among the Indians of Brazil and Paraguay, and fueled one disastrous European expedition after another. These continued long after Pizarro's triumph, when it should have been obvious that the stories actually referred to the Incas and their llamas. From Mendoza to Raleigh, dozens of adventurers desperately sought to mend their fortunes in the forests of Colombia, Brazil, Paraguay, Guiana—anywhere but Peru, where the "white king" had already yielded up his ransom and been so expediently strangled.

During the seventeenth century, as the dream of a material paradise slowly faded, the image of the Indian underwent a subtle transformation. Previously characterized as savage, ignorant and satanic, they now appeared to some commentators to represent a "natural" state of man, untainted by the corruptions of civilized life. Not everyone, of course, was prepared to accept the Amazon as the Garden of Eden (the question of how Adam crossed to the Old World was one of the obvious difficulties of the theory). Nevertheless, many authors began to contrast the innocence of the Indian to the greed and cruelty of the civilized Spanish.

Already, in his influential *Essays* of 1580, the philosopher Montaigne had denounced Pizarro for his treachery in executing Atahualpa. The good faith and reasonableness displayed by the Inca ruler exposed the corrupt motives of his captors. Moreover, Montaigne asserted, the achievements of the Inca road builders had surpassed those of the civilizations of Greece, Rome and Egypt. As if to illustrate this judgment, the popular German artist Theodore De Bry portrayed the Incas as tall, naked and fair-skinned; in his engravings, they look like the idealized muscular models of Greek and Roman sculpture.

The changing image of native South Americans, opposite. The German woodcut, top, dating to 1505 (barely five years after the Portuguese discovery of Brazil), shows savage Brazilian Indians roasting human flesh. By the time of De Bry's engravings of the Incas a century later (below left), the savages had become noble, athletic figures. And in the following century the Incas were idealized as virtuous lawgivers (below right), in this plate from Marmontel's romantic novel, The Incas, published in 1777.

Indeed, certain outspoken authors, notably the Mexican Bishop Bartolomé de Las Casas, had called for a complete reversal of the moral judgments that had been applied to the Indian. Las Casas described how God created them "to be the happiest in the world." He compared their virtuous nature, "very simple, without subtlety, or craft, without malice, very obedient, and very faithful," with the vices of the conquerors, who entered the New World "as wolves, as lions, and as tigers most cruel of long time famished." In writing to the king about his majesty's Spanish subjects, Las Casas roundly declared that "in those regions there are not any Christians, but devils."

The distinction between depraved Europeans and virtuous Indians was emphasized even more during the eighteenth century, as the theme of the "Noble Savage" spread among artists and writers. They increasingly depicted the Incas as models of reasonable and just behavior. In fact, in his long-winded novel *The Incas,* published in 1777, Jean François Marmontel claimed that their laws "protected modesty as something inviolable and holy; liberty as the most sacred thing in nature; innocence, honor, and domestic peace as the gifts of heaven that must be revered." While few writers indulged in such rhapsodies, many philosophers did turn to the Incas as an admirable example of a well-ordered society. Naturally their opinions were colored by their individual political outlook: if a commentator was caught up in the ferment of revolution, it was the collective basis of Inca society that counted. More conservative authors, on the other hand, emphasized the "enlightened despotism" exercised by the Inca ruler.

Interestingly, similar contradictions arose when the Incas were again widely discussed during another period of radical dissent, this time in the 1930s. It became fashionable to depict the Incas as successful socialists, largely because the chroniclers had mentioned how the elderly and incapacitated were granted relief from the state's warehouses. Many writers suggested that the Inca rulers deliberately concerned themselves with assuring the well-being of their subjects, and, in doing so, foreshadowed the principles of the welfare state. A well-known American historian, Arthur Morgan, claimed that the Incas "succeeded more completely than any nation before or since" in ensuring the economic security of all. However, the authors of some popular books of the 1930s painted a totalitarian image of Inca rule; Gregory Mason, for instance, wrote unfavorably of pre-Conquest Peru as a "Socialist Utopia," and charged that "the rulers of modern Soviet Russia seem to be trying to build up just such an imperialism of communism as the Inca emperors built."

Regardless of political sympathies, the comparisons with socialism were all equally misguided. A deeper understanding of the issue of "Inca welfare" emerged only in the 1950s, when a new generation of scholars reexamined the testimonies of the Spanish chroniclers more critically. If the personal background of each sixteenth-century author is carefully weighed, it becomes obvious that some gave fairly dispassionate accounts. Others, though, had as much reason to distort the facts about the Incas as any writer of our present era.

In general, the welfare function of the state warehouses is mentioned only briefly, if at all, by most of the chroniclers. Relief was apparently given only in exceptional circumstances. By contrast, details about the provision of state grain to the military, the priests and the state's labor forces are constantly described.

Indeed, when some Spanish writers *did* refer to state support of the needy, they may have confused it with the obligation of the Inca emperor to feed his own immediate entourage, the royal families who lived in and around the capital, Cuzco.

Abandoned Inca houses and cultivation terraces in the Colca Valley. Under the management of the Incas, the agricultural landscape became extraordinarily productive, but the question of how oppressive their rule was still generates controversy.

Whether relief was regularly provided to communities outside is much less clear.

Undoubtedly the inhabitants of small villages in the high Andes followed a basically communal existence, much as they do today, sharing the ownership of land and the care of the sick and elderly. However, the roots of this ancient pattern of peasant life stretch much further back than the Incas. When they eventually came to power in the fifteenth century, the Incas wisely chose not to interfere with the fundamental basis of traditional life. Instead, they merely organized a proportion of each community's labor to benefit the state. In many cases, they also reinforced the petty power of local chiefs over the ordinary population.

These arrangements were evidently very far removed from socialism. Indeed, the Inca ruling class probably didn't trouble itself much with the affairs of local communities. They were concerned, of course, with the necessities of collecting tribute, as well as with encouraging the spread of Inca laws, language and culture. Yet their general policy seems to have been merely to adopt age-old practices of Andean labor and organize them efficiently for their own ends.

In hindsight, once the Spanish had begun to abuse the traditional labor system so cruelly, Inca rule probably seemed like a golden era. But if we bear in mind all the wishful thinking and bias present in the historical records, it is difficult to know exactly how oppressive the Inca system really was. For instance, one reliable commentator, Cieza de León, asserts that the work periods contributed to the state by the ordinary farmer were so short that "they felt the labor little." Others emphasize how constantly the populace was kept busy at their official chores. And sometimes, when the rulers were faced by an excess of labor, they even devised unnecessary job schemes, such as hauling stones from Quito to Cuzco for no practical purpose.

However the laborers may have felt about their masters, there is no evidence at all that the Incas were altruists, intent on creating a just society. Such a notion belongs firmly to the modern fantasy of Inca socialism, one of the many persistent myths about the Peruvian past.

White Gods and Supermen: The Racial Delusion

WHILE THE ACHIEVEMENTS OF THE INCAS naturally excited much speculation, a special aura of mystery grew up around even earlier periods of prehistory. A century or more ago, engravings in popular travel books often endowed pre-Inca ruins with a romantic grandeur, as if their stones were hewn by superhuman forces.

In fact, the earliest theory circulated among the Spanish attributed the construction of many such monuments to an unknown race of giants. This theory was seemingly supported by chance discoveries of huge bones belonging to extinct animals. Evidence in its favor also came to light when travelers described the monoliths of Tiahuanaco. These immense stones were carved in a rigid and austere style to represent effigies of gods

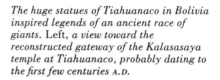

The huge statues of Tiahuanaco in Bolivia inspired legends of an ancient race of giants. Left, a view toward the reconstructed gateway of the Kalasasaya temple at Tiahuanaco, probably dating to the first few centuries A.D.

in human form. The Jesuit Father Bernabé Cobo, writing in the early 1600s, was particularly impressed by these statues as proof of the popular "giant" theory:

> Not only in the size, shape, and features of the face do they prove to be figures of giants, but the fact that their garments,

headdresses, and hair are of a very different style from those of the Indians is no small indication that these statues were made by other people. If the statues had been done by Indians, they would have had the Indians' stature and dress, as do many other statues that we find in other places.

Here we encounter one of the most deep-seated popular myths about ancient Peru: the idea that its spectacular ruins could not have been built by the ancestors of the Andean peoples, or even by the human race itself.

The temples of Tiahuanaco owe much of their awe-inspiring character to their setting on the desolate Bolivian altiplano near Lake Titicaca. The presence of a high civilization in such bleak surroundings still fuels the imagination of visitors to the site today. It is scarcely surprising, then, that the ruins have always been linked to fantastic theories and folktales.

When Spanish friars questioned their native informants about the creation of the world, nearly every story they recorded began at Lake Titicaca. According to one of the more reliable accounts, the creator god, Kon-Tiki Viracocha, emerged from the lake with his retinue, then proceeded to Tiahuanaco; here he made the sun in an instant, followed by the moon and stars.

Many scholars echoed this notion of Tiahuanaco as a city nearly as old as time itself. In 1875 a distinguished Bolivian linguist, Villamil de Rada, claimed that the Aymara language of Bolivia was the earliest human tongue; by implication, Tiahuanaco was therefore the world's oldest city.

Much the same conclusion was reached by Arthur Posnansky, an Austrian naval engineer who emigrated to Bolivia at the turn of the century. Posnansky devoted many years to pioneering surveys and excavations of the ruined city. Much of the information he amassed was invaluable. Yet, even in 1945 he still clung to his conviction that Tiahuanaco had been built as early as fourteen to fifteen thousand years ago. (This would have been in the middle of the last Ice Age, when the high-altitude plateau must have been uninhabitable. Subsequent archaeological work, supported by over thirty radiocarbon date measurements, established that occupation of the site actually covered a much more recent period, from about 100 B.C. to A.D. 1000.) There were also racist overtones to Posnansky's beliefs: in his view, the superior mental faculties of the Tiahuanaco people allowed them to enslave inferior breeds and to spread civilization throughout America.

Other researchers inclined to believe in a Peruvian "master race" seized upon the tradition that Kon-Tiki Viracocha, the creator god, was bearded and white. For instance, the Norwe-

those who come from the Pleides?

gian explorer Thor Heyerdahl devoted much attention to these references to a white god. He interpreted them to mean that an alien race of Caucasoid origin was originally present in Peru. Since the creation myths end with Kon-Tiki and his followers putting out to sea and vanishing across the Pacific, Heyerdahl supposed that his superior beings eventually emigrated on balsa rafts to colonize Polynesia. This idea led to his daring voyage on a similar raft in 1947, described so vividly in his book *The Kon-Tiki Expedition.*

His theory, however, was more or less pure fantasy. Heyerdahl relied heavily on the accounts of certain Spanish priests who were clearly attempting to assimilate native beliefs into the Catholic faith. Such sources portray Kon-Tiki as a bearded individual clad in white robes. In fact, some descriptions of this benevolent personality, who wanders through the Andes performing miracles, quite obviously echo the stories of Catholic saints.

If we take into account the full range of more authentic sources, the Viracocha of native tradition emerges quite differently. In the Andean mind, Viracocha was never a single well-defined person or god. Instead, the creator concept embraced a host of loosely defined supernatural powers and meanings. The deity who rose from the lake near Tiahuanaco was both the sun *and* the superhuman hero Kon-Tiki: they were interchangeable figures, one and the same. Furthermore, the identity of Viracocha also included other ancient deities who controlled weather phenomena such as thunder and hail.

Though the contradictions puzzled the Spanish friars, many of whom simplified the stories to their own taste, the original Andean myths were subtle and complex. If we look no further than Heyerdahl's crude literal reading of the legends, we never become aware of the richness of the original traditions. The genuine, intricate meaning of the Viracocha myth is amply documented by several of the more reliable chroniclers.

As for the intriguing detail of Kon-Tiki's white and bearded appearance, these same sources indicate that his "whiteness" stood for the dazzling light of the sun. In addition, the many-sided aspects of the god included a "junior" and a "senior" sun; these different solar identities were evidently linked to the progress of the sun through the sky during the seasons. Viracocha was particularly associated with the mature, aged sun of midwinter, a time when the sun's rays are at their feeblest; hence the appropriateness of the bearded image. Moreover, within recent memory, the Aymara speakers of the Titicaca region used to refer to the sun's rays as his beard. Though unusual, facial hair is by no means unknown among Native

Americans, and indeed was probably considered a mark of authority or divinity by the Incas. Not a shred of genuine evidence, anatomical or otherwise, supports the notion of an alien race present in ancient Peru.

Nevertheless, many popular writers still assume that the native Peruvians were incapable of developing civilization on their own without the aid of voyagers from afar. Dozens of different candidates have been proposed for these enlightened mariners. These have ranged from the Lost Tribes of Israel to the people of Atlantis, not to mention the early Chinese in their junks and reed-boat sailors from Africa. However, in recent years, no point of origin has proved quite so popular as outer space.

Chariots of Fantasy

THE ONE NAME popularly associated with Nazca and with the idea that ancient astronauts visited the earth is of course that of the Swiss author Erich von Däniken. While he was phenomenally successful at publicizing the notion of the Nazca lines as an airport for extraterrestrials, von Däniken was by no means the first to think of it. In fact Harold T. Wilkins, a British writer on UFOs, anticipated the argument in his book *Flying Saucers from the Moon*, published in 1954. Here Wilkins states that the lines might have been "indications to an interplanetary space ship where to land." Six years later, George Hunt Williamson's *Road in the Sky* appeared with a complete chapter on Nazca entitled "Beacons for the Gods." Indeed, so much of von Däniken's best-seller *Chariots of the Gods?* was lifted from previous books that one aggrieved publisher contemplated a plagiarism suit.

In any case, eight months after *Chariots* first appeared in Germany in 1968, von Däniken did appear in court, charged with embezzlement, fraud and forgery. His jaunts to remote ruins had strained his finances to the point where he falsified the books of the hotel he managed in Switzerland.

A similar lack of scruples is evident in the research methods he applied to his own books. Throughout his writings, archaeological information is constantly suppressed or distorted. Substantial items of evidence are now known to have been completely fabricated (notably the visit to the Ecuador caves described in *The Gold of the Gods*).

Nowhere are the inconsistencies of von Däniken's approach more obvious than in his arguments about Nazca. In *Chariots*, he begins his case by deriding the "preposterous idea" of archaeologists that the lines are Inca roads. As he correctly observes, *some* of the markings are indeed ill-suited for roadways: for instance, the geometric figures that start and stop in the middle of the open desert. However, it was not archaeologists who adopted the term "Inca roads," but local farmers in the Nazca Valley. This was explained in one of the first articles on the lines to appear in print, written in 1947 by Paul Kosok and Maria Reiche (whose work is fully discussed in Chapter 4). In this influential piece, the authors specifically refute the "Inca road" idea and point out how impractical some lines are for ordinary purposes of transportation.

Nevertheless, meandering sunken trails *do* exist inside a great number of the narrow, single straight lines. These indicate that certain types of lines were indeed used as pathways, though obviously not for everyday travel. The possibility that they were routes for ceremonial activities or pilgrimages is discussed in detail later in this book.

It is certainly less obvious how the markings could have been used as landing strips, despite the superficial resemblance of the trapezoids and triangles to airport runways. In many parts of the pampa, the surface is so soft that any vehicle without four-wheel drive soon becomes stuck in the sand. Anything more substantial than the smallest light aircraft could attempt a landing only at severe risk. ^check into woman's journey book I read last year - hideaways

In any case, we might reasonably expect any visitors who had mastered intergalactic travel to have developed a more sophisticated takeoff and landing technology than our own. Nor does von Däniken help his argument by reproducing a photo of a Nazca "runway" with "parking bays," again resembling a modern airport. What he neglects to tell his readers is that the markings actually belong to the outline of a giant bird; in reality, the "parking bays" are the creature's right knee and its four claws. Von Däniken was directly challenged about his use of this photograph in a documentary entitled *The Case of the Ancient Astronauts*, produced by the BBC in Britain in 1978 and featured on the American *Nova* series. During an interview shown on the program, he freely admits that the picture was a "mistake" on his part. Nevertheless, he permitted it to reappear in subsequent editions of *Chariots* published after 1978.

← related to circles now appearing near stonehenge? - especially the new ones (1990) appearing w/ appendages?

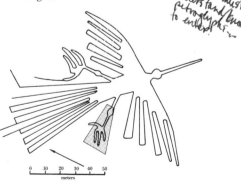

in the mtns. impervious/sheeled to others

Photo reproduced in Erich von Däniken's Chariots of the Gods? *compares these outlines to "parking bays" at a modern airport. In reality, below, they belong to a leg of the giant bird beside the Great Rectangle.*

Can only crack w/ code-must understand/know to enter this~

0 10 20 30 40 50
meters

No hardware to be seen — different dimensionality.

This is not an industrial technology as we know it.

If Nazca really was a place of contact with an alien technology, it is strange that no one has ever encountered extraterrestrial hardware of any kind along the lines, even though most have now been surveyed by archaeologists. "Surely this was the cleanest airport in the world's history!" exclaims Peter White, the Australian author of *The Past Is Human*. "Where are the foundations of the control center? Where the dropped bolts, spanners, odd bits of junk, thrown-away food wrappings, and all the other litter that industrial technologies produce?"

In the face of such criticisms, von Däniken soon revised his theory to make it a shade more plausible. In *Return to the Stars*, published in 1970, he claimed that the space visitors "built an improvised airfield." However, by the time of his appearance in the BBC/*Nova* documentary of 1978, he denied he had ever said that the extraterrestrials needed runways. Instead, he supposed that "a small vehicle . . . landing with an effect maybe even of an air cushion system" blew away the surface of the desert to create tracks as it took off and landed. He went on: "Later the natives came and saw these two lines, and they would whisper, 'The fiery gods rode on these lines.' Only now they start to protect the lines, and maybe in later generations, to make new lines . . . some directed to stars because they feel or they saw that the gods have come from the stars." He imagined that when it eventually became clear that the "gods" would not return, the "natives" resorted to drawing pictures of birds (symbolizing the flight of the gods). Later still, they outlined other animals; he does not mention spirals, zigzags or other geometric figures.

Unfortunately, von Däniken's fantasy reverses the probable sequence of the markings, since animals are probably among the earliest designs (see p. 131). It also attributes a childlike simplicity to the thinking of the "natives." If we merely glance at photos of some of the more complex interconnected figures, it should be obvious that von Däniken's fairy tale is wholly inadequate to account for them.

In his books, von Däniken also discusses another mysterious ground drawing, the so-called Trident of Paracas. This immense figure overlooks the Pacific on the northern edge of the Paracas peninsula, about 100 miles north of Nazca. The three-pronged design is over 600 feet high and nearly 200 feet across. The "trunk" emerges from a rectangular base, while the "arms" are embellished with curious, petal-like designs. Unlike the majority of Nazca markings, which were formed by the removal of a shallow surface crust, the Trident actually consists of trenches dug down into the firm, salty crust of a sloping dune. Some of these trenches are well over three feet deep. Von Däniken

claims that the figure is made of "phosphorescent blocks . . . as hard as granite," but in reality the material is only sand, while the salt crystals explain its supposed phosphorescence.

Von Däniken believes that the Trident functioned as a navigation beacon for UFOs heading south to Nazca. Unfortunately, the orientation of the figure (about 5 degrees west of north) would cause any airborne ET to miss Nazca by a good 150 miles. A more reasonable explanation is that it was intended as a landmark for sailors entering the excellent harbor afforded by the Bay of Paracas. Despite von Däniken's statements to the contrary, the Trident can be seen by anyone approaching the bay on a clear day from as far as fifteen miles out to sea. One possibility is that it represents the constellation of the Southern Cross, a star pattern known to have been important in the traditional navigational and calendrical lore of Peruvian fishermen.

Furthermore, only six miles from the Trident lies the remarkable prehistoric cemetery of Paracas, described in Chapter 8. Over two thousand years ago, this cemetery must have been one of the most sacred sites of the Peruvian coast. As well as being a practical landmark, then, the Trident may also have functioned

The Trident of Paracas, a 600-foot-high ground drawing of uncertain age and meaning.

✓ on Lynn Andrews aboriginal interpretation of the Southern Cross in Australia. — & dolphins, too.

← ETs were buried there a la Cocoon... ancient knowledge as well.

as a religious symbol. The magnificent textiles of Paracas frequently depict mythological creatures or human warriors bearing sprouting plants (see page 148). The choice of design for the immense Trident may well have been influenced by religious symbolism of this kind.

Though the prehistoric origin of the Paracas Trident seems plausible, the local people of Paracas regard it as a Catholic image of recent date. In fact, each May it is customary for them to gather at the drawing to free its outlines from the sand. (This is not particularly hard work, since the fierce winds of Paracas normally perform the job quite well.) Some researchers believe that the design could have been executed as a protection against evil spirits sometime during the sixteenth or seventeenth century. This was a period when local priests are known to have made great efforts to stamp out the pagan rituals that lingered on at Paracas. Interestingly, a record exists of a ceremony conducted at the Trident in 1898 by three Franciscans who were firmly convinced of its Catholic origin and significance.

While the Trident remains a mystery, any of the earthbound explanations are surely more plausible than von Däniken's arguments. He has certainly done much to whet the public appetite for popular coverage of prehistory—a demand often ill served by academic archaeologists. Nevertheless, much of his appeal can be attributed to our modern obsession with high technology.

Though it may be comforting to picture benign extraterrestrials who long ago managed to evolve beyond the present-day realities of war, pollution and world hunger, the genuine achievements of the Andean peoples represent a far more interesting story. Much of von Däniken's writing implies a patronizing, if not overtly racist, superiority to the "natives," who were supposedly too stupid to create anything by themselves.

The Technological Obsession

BESIDES VON DÄNIKEN'S "SPACEPORT," there are countless other fanciful explanations for the lines, most of them equally colored by twentieth-century preoccupations. To mention only a few, one researcher argues that the lines were racetracks for a prehistoric Peruvian version of the Olympics, while another maintains that they were created as a memorial to a primeval atomic war. Or could they have been set out by ancient Peruvian "chain gangs" serving a sentence of hard labor?

A frequent characteristic of such theories is the idea that the lines must have been built to facilitate some practical everyday task, like modern labor-saving devices. For example, one well-known Peruvian archaeologist, A. Rossel Castro, believes that the large cleared areas are actually the remnants of cultivated fields. He suggests that the raised edges of the clearings helped to retain moisture, while the interiors were piled high with humus, guano, seaweed and llama dung as fertilizer. Considering how many of the clearings are located on the highest and most arid ridges overlooking the valleys, this is almost as fantastic a proposition as von Däniken's spaceport.

Still another "practical" use for the clearings attracted considerable media attention in 1983. This equally farfetched proposal was advanced by Henri Stierlin, a Swiss author of several

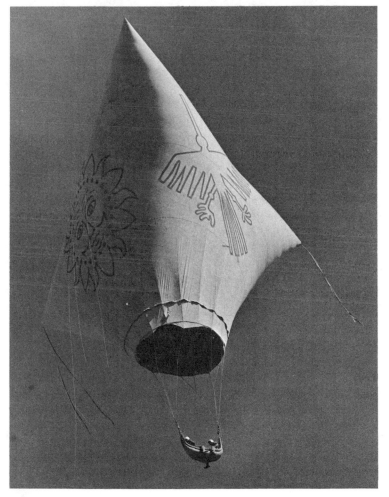

Explorer Jim Woodman and balloonist Julian Nott flying over the Nazca pampa in their hot-air balloon, Condor I, *on November 28, 1975.*

Jim Woodman's photo of a "balloon"
design on a fragment of Nazca pottery,
left, *can be interpreted more convincingly*
as one of the sprouting beans so frequently
depicted in Nazca art; compare the image
of the agricultural deity, right, *traced from*
a Nazca pot.

admirable books on ancient art. According to him, the vast clearings were used as textile workshops. Immense strands of cotton thread, some dozens of miles long, were supposedly stored there as they were woven into the huge burial shrouds that have been discovered from the earliest stages of the Nazca culture. True, the weaving of these enormous shrouds poses an interesting technical problem; on the other hand, Stierlin ignored recently published evidence about how it was probably done (described on page 150). Anyone who has personally experienced the extreme heat and high winds of the open pampa would find the notion of prolonged weaving projects in such a location difficult to take seriously.

One of the more superficially appealing ideas is that the line builders actually succeeded in flying over their designs. Of course, our impressions of the markings are deeply influenced by photographs taken from modern light aircraft. Some writers on Nazca, such as Jim Woodman, are convinced that the ancient drawing activity would have been pointless if the artists had been unable to share the impressive air views available today. In his book *Nazca: Journey to the Sun,* Woodman comments: "I'm sure Egypt's pyramid builders could never have worked blindfold—never having been able to stand back and admire their work. I felt the people who built Nazca had to have seen it. It is all just too incredible to have never been seen or admired by its creators."

To support his conviction that the Nazcans must have flown, Woodman and a British balloonist, Julian Nott, successfully piloted a crude hot-air balloon over the pampa in November 1975. The balloon was constructed from materials readily available to ancient Peruvians, including reeds for the basket and cotton for the envelope similar to that of the finely woven shrouds recovered from Nazca graves. To inflate the balloon, Woodman's assistants dug a substantial fire pit, with a long smoke tunnel leading off to one side, lined with mud bricks. With the help of tall eucalyptus poles and hundreds of feet of rope, the immense seven-story-high balloon was maneuvered into position over the mouth of the smoke tunnel. The dramatic account in Woodman's book makes it obvious how tricky the inflation procedure proved to be: the entire envelope could have caught fire from a single spark. Eventually, however, the balloonists managed a brief hop of about two minutes, reaching a height of 300 feet—enough to convince them that flight in ancient Nazca times was at least a theoretical possibility.

But is there any positive evidence of such flights? Traces of massive sunken furnaces surely would have survived on the open pampa. Despite Woodman's assertion that "burn pits" with "charred rocks" are to be seen at the end of many of the cleared areas, no such evidence of substantial fires has ever been recorded by surveyors or archaeologists.

His own account leaves little doubt of the hazards involved in experimental flying on the pampa, where afternoon winds of up to 25 knots are common. Even in the comparative calm of early morning, unpredictable gusts would be an ever-present risk. A reconnaissance balloon operated by a highly experienced team from the University of Minnesota was wrecked by such gusts during its initial morning flight at Nazca in June 1984.

Woodman denounces von Däniken's spaceport as a "blasphemous" theory that denies the intelligence of ancient man. Yet his own balloon experiment represents just another simple-minded technical solution to the Nazca mystery. Like so many of the other unsubstantiated "practical" theories, it does little to illuminate the actual purposes behind the drawings. In fact, in its insistence on the importance of our modern airborne experience of the lines, Woodman's view is nearly as arrogant and as limiting as von Däniken's. It excludes the possibility that the Nazcans may have "experienced" their drawings in other ways —as ceremonial pathways, for example, or as "messages" directed to sky deities. These possibilities need to be explored if the study of the Nazca lines is to achieve anything more than a mere confirmation of the outlook and prejudices of our own age.

CHAPTER 3

MASTERS OF THE SEA AND RIVERS

The Unknown Wonder: The Canal of La Cumbre

THE TECHNOLOGICAL FANTASIES ABOUT NAZCA seem trivial compared to the results of recent research on ancient Peru. For instance, we now know that Andean peoples coped with their unstable surroundings by developing a technology quite as successful as anything offered by the modern world.

Some of the catastrophes they experienced were so great they can scarcely be imagined, even in terms of the floods and earthquakes of the present century. For instance, new evidence indicates that probably the most severe El Niño of all struck the coast of Peru long before the arrival of the Spanish. Though there are no written records of this event, the floods of around A.D. 1100 left a trail of damage along the northern river valleys that has been carefully traced by archaeologists and geologists. A team of experts from Chicago's Field Museum spent over two years examining the evidence of flood damage visible in ancient canal profiles and in air photographs of landscape features.

This study was unusual in that geologists normally concern themselves with long-term changes rather than with single events, and its conclusions pointed to a disaster of staggering proportions. For the sake of comparison, the researchers traced the effect of the 1925 El Niño, believed to have been the worst in the past four centuries. In the central portion of the broad Moche Valley near the city of Trujillo, the 1925 event resulted in flooding to depths of about ten feet. An "extremely conservative" estimate of the A.D. 1100 event suggests that then the floods reached depths of fifty feet or more. The swollen Moche River carved a channel over two miles wide. This is astonishing if we consider that the average rainfall in this area is less than half an inch a year!

Though its date cannot be fixed precisely, the pre-Columbian flood happened during an era of crucial changes among the peoples of the north coast. The inhabitants of the Moche Valley had been drawn together under the rule of the Chimú, a new dynasty that was to engage in wide-ranging campaigns of foreign conquest. From their capital, Chan Chan, founded on the northern edge of the valley close to the ocean, the Chimú eventually ruled over an empire second only to that of the Inca, who ultimately defeated them around A.D. 1460.

Back in the 1100s, however, the Chimú rulers were still concerned with consolidating their power in the local Moche Valley. During this early phase they embarked on a massive project to extend the irrigation systems already present there. The plan included a complex of new roads and settlements that entirely altered the landscape of the valley; its overall impact was to bring about 40 percent more land under cultivation than is farmed at the present day. Then the great El Niño struck, and the entire irrigation system suffered massive damage.

The disaster by no means crippled the ambitions of the Chimú dynasty, however. The canal system was rebuilt with improvements in design that probably reflected careful observation of the damage caused by the flood. Furthermore, the influence of Chan Chan as an imperial power seems to have grown stronger. The plans of the royal palaces grew ever more ambitious with each succeeding ruler.

Subsequent El Niños may even have assisted the Chimú in their campaigns of conquest. According to legends recorded by the Spanish in the Lambayeque Valley farther north, the power of the local dynasty there disintegrated after their king, a man named Fempellec, was seduced by a temptress in a vision. Fempellec thus angered the gods, and it rained for thirty days. The crops were devastated, and during the subsequent famine the high priests assassinated Fempellec. If the legends are to be trusted, the resulting power vacuum enabled the Chimú to extend their control over Lambayeque, and hence over most of the major valleys of the north coast.

Seemingly undismayed by periodic floods, the Chimú rulers planned irrigation schemes in their newly acquired lands on an extraordinary scale. Indeed, their vision was so ambitious that eventually it led to a "megasystem" of linked water resources,

Flooded streets in Trujillo during the severe El Niño of 1925.

A golden Chimú mask from the north coast.

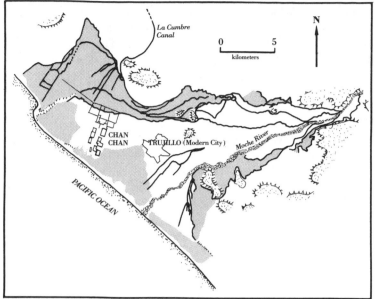

Traces of ancient irrigation canals in the desert beside Chan Chan, capital of the Chimú empire on the north coast.

Archaeologists have plotted a sequence of elaborate canal networks surrounding the ruins of Chan Chan, reflecting the rise and fall of Chimú power. Shaded areas on the map, above right, indicate irrigated land that was never again reclaimed for agricultural use.

combining more than one drainage in a single land reclamation network. Eventually giant intervalley canals linked together all five major rivers of the Lambayeque region. If the area watered by this one megasystem had been farmed efficiently, it would have accounted for one third of all the land *ever* cultivated along the entire Peruvian coast.

Such grandiose plans imply a remarkable degree of social and technical confidence. Yet the Chimú planners did not stop there, for traces exist of a channel that would have connected the huge Lambayeque network to another multivalley system located in the Chicama and Moche valleys forty miles to the south. Though this second system watered a smaller area than the Lambayeque one, it incorporated what was probably the most audacious hydraulic engineering project ever undertaken in the ancient New World: the remarkable La Cumbre canal.

Following the great flood of the 1100s, the inhabitants of Chan Chan had successfully reconstructed their own local canal system. However, over the course of many decades, they faced a steadily deteriorating water supply. The deterioration was almost certainly due to the subtle long-term process of coastal uplift. This had caused the rivers to cut deeper into their beds, lowering the water table and leaving the canal intakes high and dry. Gradually the gardens of Chan Chan shrank back toward the ocean, while the city's numerous walk-in wells were driven ever deeper to reach moisture.

These developments must have led the Chimú rulers to conceive of their boldest plan of all. This called for a 50-mile-long canal that would collect water from the neighboring river to the north, the Chicama, and deliver it to the Moche Valley, close to the capital itself. The requirement that the canal should service the city as well as fulfill agricultural needs imposed severe design problems. The chief obstacles were a sand dune and the rocky Andean foothills that separate the two valleys.

To get the canal through this rugged terrain, the Chimú had to design embankments and aqueducts on a monumental scale. Though the materials were simple—soil and cobbles hauled up from the plain below, together with fire-quarried rock from the surrounding slopes—each section of this elevated watercourse required extraordinary forethought and planning. There are

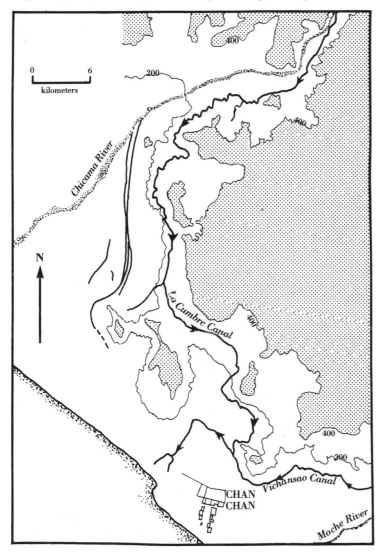

Plan of the La Cumbre canal.

The canal of La Cumbre on Peru's north coast was one of the most ambitious of all ancient engineering projects. Immense ruined stone aqueducts up to seventy feet high snake their way around the flanks of the Andes. Designed to transport water some fifty miles from the Chicama to the Moche Valley, La Cumbre is thought to have absorbed two centuries of construction and a labor investment perhaps ten times that devoted to Egypt's Great Pyramid. Problems created by geological uplift almost certainly led to its final abandonment in the fifteenth century A.D.

few more stirring sights in Peru today than the ruins of this abandoned channel winding around the 60-degree mountain slopes. In some places the mighty embankments supporting it are ten stories high. Astonishingly, this awesome monument is rarely visited and remains entirely unprotected on private land.

For all the vast labor expended on it, La Cumbre never delivered a drop of water to Chan Chan. In fact, the northern half, the part running through the most difficult terrain, was the only section successfully completed. The refinements visible here suggest that parts of the canal were flow-tested as the construction proceeded to enable the builders to fine-tune the design. Irrigated fields were also laid out in some places, as if the practical operation of the system were only a matter of time. But then, at the point where the channel finally emerges from the foothills, it looks as if the incentive for the grand scheme fell through. What happened to discourage the designers?

The technical expertise involved in the canal's construction was unknown until the early 1980s when an American engineer, Charles Ortloff, joined forces with the Chicago Field Museum archaeologists investigating the ruins of Chan Chan. To explore the intentions of the Chimú architects, Ortloff built a 15-foot-long scale model that precisely reproduced the contours of part of the ancient canal. In addition to observing the flow of water through the model, he developed a computer graphics program to use in simulating an entire mile-long section.

Ortloff's tests indicated that the canal was not designed haphazardly as the work progressed, but had followed a unified, preconceived plan. In every section he studied, the channel had been designed to maintain the most efficient delivery of water possible. In fact, the calculations from his model were virtually identical to the so-called near-critical flow rate that a modern hydraulics engineer would have incorporated into such a project.

To achieve near-critical flow, the Chimú ingeniously modified the channel, altering its profile to speed up or slow down the current of water as needed. They also varied the texture of the canal wall. For example, a rough surface would be used to decrease the speed of the water as it approached a curve. Similarly, they incorporated what modern engineers refer to as hydraulic jumps; these were boulders placed on the channel bed, intended to slow down the flow just before a vulnerable structure such as an aqueduct.

In Ortloff's view, the refinements of the channel reveal an understanding of surveying and hydraulics not equaled in the Old World until the late nineteenth century. Indeed, to maintain the constant gradients necessary for such an even flow of

Charles Ortloff's reconstruction of a possible Chimú surveying instrument. First he levels the clay bowl by filling it with water up to a series of holes pierced through its sides; then he uses the holes as sighting devices.

water, the builders would have had to survey lengths of the channel to within one-half degree of accuracy. (To provide a possible explanation for how this was done, Ortloff devised a simple, ingenious surveying device based on a curious Chimú artifact of unknown use.) Furthermore, the designers would have needed to calculate the absolute height above sea level of both the intake in the Chicama Valley and the outlet near Chan Chan. Even with the latest equipment, a present-day engineer would find it tricky to trace a course through the difficult terrain separating these two points.

Yet all this Chimú expertise was to no avail. By the time construction began on the southern segment of La Cumbre—perhaps as much as *two centuries* after the project had begun—tectonic movements had already upset the careful planning of the designers. Today some sections of the channel actually run uphill. Geological displacement is almost certainly responsible for these, rather than lack of skill on the part of the builders. Meanwhile, in the southern half of the project, the remains of many incomplete channels suggest that repeated efforts were made to overcome the shifting of the landscape. Ultimately, restless earth movements proved too much even for the persistent Chimú.

Though it must be termed a failure, the La Cumbre canal illustrates the fact that ancient Peruvians were anything but helpless victims in the face of catastrophic events. On the contrary, they devoted their sophisticated skills to developing and carrying out schemes that defied the instability of their natural surroundings.

In any case, it is perhaps wise to reserve judgment on the Chimú until the success of recent irrigation projects on the Peruvian coast becomes clear. One such project, requiring a minimum investment of nearly $400 million, was designed to revive a small part of the Lambayeque megasystem. This modern intervalley canal is intended to bring water from the Santa River Valley more than sixty miles to Trujillo. Along the way, the channel runs through two tunnels through the mountains, each almost twenty miles long. This project must operate successfully for a century or more if the benefits of agricultural production are to cancel out its initial development costs. Will modern planners find themselves repeating the lesson learned by the Chimú some six centuries ago?

Peruvian Genesis: The Rise of Civilized Life

BESIDES THEIR KNOWLEDGE OF SURVEYING AND IRRIGATION, ancient Peruvians undoubtedly developed an acute awareness of their surroundings. Such an understanding must have helped them to prepare for periodic natural disasters.

Coastal dwellers would surely have detected many different warning signals, since normal weather patterns are disturbed long before the onset of an El Niño. For instance, the winter preceding the 1983 floods was unusually dry and clear along the coast. As a result, the vegetation normally dependent on fog-borne moisture failed to develop properly. This was a full six months or more before the rains began.

Observant fishermen would also notice unusual behavior among seabirds and fishes. At the time of a severe El Niño, warm ocean currents disrupt the normal habitats of fish, so that immense shoals are sometimes driven in toward shallow water or become stranded on beaches. Meanwhile, seabirds, weakened by hunger, are equally easy to catch. Even though the ultimate result is a catastrophic death toll of marine animals, some human populations temporarily benefit.

Furthermore, after the rains arrive, vegetation inland flourishes (sometimes for several years after a single El Niño). In addition to falling back on plant resources, coastal dwellers may also have relied on dried foods. Though evidence of storage facilities rarely survives in Peruvian coastal sites, some interesting discoveries emerged from recent excavations at Paloma, a site in the Chilca Valley dating back to at least seven thousand years ago. Here archaeologists found a number of grass-lined pits that are likely to have been used to store marine foods fetched from the beach two miles away. These foods probably included roasted mussels, dried anchovies and fish meal.

Furthermore, the coastal dwellers were probably not solely dependent on their immediate surroundings for food. Potatoes and other root crops that do not thrive on the coast have always been a traditional item of exchange with communities in the high Andes. Traces of such imports are present at coastal sites that date almost as far back as Paloma. In return, dried seafood and even algae may well have been carried to the highlands, as we know they were during Inca times, just prior to the arrival

Plentiful marine food resources enabled Peruvian coastal dwellers to lead a settled way of life long before they depended on agriculture. At Paloma, in the Chilca Valley, a village dating back to 6000 B.C. has been investigated by an archaeological team led by Robert Benfer of the University of Missouri. Air view of the site, opposite, top right, shows its location about two miles from the beach. Over 200 burials were uncovered among the remains of 55 wood-framed houses. Among the finds were stone beads, above. Examination of human bones from Paloma suggests a gradual improvement in diet and health over the centuries.

of the Spanish. Such a network of exchanges could have provided an extra measure of security against the risk of famine.

Indeed, the richness and relative stability of resources along the coast help explain several of the unique characteristics of Peruvian civilization. To begin with, there was no "agricultural revolution," as scholars a generation ago used to define it: an abrupt transition from nomadic hunting and gathering to sedentary farming. On the contrary, the development of a settled way of life in Peru extended over several thousand years of prehistory. Surprisingly, knowledge of farming played only a minor part in this development.

Though the first remnants of cultivated plants in Peru have been found at archaeological sites dating back to around 10,000 B.C., their presence did not instantly transform the old pattern of life. Instead, small groups of hunters near the coast maintained their routine of shifting seasonal activities. For part of the year they camped in the so-called fog oases (also known as *lomas),* watered entirely from the mists that roll off the Pacific during the winter months. These luxuriant, though temporary pockets of vegetation provided the hunters with abundant roots, seeds and fruits, and also attracted llama and deer down from the highlands.

When summer arrived and the *lomas* began to dry out, the hunters headed down to the river valleys. There they pursued small game and collected wild grasses from the riverbank, as well as shellfish from the shore.

When their way of life *did* begin to change, it was not because of the plants they had already cultivated for centuries. Instead, they learned to rely increasingly on the abundance of the sea, particularly anchovies, sardines and shellfish, which could be procured with much less effort than small game. (Today, it takes skilled Peruvian divers a mere half hour to collect 100 pounds or more of deep-water mussels.)

By about 3000 B.C. the hunters no longer moved to the *lomas* areas in the winter, but began to congregate at year-round settlements closer to the coast. Here layer after layer of discarded mollusk shells piled up to form extensive mounds, or middens. In among the shell refuse, archaeologists often encounter human burials. They have also found traces of houses with stone foundations and walls improvised from cane, reeds, willows and whalebones.

Of course, inland expeditions were still undertaken to gather particular foods, including crops cultivated in the floodplains of the rivers. But there is no question that marine resources became the mainstay of these early coastal dwellers. At Paloma, studies of male skeletons revealed many cases of unusual bone

growths in the inner ear (known technically as auditory osteomas). These were almost certainly caused by repeated diving in cold water for shellfish. Analysis of human bones at Paloma also showed high levels of strontium, reflecting a heavy consumption of seafood.

Their technology scarcely needed any elaboration beyond the rudimentary shell fishhooks and cotton netting present in the earliest levels of the sites. Most of the nets were woven with a fine mesh; these were obviously designed for use with floats in shallow waters, to catch small fish such as anchovies and sardines. The bones of large deep-water species, including shark, mackerel and bonito, are also present at the sites, though no evidence of oceangoing boats has survived.

Fishing and netting became so productive that there must have been a considerable demand for cotton cordage. Indeed, one estimate suggests that a prehistoric coastal village of fifty families would have required over 7 miles of cotton thread simply to clothe themselves. So the major reason why Peruvians expanded their early agricultural practices was probably industrial needs, not food requirements.

Moreover, in an economy that functioned without any form of money, cloth soon became a valuable commodity. It acquired importance not only for everyday exchange but also as a focus of ceremonial, religious expression. Andean peoples still regard spinning and weaving as partly sacred occupations; such an attitude may well go back at least four thousand years, to the period when spinning was so essential to the livelihood of the coastal communities.

Even then, textiles had already become a major medium for expressing religious ideas. Unfortunately, the colors of the earliest textiles have long since faded, so individual designs must be patiently reconstructed. This is done by tracing each dyed thread as it passes through the pattern. The motifs that finally emerge from such painstaking studies consist of a wide variety of geometric as well as animal patterns, including designs based on birds, serpents, crabs and fish. More startling images consist of fantastic creatures made up of parts from different animals. These show that the Peruvians had already begun to endow animals with mythological qualities. Many centuries later, this rich store of animal symbolism was to influence the artists of Nazca as they created their immense outlines of birds, whales and other beasts on the desert floor.

The religious impulses of the coastal dwellers were also channeled into the construction of large ceremonial mounds. In many cases, these monuments started off as a series of substantial masonry rooms built at ground level. Then the rooms were

A reconstructed textile from Huaca Prieta depicts a condor with a serpent curled inside its body. Such textiles suggest that symbolic animal designs already held a special meaning for coastal Peruvians as early as 2000 B.C.

the qualities were already there!

in Peru - along the coast

deliberately filled with rubble to create an elevated platform for a new series of interconnected rooms. Sometimes there were as many as half a dozen successive enlargements and rebuilding operations at a single mound. The massive stone constructions on top of the mounds form a dramatic contrast to the thin cane walls of ordinary houses; these special rooms were obviously not intended for everyday activities.

earth energy work

where (on site) did the figurines come up?

When a large mound at the site of Aspero was explored by Chicago archaeologist Robert Feldman in 1973–74, he discovered a little group of clay figurines concealed beneath the floor within the final stage of buildings. The surrounding walls were carefully plastered and arranged in a plan suggestive of a temple or shrine. A large enclosed area, most likely an open courtyard, led to a series of little rooms with progressively narrower doorways. Only a single person could squeeze through the final ornamental doorway of the innermost sanctuary. Little niches in the walls may have held offerings or images of the gods. In another of the Aspero mounds, Feldman excavated the remains of a child buried beneath a carved stone basin. This child, together with an adult whose remains were found in a nearby room, may have represented a sacrifice offered up to the powers that presided over the shrine.

Such temple mounds mark the beginning of a long tradition of Peruvian ceremonial architecture. General features of the Aspero mounds reappear at ritual platforms built along the coast many centuries later. The successive remodeling phases, the layout of rooms resembling shrines, the dedicatory burials —all these features were typical of Peruvian monument-building practices that were to endure until the arrival of the Spanish.

Obviously, the people of Aspero already belonged to a com-

Reconstruction of a clay figurine that was buried under a clay floor on top of a ceremonial mound at Aspero on the central coast.

Exterior view of a reconstruction of one of the vast room complexes at El Paraiso on the central coast. The terraces are several stories high and surround a series of interior rooms and courtyards.

It is important how they are built around the central mound.

plex social world. During the period the mounds were in use, between about 2800 to 1900 B.C., there were perhaps as many as two or three thousand inhabitants crowded into the huts surrounding the site. The burial practices of these people reflected a number of sharply drawn social distinctions, notably between the sexes. Women were usually buried separately, often with fewer grave goods. Status differences are also apparent, since a small number of males received unusual quantities of textile offerings. Infants or small children were rarely given any kind of burial.

Strangely enough, mummified severed human heads were also discovered at one of the early coastal sites known as Asia. Were these the product of raids against hostile communities? The heads may well have had a sacred meaning, since a cult of severed heads was later to emerge as one of the central religious preoccupations of Nazca and the other cultures of the coast.

If warfare existed so long ago, so too did strong principles of cooperation between different communities. This is implied by the enormous size of several early ceremonial buildings, which must surely have involved labor resources drawn from a wide area. For example, at the site of El Paraiso, nearly 100 miles south of Aspero, archaeologists uncovered only a small area of refuse resulting from everyday occupation, covering no more than half an acre. The ruined building complexes also present at the site cover an area three hundred times larger! When the French archaeologist Fréderic Engel arranged for the reconstruction of just *one* of the eight or nine complexes, it involved transporting some 15,000 tons of rock to the site. Clearly, nonresident laborers must have contributed to these structures, another element typical of much later Peruvian monuments.

Around 2500 B.C., when the Great Pyramid of Egypt was only a century old, ancient Peruvians already displayed many of the attributes we associate with civilization. They were living together in large permanent settlements and had developed differences in social status. They had also acquired artistic and religious values and were capable of organizing massive construction projects. The fact that all this had happened *before* they became dependent on agriculture—indeed, before they had even begun to make pottery—took an entire generation of scholars by surprise. Most researchers had expected Peruvian civilization to follow much the same course as the prehistory of the Old World. They had assumed that pottery skills and facilities for storing surplus grain were essential for a high culture.

This assumption meant that the simplicity of life among the early coastal dwellers of Peru was taken for granted. It was so difficult to conceive of elaborate ceremonial activities in such a setting that the mounds at Aspero were at first assumed to be natural hillocks. Even though surveys and excavations of the site had taken place in 1905 and again in 1941, it was only in 1971 that the mounds were recognized as artificial! Evidence accumulated for decades before archaeologists finally reached the inevitable conclusion: Peruvian civilization had been based upon a unique foundation of ocean resources.

Indeed, the sea provided such an abundant and secure way of life that we may wonder why the Peruvians should ever have been motivated to reclaim the desert. After all, there was nothing inevitable about the development of irrigation, even though it made the coast more productive. The technology involved in canal building required special knowledge and a great deal of labor. It was certainly harder work than digging for clams. What, then, can have disrupted the Peruvians' maritime existence?

Could a single severe El Niño have prompted the coastal dwellers to intensify their farming in the valleys? This seems highly unlikely. During such a disaster, fields watered by canals were even more vulnerable to damage than the natural food resources of the coast.

An alternative explanation may lie in the other major source of natural upheaval in Peru: the normally invisible force of tectonic uplift. A major earth movement might have stranded local shellfish beds above the tideline and could also have disrupted the rich habitat of lagoons along the shore. On the other hand, episodes of uplift probably had little impact on shoals of anchovies and other fishing resources. It is difficult to believe such incidents alone would be enough to encourage the rapid shift toward the valleys that took place in the course of just a few centuries after 2000 B.C.

Instead, it is more likely that human affairs played a crucial part. By this time the coastline was densely settled; many communities probably had populations numbering in the thousands. This may have put pressure on the inhabitants to expand the agricultural activities that were already a traditional part of their way of life. Settlement in the river valleys could also have been encouraged by the territorial ambitions of petty chiefs. Yet another factor may have been widening political contacts or conflicts with the people of the highlands.

Though we may never know all the circumstances, we can be sure that Peruvian civilization was essentially a homegrown affair. The highly distinctive character of the maritime sites seems to have resulted from at least four to five thousand years of gradual development. When important innovations did occur (for example, the first appearance of cotton textiles, around

If they had been guided to do so, then that's what they would have done.

3600 B.C., or pottery making some fifteen hundred years later), it was never with the abruptness that might suggest a dramatic turn of events, such as an invasion from outside.

As we have seen, many writers have advanced the romantic notion that "high culture" was imported to Peru from afar. At the present time, however, no reliable evidence exists that early Peruvians were ever influenced by the arrival of voyagers from other lands. This does not mean, however, that the early Peruvians were cut off from the outside world. Certain fundamental aspects of belief seem to have been shared by the civilizations of both Central America and the Andes, particularly the worship of supernatural felines. Quite possibly these beliefs go back very far indeed, to the primitive cults that hunter-gatherers brought with them when they first entered the Americas, well over twenty thousand years ago.

More recent links are indicated by research on the origins of domesticated plants. Virtually all the crops cultivated along the Peruvian coast were introduced from elsewhere, some from as far away as Mexico and Argentina. Maize, for example, appeared in Mexico several thousand years before it is first recorded in Peru. Other likely imports from Mexico include items still highly valued in the Peruvian diet today, notably avocados, chili peppers and certain varieties of squash.

The spread of new plants also occurred in the reverse direction. Thus cotton and certain varieties of beans are believed to have originated in Peru and migrated northward. Many experts believe that the tropical eastern fringes of the Andes were a key area for early experiments in domestication; this may have been the place where farmers first cultivated lima beans, sweet potatoes and guavas (to name just a few).

Above all, we can be sure that the development of agriculture was not due to the intervention of an alien race armed with superior knowledge. Once again, we must remember that there was no single agricultural revolution. The new crops did not appear overnight as the result of a single breakthrough; the Peruvians adopted them in a seemingly haphazard pattern over the course of more than three thousand years. Indeed, civilization began long before irrigation and maize growing figured prominently in the lives of the coastal people. It was no accident that the Peruvians referred to the ocean as *Mamacocha,* or Mother Sea. Without the resources of the sea and the heritage of the early maritime peoples, Peruvian culture might have remained as impoverished as so many areas of the coastal desert appear today.

It is ironic that so many recent popular writers should seek to explain the Nazca lines and other Peruvian monuments as the

lot of energy from the water

Gold cup in the Chavín style, the earliest fully developed art style in ancient Peru, dating back perhaps as far as 1000 B.C.

product of a "lost" high technology. Recent research suggests exactly the opposite. The tools and materials of the coastal peoples were of the simplest kind: it was skills and knowledge, not equipment, that enabled them to overcome their unstable environment. Indeed, the character of their civilization was so original that it is perhaps not surprising to find their descendants engaged in building those most extraordinary monuments of all: the Nazca lines.

CHAPTER 4

MARIA, SOLITARY WOMAN OF THE LINES

They Call Her Saint Maria

THE WAITER PAUSES while laying out the tables for dinner and whispers to me "Santa Maria," nodding toward the other end of the hotel terrace.

At that moment Maria Reiche, a stooping figure with a commanding gaze and a shock of white hair, emerges from a passageway, supported on the arm of her younger sister, Renate. Each night their routine is the same: slowly they make their way to a circle of chairs on the terrace, where a group of tourists gathers to hear Maria speak. Though trembling from the effects of Parkinson's disease and nearly blind from glaucoma, this eighty-four-year-old ex-teacher of mathematics delivers a lecture in one of five languages, depending on the nationality of her audience. At the end of her talk, her listeners are invited to buy copies of her book, *Mystery on the Desert*. The proceeds from the book pay the salaries of four guards whom Maria employs to watch over the Nazca lines. Since a single car or jeep driven across the pampa can destroy the ancient lines etched on the desert surface, the guards are a vital safeguard. Had Reiche not persisted in her efforts to protect them, many of the figures would have been erased by tire tracks long ago.

It is not surprising, then, that local people who work in Nazca's hotels and restaurants should know her as Santa Maria. Their affection for Reiche seems genuine, but if you ask Maria

Maria Reiche on a visit to the Nazca pampa in 1984.

herself about the school and the street named in her honor, or the fiesta held each year on her birthday, she laughs sardonically. "It's just business, that's all," she says. "Twenty years ago it was different."

She remembers with fondness the time before the tourists came, when she was a recluse on the arid pampa above the town, living in a car and subsisting on a diet of nuts, bananas and cheese. In those days the people of Nazca assumed her to be mad or a witch, and left her alone to pursue her solitary study of the lines. Because the desert markings are so difficult to see from the ground, for years many local people had little respect for, or even awareness of, their existence.

If any legends still lingered about the lines at the time the Spanish arrived, they did not survive the wave of violence and disease that accompanied the Conquest. With the population of many south coast valleys virtually wiped out, the Spaniards had little opportunity to collect native folklore even if they had been so inclined. A few early Spanish writings mention roads in the vicinity of Nazca, but these may well be the Inca roads that connected Nazca to the neighboring valleys and the coast.

In one of these accounts a local magistrate, Luis de Monzon, recorded a tradition that could conceivably refer to the lines and clearings on the pampa, though it has the air of a half-remembered fairy tale. Apparently, in the 1580s, old people near Nazca used to speak about the "ancient times" before the Incas ruled over them, when "there came to that land another

CIVDAD
LAVILLADESTIAGO DE
LANASCA

*The earliest view of the town of Nazca,
from a woodcut by Poma dating
to about 1600.*

people they call Viracochas, not many of them, and they were
followed by Indians who came after them listening to their
word, and now the Indians say they must have been saintly
persons. And to them they built roads, which can be seen to this
day, as wide as a street and enclosed by low walls from one side
to the other."

While the activities of the pre-Inca inhabitants of Nazca were
clearly a mystery even in local minds, the Incas themselves had
left unmistakable reminders of their presence. Besides the road
system, they had founded their town of Kashamalka, with fine
houses of sun-dried mud brick and worked stone, on the southern edge of the Nazca Valley.

At the time of the Conquest, this town had become known as
Nanasca, supposedly after the name of a local chief (or cacique,
the term applied to these native rulers by the European invaders). Another legend relates the name Nanasca to *nanay*, the
word for pain in Quechua, the language spoken by most of Peru's indigenous population. According to this story, during a
terrible drought the suffering of the Nacza people caused them
to cry out "Nanay!" until finally their creator god, Viracocha,
was so moved with pity that he restored the flow of water to
them with his tears.

In 1549 the Spaniards founded their own village of Santiago
de la Nasca beside the river about a mile north of the Inca site,
under the auspices of the military order of Santiago, or Saint
James. The earliest known drawing of the monastery and houses
of Santiago de la Nasca depicts it as a quaint country village
surrounded by fruitful vines.

Rarely has the reality of life in Nazca matched this image of
prosperity. In an ordinary year no rain at all falls in the region.
The dense fogs that cling to the coast and dampen the soil never
reach as far as the Nazca Valley, some 30 miles inland. Instead,
a low range of hills near the sea acts as a barrier, shutting off
both the inland valleys and the expanses of open pampa around
them from any sources of airborne moisture.

As a result, the skies over Nazca are often free of the depress-
ing gloom of the coast, but the sun beats down fiercely. (Shade
temperatures are usually in the nineties during the summer—
January to March—while they rarely drop below 60 degrees in
the winter.) Nor is there much shade to be found if one ventures
outside, since the red-brown foothills of the Andes sweep down
to the valleys without a trace of vegetation. Only in the narrow
basins has farming been possible, centered on one or two small
towns in each valley.

As one might expect, water resources in these valleys are severely limited. The river system of the Río Grande de Nazca

consists of two branches: one, the Río Grande itself (including several tributaries such as the Ingenio, Palpa and Viscas), normally contains a permanent flow because it originates high in the mountains. The other, farther to the south and with sources much lower in the Andes, consists of the Nazca River and other smaller streams such as the Socos, Aja and Kopara. The two major branches meet about halfway between Nazca and the sea.

At present, water runs in the Nazca River about once every five years; the rest of the time the major users of the stony riverbed are children from the town of Nazca, dozens of whom gather there each evening to fly homemade kites. Without a reasonably predictable flow of underground water, channeled to the fields along subterranean canals, farming in Nazca would be impossible.

Air view of the Nazca River during an unusually wet spring in April 1985, left. The riverbed is often completely dry for as much as five years at a time, so farmers rely on modern wells and ancient underground canals.

To explain the achievements of the prehistoric inhabitants, many have assumed that there was more water in these valleys two thousand years ago than today. Certainly, throughout recent history the environment has steadily deteriorated, as more and more arable land has been abandoned in the face of windblown sand and saline soil. During the eighteenth century, good harvests were reported in parts of the coastal valleys that have now turned to useless expanses of salt because of intense evaporation.

To survive in such an environment, farmers must have an intimate knowledge of local water sources and crop requirements. They must adjust their cultivation plans from one season to the next in response to the amount of underground water available. Two separate summer and winter plantings of cotton are usually attempted; during winter, they grow maize alongside the cotton. Sweet potatoes and beans supplement the main

Street scene in Nazca during the presidential election of 1985.

During the election campaign, political slogans appeared alongside Nazca animal designs on house walls.

The "control tower" at Nazca's airstrip.

crops, while orchards of gnarled carob trees, grown for their chocolatelike fruit and iron-hard wood, offer patches of shade in parts of the valley.

Even if we suppose that such crops were grown under more favorable conditions in the ancient past, it is still hard to imagine the valley as an oasis. The French archaeologist Fréderic Engel, who spent many years prospecting for sites along the Peruvian coast, concluded that "Nazca . . . must have been an ecologically poor basin. It may have gone through episodes of hunger and misery, and the inhabitants must have been physically strong and morally persevering to survive as a society that lasted for some 1,000 years and which left indications of its influence over some 750 km [450 miles] of coastal stretch."

The vitality of the modern town of Nazca stems not from its natural surroundings but from its position as a major stop on the great Panamerican Highway, which runs the entire length of South America's Pacific Coast. Street vendors are stirred into flurries of activity as trucks and buses pass along this highway through the town. In fact, most commercial life revolves around two economies, one geared to the tourists and the other to the local Nazcans.

At the dirt airstrip nearby the gleaming Cessnas stand poised to give visitors either an exhilarating or stomach-churning ride over the ancient lines; meanwhile, the locals pass by on donkeys and on every conceivable homemade variation of the bicycle. The main hotel, the tiles of its pool and passageways polished to a mirror finish by its attentive staff, is divided off from the dusty town by a high barbed-wire fence like a prison. Tourists contemplate buying souvenirs such as crudely painted imitation pots and Nazca line designs etched on pebbles while young children peddle candy on the street to each other for fractions of a cent.

These ironies are not lost on Maria Reiche. Since the tourist buses began to arrive at Nazca in earnest only about a decade ago, she is acutely aware of the change in attitude toward her in the town, as she told me: "Without the drawings, Nazca would be completely dead, particularly because we have had so many years of drought recently. Nazca has come to life with all those hotels. And they have seen me before all those years, considering me as mad or as a witch—now they realize there was something in it. Now they use me as a form of tourist propaganda." Nevertheless, she recognizes she must play this role in order to publicize the lines and fight for their protection.

Her celebrity status is as recent as the arrival of the tourists. But how did it feel to live in Nazca for three decades before she was taken seriously?

Rebel and Bookworm: Maria's Childhood

LIKE MANY WHO REBEL against conventional values, Maria Reiche comes from a solidly upper-middle-class background. Born in Dresden on May 15, 1903, she came from a line of well-known judges on her mother's side, and her father was also a judge. Maria believes that her father's orthodox outlook would have shaped the course of her life quite differently had he not died fighting in the Battle of the Somme in 1916, when Maria was thirteen. "If he hadn't died," she comments, "I'd have been a little German bourgeois. I would *never* have escaped to the pampa."

Maria Reiche and her younger sister, Renate, photographed with their mother around 1906.

Maria's mother set a more unusual example. A woman with strong intellectual interests, she read theology at Berlin and English literature at Edinburgh University; she was also one of the first women to ride a bicycle through the streets of Berlin. She supported the family by taking teaching and social work jobs all through Maria's student years. Maria's younger sister, Renate, believes that Maria's relationship with her mother remained a close one, even though Maria blames part of her eventual decision to leave Germany on tensions within the family. Certainly Maria acknowledges the influence of her mother's pioneering feminism on her own attitudes.

The children grew up in an intellectual atmosphere; their house was full of books in both English and German, and Maria spent most of her childhood reading. Long before studying English in school, she had already gone over each page of her mother's English literature books three or four times till she grasped the meaning. This early practice awoke a lifelong love for Shakespeare. (Indeed, to keep herself company on the Nazca desert, she often used to recite long passages from the plays.)

Renate and Maria in 1910.

As the eldest child, with a strikingly pretty face and natural curls, Maria was spoiled, "*terribly* spoiled. Then three years later my sister came along and they said, 'Oh, another girl,' and they didn't give her any importance. Her character was shaped by this experience. But she got very important in the family; she was the *most* important because she kept the whole household going. I just did what I liked and read." Maria remembers admiring her sister as a small child when Renate hauled up coal from the cellar each morning, yet Maria never volunteered to help her.

In her own words, Maria "suffered terribly" when her brother was born, pushing her off her "throne"; on one occasion, she had a jealous tantrum so extreme that her parents called a doctor. Her own vanity as a child (she recalls her father's fury when he caught her admiring her curls in a mirror) was clearly something she reacted against later. Now she says, half seriously, that there shouldn't be any mirrors in a house. And she earnestly believes that women who spend time making up their faces are simply wasting their efforts in a world dominated by men.

Maria was apparently a lonely child, lost in a world of books and never popular at school. Nor were the Reiche sisters known as outstanding students, perhaps because of their reputation for mischievousness. Maria had a strong curiosity about the natural world, though, and she experimented with her own scientific instruments made of matchboxes, string and knitting needles. Her passion for mathematics was so great that she would perform calculations secretly under her desktop during history lessons.

After studying at both Hamburg and Dresden universities, Maria worked as a teacher until the early 1930s, when the political situation in Germany and the tensions within her family grew worse. After she was laid off from her job, she looked for an escape, and answered a newspaper advertisement for a private teacher in Cuzco, Peru. Though seventy-nine others applied for the job, she was the lucky one chosen, and in 1932, at the age of twenty-nine, she set off for South America. During the long ocean voyage, a man proposed to her, but she turned him down: ". . . luckily my reason got the upper hand. He was a very dull man. German men are impossible. They can't stand independent women." Arriving in Cuzco, she took up her post as a governess to the two children of a brewery manager. When this job proved unsatisfactory, she managed to support herself in Lima by translating scientific papers and teaching languages and gymnastics. Through this translation work at Lima's University of San Marcos, she came into contact with several academics, one of whom was to alter the course of her life.

Paul Kosok, the ebullient American historian who pioneered the study of ancient Peruvian canals and was also the first academic to investigate the Nazca lines.

A Fateful Sunset

Paul Kosok was an ebullient native New Yorker with far-ranging interests. Besides teaching history at Long Island University, Kosok was a passionate musician (at one time, a conductor of the Brooklyn Civic Orchestra). After extensive travels in China and the Near East, he became absorbed by the question of how and why civilizations and empires first arose.

Kosok was particularly impressed by the important role that irrigation agriculture had played in ancient Egypt and Mesopotamia; in those cultures, the maintenance of large-scale canal systems must have called for bureaucratic management and control, leading directly (so Kosok and several other historians believed) to an oppressive system of slaves, priests and kings. Wherever elaborate waterworks appeared, slave gangs and overseers must have existed. This "totalitarian" image of the ancient world, so strongly linked to the importance of such basic resources as water, had an obvious relevance for Kosok and his contemporaries in the political climate of the 1930s.

Kosok first visited Peru in 1939, a period when scholars had not yet realized the full extent of the vast canal systems of the north coast. Here was an ideal testing ground for his theories about the rise of civilization: if it could be demonstrated that networks of canals had appeared at the same time as other structures suggestive of an oppressive regime, such as giant pyramids or splendid palaces, then the "waterworks" theory would triumph.

Kosok tackled his project enthusiastically, embarking on a survey of twenty-two valleys and almost five hundred miles of the Peruvian coast. To cope with this nearly superhuman task, Kosok pioneered the use of aerial photographs to help trace the faint lines left by abandoned irrigation ditches across the desert sand. In many cases this bird's-eye view was later followed up by visits on the ground, both to help confirm the existence of canals and also to explore their connection with nearby settlements and pyramid mounds.

At the time of his death in 1959 Kosok had published few results. Nevertheless, his popular book *Life, Land and Water in Ancient Peru* (published posthumously in 1965) instantly became one of the classic books of archaeological discovery. His lively narrative and magnificent aerial photos drew attention to the extraordinary scale on which the ancient Peruvians had reclaimed the desert.

Kosok was first attracted to Nazca in the summer of 1941 after hearing rumors that abandoned canals were to be seen on the surface of the surrounding pampa. He quickly realized that the canals were really giant desert drawings. Kosok was not the first to discover their existence, however. When regular commercial flights began in the 1920s between Lima and Arequipa in the south, Faucett Line pilots and passengers were often surprised by glimpses of the large cleared geometric areas in the Nazca region. In fact, the nickname "prehistoric airstrips," which was

The first animal figure discovered by Kosok was this outline of a bird with an immense tail over 160 feet long, situated above the Palpa Valley. The bird's head and part of its outstretched wings are obliterated by one end of a huge cleared geometric figure.

to become so popular after von Däniken's books, was already circulating in Peru at least twenty-five years earlier.

The first person to study the lines was a well-known Peruvian archaeologist, Mejía Xesspe, who explored the pampa in 1927 while assisting with excavation work in the Nazca region. Xesspe waited until 1939 to publish a brief account of his work, consisting of a simple description and schematic plan of thirteen major concentrations of drawings. These he explained as ancient roads of a religious or ceremonial nature; to refer to them, he used the word *sege*, a traditional term for the invisible sacred pathways that had once radiated in every direction through the Inca capital of Cuzco (described in detail in Chapter 13). Xesspe's paper barely discussed why he thought the lines were pathways, and his suggestion attracted little attention at the time.

Kosok's 1941 visit proved to be a turning point in the search for explanations. Near the end of June he and his wife, Rose, decided to follow an impressive cleared avenue that led vertically up the slope of the Palpa Valley. Eventually it reached a level, stony plateau, where it ended in a central spot from which many other straight lines radiated in different directions. The plateau stretched away from this center for several miles to the east, and there they discovered more lines and several large cleared rectangular shapes. Adjoining one of these was the faint outline of an enormous drawing, 150 feet across, later plotted on paper and recognized by Kosok as a strange, stylized image of a bird. This was the first of the animal figures to be discovered.

As dusk approached, the couple returned to the central spot to watch the sunset; as Paul remembered, their minds were

[handwritten margin notes: maps? (to the stars?) this is significant ← direction will tell which star system & what animal figure is associated with it.]

"whirling with endless questions about these strange and fantastic remains." According to Rose, she then noticed that the sun was setting almost exactly over the end of a line. Suddenly they recalled that the date was June 22, the shortest day of the year in the southern hemisphere and the day when the sun rises and sets at its northernmost point along the horizon. "With a great thrill we realized at once that we had apparently found the key to the riddle!" Paul recollected, ". . . for undoubtedly the ancient Nazcans had constructed this line to mark the winter solstice. And if this were so, then the other markings might very likely be tied up in some way with astronomical and related activities. . . . With what seemed to us 'the largest astronomy book in the world' spread out in front of us, the question immediately arose: How could we learn to read it?" The answer, Kosok decided, was to acquire an overall impression of the

This air photo taken by Peru's National Air Photography Service shows the major concentration of markings overlooking the Ingenio Valley. It dates to the early 1940s, when Kosok and Reiche had just launched their first investigations of the Nazca lines.

markings with the help of aerial photographs taken from a Faucett Line plane. The aerial views helped him to pinpoint about a dozen of the "radiating centers," from which lines fanned outward across the pampa like the spokes in a wheel.

With only a few weeks of Kosok's field season left, a systematic study was impractical, so he contented himself with compass readings of lines taken at just a few representative centers. These rough measurements convinced him that more solstice lines existed and that certain orientations were repeated at different locations. Though he had only scratched the surface of the problem, Kosok satisfied himself that he had found the right approach and looked for someone else to continue the investigation there while he returned to his work on the north coast.

Maria the Outcast

THAT SOMEONE ELSE WAS MARIA REICHE, whom Kosok had met in Lima when he hired her to translate an academic paper into Spanish. Originally he thought that a year of continuous fieldwork might yield the answers he was looking for; he could scarcely have imagined that Reiche would devote the rest of her life to the problem. But Maria had been waiting for years for a project of some kind that would fully engage her intellect. She makes it clear that from the start both the desert landscape and the lines made a deep impact on her. To this day, she still speaks of her enjoyment of the solitude of the desert and the beauty of the soft red-brown colors of the mountain slopes.

Maria visited Nazca for the first time in December 1941, when she confirmed the apparent astronomical connection of certain lines by observing the sun set along them around the time of the solstice, just as Paul and Rose had done earlier the same year. (This solstice was on December 22, the longest day of the year in the southern hemisphere, when the sun rises and sets at its farthest south along the horizon.) Because of her nationality, Maria was not allowed to live outside Lima until the end of the war, so that she was unable to begin her study of the lines in earnest until 1946.

She had set herself an enormous task. The main area of the pampa begins about a dozen miles north of the town of Nazca, and covers an area of some 150 square miles. Much of this great expanse appears absolutely flat and featureless to the eye, though in reality it undulates gently down toward the west. Its shape is very roughly that of a triangle, with the river valleys of the Nazca and the Ingenio on two sides, and the mountains on the other.

To the east, the pampa is bordered by the foothills of the Andes, which end in numerous little hillocks projecting out across the surface of the pampa like promontories on a rocky coast. To the south, the pampa turns into a series of low terraces overlooking the Nazca River. The northern end is much more dramatic, plunging abruptly toward the Ingenio far below; beside this border is the greatest concentration of markings, crowded alongside the steep escarpment.

Apart from the hundreds of lines and geometric shapes clustered here above the Ingenio, many other major groups of markings exist on similar level expanses farther north, overlooking the Viscas and Palpa valleys. In fact, practically every available drawing surface for thirty miles is covered with designs. A few triangles and rectangles can even be glimpsed on landing at the Nazca airstrip, right in the suburbs of Nazca itself. Others are perched on isolated mountaintops that from the air look quite inaccessible.

Most of the Nazca pampa is a level, stony wilderness, devoid of water or vegetation.

The main pampa is about 1,500 feet above sea level, and in an ordinary year receives virtually no rainfall. The lack of rain is,

of course, the main reason why the markings have survived for so long. In the event of a strong El Niño, streams will flow briefly over the bone-dry surface, leaving behind swirling patterns that contrast with the man-made designs and in places have obliterated them.

The geological events that shaped the pampa happened in a different climate far back in the Ice Age, long before any human settlement in the area. At that time, a basin existed between the mountains and the low hills near the coast. Then it slowly filled up with a huge fan-shaped deposit of volcanic rock, clay and calcite washed down from the Andes. For thousands of years this deposit has remained substantially unaltered. The only changes have come about as a result of the main rivers carving out their valleys, and through the action of the wind. This has blown most of the fine particles away, forming a stable, level pavement of pebbles and rocks on the surface.

The considerable difference in temperature between night and day has caused many of these rocks to split and shatter into smaller fragments. At the same time, their constant exposure to sunlight during the daytime has led to the formation on their top surfaces of a brown-black layer that geologists call desert varnish. This coating is very obvious when you turn the stone over, since the surface underneath has the lighter, red-brown tone of the natural rock. The varnish is actually caused by the very slow decomposition of the rock surface, together with the deposition of oxides on top of it.

So a dramatic color contrast results from removing the pampa's upper crust of rocks and pebbles. Trapped beneath these dark surface rocks are finer particles that the wind has been unable to blow away. The particles actually have the consistency of coarse sand, and are formed of a mixture of whitish-yellow clay and calcite. This was the color contrast that the ancient Nazcans exploited to produce their images: the light subsurface soil of a cleared line or area stands out against the dark accumulation of stones all around it.

Many of the narrow lines have grown quite faint over the centuries. This has happened because the wind has swept away the exposed light-colored subsoil, gradually creating a new stable layer of little dark pebbles beneath. The wind also blows in small stones from the outside. As a result, the color of the soil within the lines has slowly tended to merge with that of the surrounding pampa.

This natural "fading" process posed a problem in the early study of the lines. When Maria began her work in 1946, only major lines, triangles and trapezoids were visible from the air. None of the animal figures could be seen because there was

animal figures only visible w/in last 35-40 yrs.

insufficient contrast between the narrow outlines and the rest of the pampa. For instance, the giant bird beside the largest rectangle could be traced on the ground but was invisible from a plane.

Maria therefore decided to clean the animal figures as she discovered them. At first she used a rake, but she found that too crude an implement for the job; one of the first animal outlines she cleaned, a giant hummingbird, still stands out more boldly than the other animals because she used a rake on it. So instead she started using a broom, lightly sweeping away the dark surface pebbles to expose fresh clay underneath. Maria insists that she did this with the utmost care, never disturbing the soil at places where, for example, one line crossed an earlier one. Often the cleaning stretched over days or even weeks, for she would return to the same figure in different light conditions to make absolutely sure she was following the true outline. When Kosok returned for his second and final visit to Peru in 1947 and 1948, his approach was much more casual: apparently he and his son shuffled along with their boots to expose a line!

By this time Kosok had already agreed that Maria should take over the detailed study of the drawings. She began her work with a grant from San Marcos University in Lima. As with the other modest amounts that she was occasionally to receive from academic sources and from her sister, she stretched this sum out over a long period and lived with complete disregard for material comfort. (This sometimes meant doing her calculations on toilet paper.) As far as many people in Nazca were concerned, she was living like an outcast: "I was socially unacceptable. I lived like an Indian, carrying everything I had with me. I was never invited into upper-class drawing rooms, fortunately. I would have had no place there."

At first she lived in an old hotel in the town of Nazca, getting up at three or four each day to hitch a ride on trucks passing through along the Panamerican Highway. This was her only way of reaching the main pampa, about a dozen miles north of the town. She had to begin work at dawn because by noon the heat out on the open desert was often intolerable. Eventually she was able to move to a room at the San Pablo ranch, located less than an hour's walk from the main figures on the edge of the Ingenio Valley. This was to be her headquarters for the next decade.

Though the ranch was in a more convenient location, conditions there were primitive. Because mice ate holes in her charts and calculations, she began to store them by fastening them with clothespins to strings hanging from the ceiling. This is still the way she stores her papers today, even in the comparative luxury of her room at the tourist hotel in Nazca.

Though Maria lived as an outcast, she nevertheless received considerable help in her work from local sources. A military surveying unit loaned her a theodolite, while the municipal authorities of Nazca arranged for her to borrow a garbage truck and the electric company's ladder. The ladder was propped against the truck to provide a platform for photographing overall views of the animal and geometric designs. Meanwhile, the Peruvian air force gradually built up an archive of aerial photos of the pampa, taken in the course of numerous training flights over the desert during the period from 1944 to 1947.

Maria Reiche describes her work to military personnel at the headquarters of the National Air Photography Service in Lima in 1947.

Maria Reiche strapped to the landing skid of a military helicopter. From this exposed position, she took many low-level photographs of the animal figures.

Still, the results were not quite satisfactory, and when eventually one of the first helicopters arrived in Peru, Maria reserved it for a flight over the pampa. Since it was difficult to take pictures from inside the cabin, she had herself strapped to a wooden board that in turn was fastened to the landing struts of the helicopter. Her flight caused a sensation in Nazca.

The Beasts of Nazca

BY THE TIME KOSOK FINALLY RETURNED to America in 1948, Maria had already discovered at least eighteen animal figures. The first one she found was a giant spider, 150 feet long,

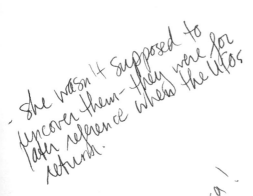

she wasn't supposed to uncover them — they were for later reference when the UFOs return.

orca!

connected to USA desert petroglyphs?

beside the largest rectangle (the so-called Great Rectangle); to begin with, she thought she was tracing the arms and legs of a human figure.

In 1952, after pilots had reported seeing something near the spider, she came across perhaps her favorite drawing, a huge monkey, over 300 feet across. Maria literally caught the monkey by its tail by first of all discovering the spiral pattern twisting round and round toward the body. As she began to make a chart of the figure, she thought it might be a frog; when the image of a monkey finally appeared on paper, she collapsed with laughter on the pampa!

Other creatures emerged one by one from the tangle of lines. There were three examples of fishes resembling killer whales, a dog, a pair of llamas and two lizards, one of them sliced in half by the Panamerican Highway. There was also a beautifully symmetrical flower motif, as well as several images resembling either seaweed or plants with thick roots or branches.

One curious design consists of a pair of outstretched apparently human hands with only nine fingers. These are joined together at the top by an outline suggesting the ears and head of a monkey. (In fact, the large monkey with the spiral tail also has only nine fingers, so the monkey identification of the hands may be correct.)

Images with human elements in them are exceedingly rare. Maria did find a few strange human figures, but these are entirely confined to the sides of steep hills and never appear on the pampa, where all the other drawings are to be seen. The half dozen or so humans also differ because of their rather crude, cartoon-like style. Perhaps they were done at some period other than that of the main drawings, or their crudity may simply reflect the difficulty of tracing a neat outline on a steep slope.

Back on the pampa, Maria found that the commonest realistic pictures were of birds; eventually she identified a total of eighteen examples. Three of these seem to show the peculiar scavenging seabird known as the frigate bird, or sea eagle. This creature has the ability to inflate its gullet to a grotesque size in midair, scaring other birds and causing them to drop any fish they may be carrying in their bills. One of these frigate bird figures was turned into an almost totally abstract, geometric pattern, with rectangles for wings and big circles for eyes; it is huge, nearly 600 feet from wingtip to wingtip. Its style contrasts remarkably with a much more realistic profile of the same bird outlined on a different part of the pampa, a mere 180 feet from beak to tail.

Perhaps the single most striking aspect of all the animals is the fact that each outline was executed with a single narrow

↑ *animal giving birth?*

The spider is one of the most perfectly executed of the Nazca animal figures. A peculiar feature is the extension of its lower right-hand leg as twin parallel lines. Astronomer Gerald S. Hawkins popularized the idea that the figure might depict an exceedingly rare creature known as Ricinulei, left. This tiny arachnid is found only in the Amazon; the male uses an organ on its extended leg for copulation. Apart from the leg, however, the Nazca outline does not closely resemble Ricinulei. A more plausible idea is that the figure depicts one of the many common spiders of the Peruvian coast, as painted on a Nazca pot, below.

Spider and squirrel monkeys abound in the Amazon forests east of the Andes, while capuchins are common in parts of the far north coast, both in the wild and as pets. Monkeys found in ancient south coast graves were probably traded from these regions. Supernatural monkey on a Nazca pot, *right*, clutches a human trophy head and a club or staff. The giant bird beside the Great Rectangle, *below right*, has a wingspan of over 350 feet; it may represent a cormorant, as seen on a Nazca pot, *below left*.

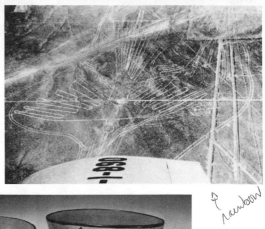

This outline of a fox or dog is about ninety feet wide. Many Andean folktales describe foxes as the servants or helpers of all-powerful mountain gods.

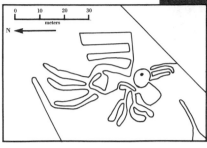

Male frigate birds inflate a balloon-like red throat patch during the breeding season. Though today their range rarely extends farther south than the Ecuador coast, they may be the birds depicted on Nazca pottery and in several desert drawings, left.

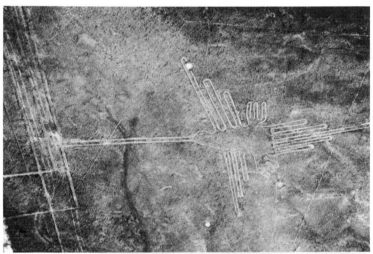

Hummingbirds are common visitors to gardens in present-day Nazca, while in Andean mythology, they figure as special messengers of the mountain gods. There are at least two major depictions on the Nazca pampa; this example has a wingspan of over two hundred feet.

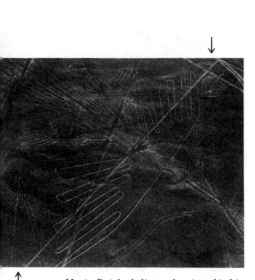

↓

↑

Maria Reiche believes the giant bird is astronomically significant because the major line that crosses it points toward midsummer sunrise in one direction and midwinter sunset in another. But are these astronomical alignments due purely to chance? And were the builders of the straight line even aware of the bird figure? In almost every case, long lines overlie animal figures and may date to a later period.

continuous line. This reminded Reiche and Kosok of a children's game in which the object is to complete a drawing without lifting the pen off the paper. Despite the varied sizes and styles of the different animal depictions, there are no exceptions to this rule, except for a small pair of llamas that were solidly filled in with stones, rather than traced with narrow outlines. In every other example, the lines forming each animal shape are never broken and never cross one another.

This immediately suggested to Reiche and Kosok that the outlines could be ceremonial pathways, laid out so that you could enter, trace the entire image of the animal through all its twists and turns, then finally exit near the original starting point. The idea that the animals represent a special kind of sacred, maze-like pathway remains one of the most promising explanations of their purpose.

Most of the animal designs are clustered together near the northern edge of the pampa overlooking the Ingenio Valley, where the thickest concentration of markings of all kinds is to be seen. In fact, the animals are vastly outnumbered by scores of geometric drawings and cleared areas, not to mention hundreds of lines running straight across the desert. These lines sometimes cut across an animal image; in some cases, Maria thought, this was not accidental but deliberate, a connection linking the figure to astronomical solstice lines or to other designs and cleared areas in a different part of the pampa.

Though it was difficult to prove, Maria also believed that several animal figures had been positioned intentionally alongside various large rectangles. For instance, the outline of the giant bird (perhaps a condor or cormorant) near the west end of the Great Rectangle begins and ends near one of its tail feathers, and one of its lines joins directly to the Rectangle. Reiche and Kosok reported that there was a break in the border of the Great Rectangle at this point, as if the builders were making a deliberate connection. The monkey is another example of an animal design that seems to be linked to geometry—in this instance to a narrow cleared avenue and a complicated series of zigzags. However, in most other cases, the relationship of the animals to geometric figures is much less clear.

Moreover, the animals are relatively few and far between, so many of the cleared areas have no creature anywhere near them. Some of these clearings are over half a mile long; Kosok noted that a modern football field built inside an ancient rectangle by people from the Ingenio Valley was dwarfed by comparison. Most of the clearings were constructed by removing the surface crust of stones and piling up the debris like a wall along the edges. When the figure was located beside the rim of the pampa,

medicine wheels of the south...

— different "medicine" for each area.

the stones had apparently been dumped down the slope into the valley.

But what was the purpose of all this labor? Kosok speculated that the trapezoids "may well have been used as special ceremonial enclosures or 'temples' by the various local kinship groups or other social units from the nearby valleys." This was *a blow to this theory* a reasonable suggestion, except that Maria found some of the quadrilaterals running up steep slopes or across uneven ground, where it was difficult to imagine large groups of people congregating. The frequent presence of low heaps of stone strewn with pottery at one or both ends of the clearing did suggest the idea of "altars" with offerings. Straight lines were often aimed across the pampa directly toward these stone heaps. *working energy?*

Viewed from the ground, the borders of the huge cleared areas resemble old stone walls, left.

In some places, Reiche found large numbers of miniature stone piles arranged in orderly rows; one long rectangle contained an estimated seven thousand of them. She speculated that they might represent some kind of recording or counting device. A simpler explanation might be that they were left over from an intermediate stage in the job of constructing a quadrilateral, interrupted before the finishing touch was added of removing all the stone debris to the borders.

The triangles and trapezoids are rarely self-contained units, closed off from the pampa outside. Instead, the cleared areas are invariably connected by their points or corners to other surrounding figures, whether these are animal designs, straight lines or mazelike spirals or zigzags. The point of connection seems to have been an important place, since the narrow end of many triangles often has a conspicuous bend or kink just as it dwindles and starts to turn into a straight line.

These "exit" points from triangles and quadrilaterals occa-

Rock cairns, sometimes strewn with pottery, are often found at junctions of lines or figures on the Nazca pampa. Similar cairns are still revered as shrines to mountaintop deities in the Andes today.

Like a giant scratch pad, the surface of the pampa was reused time after time. This air view shows a pair of superimposed cleared areas. Right, a spectacular giant triangle on the Nazca pampa.

to land different kinds of ships

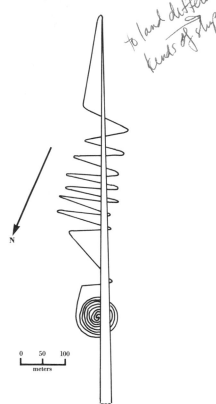

0   50   100
meters

Maria Reiche's survey of the huge "Needle and Thread" drawing at Cantalloc, east of Nazca. Several other designs nearby suggest a connection with weaving; the Quechua place name Cantalloc means "place of weaving."

sionally form Kosok's "radiating centers," spots where a number of lines fan out in many directions across the pampa. In other cases, the patterns that emerge from the cleared areas are more complex. One remarkable example is a figure in the Nazca Valley nicknamed the Needle and Thread. Here an immense needlelike triangular design about a quarter of a mile long ends in a straight line that subsequently bends around and forms a huge zigzag. The zigzag crosses back and forth under the cleared triangle some sixteen times before turning itself into a double spiral.

Spirals, in fact, turned out to be the commonest of all the single-line figures; Maria eventually found over a hundred of them. They range from crudely executed "squashed" shapes to admirably regular examples such as the great double spiral at the edge of the Ingenio Valley; its diameter is about 300 feet and each turn is nearly 10 feet wide. Near the middle of this spiral, Maria discovered an upright stone about 16 inches high, engraved with a design of a serpent and a severed human head. This and other comparisons led Maria to suggest that the Nazca people associated all their spirals with serpents. Whether or not this is correct, a basic similarity to the animal figures *is* suggested by the frequency of double spiral patterns. Like the single-line animals, you could walk along the entire length of a double spiral to its center and then out again without stopping or crossing over any paths.

Kosok and the Theory of Priestly Power

The precision of the geometrical figures varies considerably, as this selection of spirals and circles illustrates.

PROCESSIONAL PATHWAYS or even racetracks were among Kosok's favorite theories for the lines. The animal designs might have represented the badges or totems of a particular ancient community, while the stone piles at the end of the quadrilaterals were perhaps altars for offerings. The great variety of different markings on the pampa prompted an equally diverse range of explanations.

Yet Reiche and Kosok both emphasized that the markings were in no sense a chaotic jumble, but revealed definite rules of organization. Besides this conviction that the lines were not laid out at random, Kosok also had very definite ideas about how and why the ancient Nazcans had begun their desert drawing practices in the first place.

These were based on his general beliefs about the rise of civilization in the ancient world, rather than on evidence drawn from the Nazca culture itself. Kosok was convinced of the important part that astronomy must have played among the ancient peoples of the Peruvian coast. Skywatching, he thought, had developed as a practical aid to survival alongside other essential practices such as irrigation. In fact, as soon as the Peruvians realized that celestial objects moved in tune with the changing seasons of the agricultural world, they must have recognized the need for an "organized science" of astronomy, or so Kosok believed. Once they actually developed an astronomical calendar, it must have helped farmers to predict the coming and going of the life-giving waters. The rites and ceremonies that grew up with the calendar must also have served to regulate their social affairs, determining auspicious and unlucky days, for example.

Only later did the ability to predict astronomical events become an instrument of power, the property of an elite specialist group—the astronomer-priests. These specialists, Kosok wrote, carefully guarded their knowledge from the ordinary population. It gave them "a tremendous control over the people—for only the priests could know and apparently influence the forces that controlled human destiny." Though skywatching had originated in the practical needs of survival, eventually, Kosok believed, it became a means of oppression. Now the priests had found a way of controlling human activities as well as anticipating the cycles of nature. Once the priests had established their power, the whole system of astronomically determined ceremonies gained a momentum of its own. The rites grew increasingly elaborate, far more so than was required for the mere task of regulating agriculture. The influence of the priests helped explain why there were so many lines and centers on the pampa.

So Kosok looked beyond his simple pragmatic suggestions that trapezoids were racecourses and that stone piles were altars. His essential idea was that all the strange features on the pampa had functioned together in a religious system that enabled a class of priests to manipulate the people of Nazca. Furthermore, Kosok was convinced that the same process of social development had gone still further in other parts of Peru such as the north coast. Eventually, power passed from the priesthood into the hands of secular, militaristic rulers. The priests and their astronomical concerns played only a secondary part within these empires, for now their activities were carefully managed by the bureaucracy of the state. Slaves toiled to erect giant mud-brick pyramids symbolizing the state's authority.

But in Nazca, far to the south, the narrow, parched valleys were never rich enough to encourage the rise of a full-fledged state. As a result, Kosok thought, these valleys, with very limited productive potentialities, in all likelihood sustained only demon-infested priest-dominated peasant societies throughout their two thousand or more years of history.

Since no great structures could be erected, the priests and the people had to content themselves with easily built ceremonial lines and centers in the adjoining deserts. As they continued to build, generation after generation, century after century, and as the dry desert carefully preserved these markings, there slowly emerged those vast networks of figures that today strain our credulity and challenge our understanding!

[handwritten marginal note: — bunk this shit! bigger is not always better! this is common male ideology]

But where was the evidence that Nazca had actually been ruled by tyrannical astronomer-priests? All that Kosok offered was his basic case that many lines were oriented to the sun or stars. And Maria Reiche never seems to have questioned Kosok's explanation. Most of her general statements on the purpose of the lines are brief, simply repeating his argument that an accurate sky calendar was essential for farmers in an environment as harsh as Nazca, and that the calendar would also have served social ends in timing fiestas and ceremonies as well. Privately she speaks of the "chiefs" of Nazca and the "slaves" who built the lines. She thinks the entire system of astronomy and geometry must have been kept secret from the ordinary population, at the same time that they were unwillingly pressed into the task of clearing the great triangles and quadrilaterals.

"Theories Are All Imagination!"

IN ANY CASE, Maria has been interested mainly in exploring and recording the lines, rather than in speculating about their ultimate purpose. "Theories are all imagination!" she declared to me emphatically. "All you can do is measure carefully and observe, and the conclusions flow naturally from that."

In the years following Kosok's departure, Maria indeed concentrated on measuring and observing, as she accumulated more and more examples of lines apparently directed toward the movements of the sun, moon and stars. She also elaborated the idea that the animal figures might represent images of specific constellations. The Nazcans, she assumed, identified animals among the star patterns of the night sky similar to those of our own modern constellations. Speculating that these animals would have been sacred deities that ruled over certain periods in the calendar, she supposed that drawing their images on the pampa might have been intended to invoke their power, perhaps so that they would send fruitfulness to the Nazca Valley.

In making her careful charts of individual animal designs, Maria noted how frequently a straight line seemed to cross over a figure and coincide with an astronomical alignment. For example, the giant bird beside the Great Rectangle was traversed by a line apparently indicating the solstices. In another case, she identified a major line running through the spider as pointing toward a group of stars in Orion. She also argued that the outline of a spider was a good match for the shape of Orion in the sky.

She was particularly interested in the monkey, for here she thought there was a connection with a number of stars in the Great Bear (the Big Dipper). Her study of the monkey (published in 1958) identified straight lines associated with it that

The monkey figure as surveyed by Maria Reiche, who believes its builders associated it with the constellation Ursa Major (the Big Dipper or Great Bear). The long avenue below the figure would have pointed to Benetnasch, one of the stars in the Dipper, around A.D. 1000, but it is likely that the monkey actually dates to a much earlier period than this.

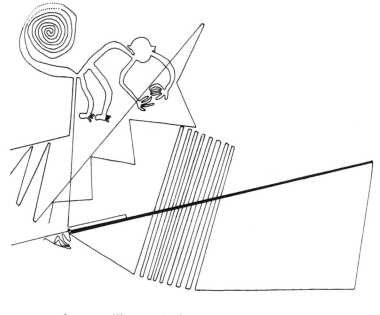

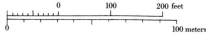

seemed to indicate one of the stars at the "tail" of the Great Bear. A thousand years ago this star would have become visible in the dawn sky for the first time about thirty days before the December solstice. This time period also coincides, in a good year, with the return of water to the rivers around Nazca. Maria's idea, then, was that a Nazca priest could use the astronomical lines associated with the Great Bear to anticipate the flowing of the rivers, and that the monkey image itself was intended to implore the deity to send more water.

Her conclusions about the animal figures also implied the existence of an elaborate, perhaps secret system of geometry. Some kind of geometry was undoubtedly necessary to set out many of the animal and spiral outlines, since they are drawn on a huge scale yet have harmonious, regular proportions. The artfulness of their design is very difficult to appreciate from the level of the pampa itself. Indeed, from the ground some animals just look like an indecipherable mass of lines. One of the whales, for instance, was thought by Maria to be a gridlike pattern of parallel lines until she transferred the design to paper. In short, the perfection of certain animal outlines could not have been achieved simply by eye alone. Furthermore, none of the animal figures is located anywhere near hills that could have given a vantage point to an ancient designer.

As Maria's eyesight began to fail during the 1970s, hindering her work with astronomical alignments, she concentrated on the detailed geometry of the figures. Today she believes that the Nazca designers used a standard uniform unit of length in setting out the figures. This basic unit of 38 to 40 centimeters she relates, plausibly enough, to body measurements of the Nazca people themselves, in particular to the distance between forefinger and elbow. A cord stretched between these points is certainly a convenient measure, and she cites its popularity in the ancient world (for example, the Egyptian cubit) and among sailors in recent history to support her case.

We might suppose that such a unit would vary from one priest to another, depending on individual physique. But Maria believes that the Nazca unit was not a rough-and-ready measure like this. In fact, she has always emphasized how accurate the designers were. Their unit of measurement varied by no more than 2 centimeters from one figure to the next—a remarkable claim, considering that some of the animal designs are over 500 feet long. Such accuracy would certainly support Kosok's idea that an organized science practiced by a select few existed at Nazca.

Maria's Mission

FOR FORTY YEARS, Maria Reiche has devoted herself to the task of charting the Nazca figures and fighting for their preservation. During that period, her ideas about the meaning of the lines have changed very little; indeed, recent statements in her lectures and in interviews with the press contain the same conclusions she had already reached in the late 1940s. She seems rarely to have wavered in her conviction that the Nazca lines were built by astronomer-priests. Only once, apparently, did she experience doubt about the validity of her ideas, wondering if she was "trying to put sense into something senseless." But this period of doubt did not last long. Another time, after her best friend in Lima died in 1960, she left Nazca briefly to teach literacy in an Andean village. Soon she found herself called back to the pampa, mainly, she says, "to satisfy curiosity. It's such an interesting subject, I feel privileged to have studied it. I forgot I was getting older. And I enjoyed the solitude: the pampa is a beautiful place. It's not a glaring desert, but a landscape of hills in agreeable shades of brown. Before there was pollution, the sky had a wonderful clarity to it, all day long."

Despite her feelings for this landscape, she nevertheless shuns romantic or mystical interpretations of what once took place there. In fact, her no-nonsense attitude toward the work that has absorbed her for so long is remarkable. Strongly antireligious in her own beliefs, Maria has consistently played down the importance of religion as a possible motivation for the lines. She prefers to see their designers as levelheaded intellectuals, methodically solving one mathematical problem after another with the patience and precision of ancient Chinese craftsmen. Despite an interest she expressed to me in the impressions of psychics who have visited the pampa and in the content of her dreams, she is nevertheless convinced that a firmly rational outlook lies behind the creation of the figures. She has obviously projected qualities of her own back onto people of the distant past.

But were the builders of the lines really such pragmatic thinkers? And is it likely that their outlook was so similar to that of a twentieth-century scientist? One drawback of Maria's fiercely guarded independence has been her reluctance to consider evidence drawn from disciplines other than her own. As will be seen in later chapters of this book, the archaeology of the Nazca

Maria Reiche in 1968.

culture and the anthropology of present-day peoples in the Andes suggest motivations for the desert drawings that would not be obvious to the modern Western mind.

Working in such isolation, Maria has had little chance to keep up with advances in the study of ancient astronomy and of the development of prehistoric societies. For instance, archaeologists now reconstruct the prehistoric social world of the Peruvian coast in a different way than Paul Kosok once imagined. Though we owe the continuing existence of the lines to Maria, together with many careful charts and surveys, her theories are the product of a narrow and limited vision of the builders' intentions.

Ultimately, Maria's theories may take second place to the example set by her dedication and independence. This, too, is what she would like to be remembered for, as she told me: "I am happy to think that I have proved to the world that a woman without the help of any man can achieve proper scientific results, without being used for the menial and dull tasks."

CHAPTER 5

CHAPTER 5

THE SKY AND THE LINES

"They've Got to Be Astronomical!"

IT WAS A RARE OPPORTUNITY: Maria Reiche had agreed to accompany a British film crew and me on a visit to a group of lines on the Nazca pampa. There we planned to film the sun setting beside one of the solstice lines she had discovered nearly forty years previously. We hoped the shot would be dramatic enough to convey something of the excitement Reiche and Kosok must have felt as they began to investigate their astronomical theory in 1941.

Tourists are now permitted to visit only one area of drawings on the main pampa: this is one of Kosok's "radiating centers." To reach it, we turned off the Panamerican Highway and followed a pair of tire tracks, twin lines of white sand cutting through the dull brown desert pavement. Recently posted signs in Spanish threatened fines or imprisonment for any person or vehicle straying from the trackway. As the Volkswagen bus lurched across the sand, Maria steadied herself by grabbing a pair of loose seat belts in front of her like reins, joking that she felt as if she were riding a horse.

Eventually we pulled up alongside a rounded hill rising abruptly about fifty feet above the level surface of the desert. I scrambled up a dusty white footpath that led to its summit. As my eyes adjusted to the twilight, I started to pick out lines and avenues fanning out from around the base of the hill. Maria had told me that she had counted about fifty lines here, but in the dusk I could see no more than about a dozen. The remarkable straightness of most of the lines impressed me, though each line was a different width and began at a different starting point around the irregular base of the hill.

That evening the pampa seemed a forbidding place to me; its absolute sterility and desolation made me think of an industrial waste site. Meanwhile, the sun slipped down toward a brown bank of haze over the distant hills. Soon the haze had deformed the sun's shape to a glowering oval of orange.

It was obvious which one was Maria's solstice line, and at first I thought the sun's path would exactly coincide with it. Then I reminded myself that I was in the southern hemisphere; the sun was sinking on a diagonal from right to left, not left to right as I was accustomed to seeing. Once I had overcome my disorientation, it was obvious that the line was in fact pointing considerably off target, and that the sun would eventually set to the left, or south, of the direction indicated by the line.

This was to be expected, since there were still three weeks left before the June solstice. During this period the sun would continue shifting northward along the horizon each day until it reached the solstice point. Then it would appear to set at the same place each evening for about a week before beginning its long march south again. If we had been able to return at the proper time, the line would probably have pointed directly toward the path of the sun.

As the pampa faded to a somber, empty expanse and the ancient scratches on its surface grew less visible, the scene became dominated by the glaring disk of the sun. One of my colleagues gasped in admiration at the spectacle. "They've got to be astronomical!" he exclaimed, pointing toward the lines. "Nobody could see this and doubt it!"

Though I, too, was impressed, there were aspects of this experience that troubled me. For instance, as the sun vanished in the haze, even the broadest avenues became progressively harder to see. When freshly made, the lines doubtless stood out as bright streaks across the landscape, yet in the twilight their far ends must have been difficult to distinguish. At night they would surely have been invisible. Lamps or torches could have been placed along the length of the lines, yet no evidence of any such objects has ever been discovered. Similarly, beacons could have been lit on top of the stone heaps positioned at the ends of many lines and quadrilaterals, yet no charred wood or ashes have been reported at these spots. (In any case, the glare of a fire would probably have interfered with night sky observation.) If the Nazcans really were concerned with watching the stars

Most of the long Nazca lines radiate from prominent hillocks overlooking the desolate pampa.

Were the straight lines intended to be pointers, indicating astronomical events on the horizon? At twilight most lines become almost invisible.

rise and set along the horizon, as Maria believes, then the lines were a curiously impractical way of marking such points.

Another problem became obvious as the evening drew in, bringing with it a blanket of clouds overhead. At present, the atmosphere of Nazca makes it one of the least favorable places on earth for an astronomer. The wind carries up fine dust particles to form a curtain of haze, and this often combines with mist generated by moisture condensing near the desert floor. At both dawn and dusk, the horizons around Nazca are frequently murky, even on days when the sky turns brilliantly blue by noon.

Maria believes that present-day atmospheric conditions are a recent product of pollution from mining operations near the coast. However, astronomer Gerald S. Hawkins reported in 1968 that misty mornings and evenings were common throughout the year, and that the local inhabitants of Nazca thought such conditions were normal. If haze was so constant a factor in ancient times, too, then Nazca skywatchers would have had a hard time keeping track of the moon, stars or planets.

I also found it difficult to shake a feeling of disappointment that the line had missed the sun by so wide a margin. I began to wonder just how close it would have to be for the alignment to seem convincing. The problem was one of accuracy: would the Nazca skywatchers have aimed their lines *exactly* at the sunset point, or would they have been satisfied by roughly the right direction, give or take a degree or two?

Some lines were so exceedingly long and narrow that looking down them at the horizon was almost like sighting through a telescopic rifle. They were so straight that the Nazcans certainly

Many lines are so straight that they seem to draw the eye toward specific points on the horizon. But was this associated with astronomical viewing, or was the extreme straightness important for some other reason?

could have used them to define points on the horizon with the high precision of a marksman if they had wanted to. But how can we be sure that this was the real reason for the extreme straightness of the lines?

This question was bound up with another even more difficult problem, the part played by chance in the layout of the lines. Because there was such an intricate tangle of lines running in every direction, it was possible that even a "perfect" match of a line with the sun might simply be a coincidence. Could the builders have had some totally different nonastronomical purpose in mind, so that the connection of the sun to the solstice line was pure chance?

The Role of Chance

THIS QUESTION must have been apparent to Maria Reiche at an early stage of her work on the pampa. As she began to survey the directions indicated by the straight lines, it was soon obvious that they ran toward virtually every point of the compass. By 1949 she had surveyed over two hundred and fifty lines and drawn up the results in the form of a chart. This shows that the lines she measured were spread out fairly evenly along the entire length of the horizon. There are no obvious dramatic clusters of markings such as we might expect if the lines were in fact directed toward particular sky events.

Nevertheless, in the article that accompanied the diagram, Maria insisted that the orientations she had measured were not merely random and meaningless. One of the most significant, she believed, was represented by over a dozen lines that pointed toward 68 to 70 degrees east of north. Her calculations showed that the Pleiades, a prominent cluster of stars, rose in this direction during the period A.D. 500–700. These centuries corresponded to the later stages of Nazca culture, according to the rough estimates of archaeologists.

The 68-to-70-degree angle came to her attention because she found it marked by the immense borders of the Great Rectangle, as well as by a number of other long lines connected to this figure or located nearby. Elsewhere on the pampa she made further discoveries of the same angle incorporated into various

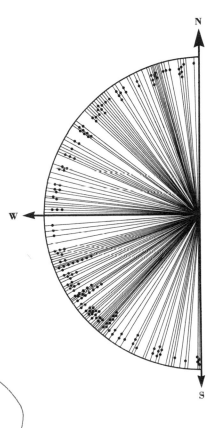

The only set of measurements ever published by Maria Reiche appeared as a diagram in a 1949 pamphlet. This diagram, redrawn here for clarity, shows the directions of over 250 lines; Maria shows these directions as reversible (i.e., a northwest line could also point southeast). The dots represent repeated cases of the same direction. Though a few clusters are apparent, numerous lines fall outside the fairly narrow band of the horizon important for astronomical events.

kinds of figures. The fact that it was repeated in widely scattered areas of the desert convinced her that deliberate astronomical planning was the only explanation.

In her search for the critical angle, Maria made no attempt to distinguish between different types of markings. This meant that she checked the angles of not only single straight lines but also the sides of broad avenues and even the detailed parts of complicated geometrical figures. Thus among the dozen or so examples of this angle, she included several lines that actually belonged to a single side of a cleared area such as a triangle or trapezoid. By treating all the figures alike, there was obviously a higher chance that she would find *some* line that fitted the angle. The fact that the examples she chose were so inconsistent was a serious weakness in her approach.

Clearly, Maria never set out deliberately to deceive anyone or to manipulate her measurements. Instead, her approach to the lines was colored by the fact that she was already strongly persuaded by the astronomical theory she had inherited from Kosok. She set forth his ideas in her early articles with scarcely any discussion. Because she was so convinced beforehand that his argument was correct, she was apparently satisfied by her sketchy attempts to prove that the lines actually *did* point to the sun, moon and stars.

Maria's early writings contain only bare references to possible astronomical alignments other than the 68-to-70-degree angle. Surprisingly, she hardly mentions the solstice lines with which Kosok's theories and her own investigations began, and only two sites with star lines are described in any detail. In no case did she publish details of the actual angles she had measured in the field. (If she had done so, it would be much easier for other investigators to evaluate her work.) To be fair to Maria, she prefaced many of her conclusions with the statement that she was still at a preliminary stage in her work and that a fuller treatment of the material would follow.

Sadly, this overall assessment of the astronomy of the lines never materialized in the decades that followed. In all her subsequent writings, Maria repeats only very general arguments in favor of their astronomical purpose, most of which she had already stated in 1949. Since then, she says she has discovered many more solar and lunar lines but has never specified the details of these new alignments. This meager output of published results is the most disappointing aspect of Maria's achievements at Nazca. Organizing and writing up her results must have represented a chore to her, a distraction from the work of surveying and preserving that she conducted so patiently and loved so much.

As a result, she neglected the general question of whether there were enough astronomical lines to rule out the possibility of chance. Instead, she concentrated more and more on just a few individual animal figures that seemed to have an astronomical connection. By focusing on these detailed cases, Maria never adequately resolved the major question of whether the alignments were deliberate or accidental.

Nazca Decoded: The Hawkins Approach

WHAT WAS NEEDED was a fresh approach. Gerald S. Hawkins, who had a background and personality vastly different from Maria's, had good reason to be concerned with the difficulty of assessing whether alignments were coincidental or genuine. In 1963 he had raised a commotion in the academic world

Gerald S. Hawkins, best known for his work on Stonehenge, conducted a survey at Nazca in 1968 with the help of Peruvian engineers.

by publishing his paper "Stonehenge Decoded" in the British science journal *Nature*. This arose from a visit two years earlier to the impressive ancient ring of standing stones on Salisbury Plain in southern England. On this occasion Hawkins, who was then lecturing in astronomy at Boston University, was struck with the idea that the layout of stones and other features at the five-thousand-year-old site might conceal an astronomical meaning.

To test the idea, he took a plan of Stonehenge and drew lines between pairs of stones, pits or posts previously identified by archaeologists. These lines were then "fed" into a computer programmed to match them against the motion of the sun and moon. Though a computer was not absolutely essential for such an operation, its use was one of the main reasons why Hawkins' work created such a sensation in the popular media. In the early 1960s computers were still a novelty; the fact that a modern machine could "decode" an ancient observatory was to many an extraordinary development.

Not everyone was impressed, however, since many archaeologists felt that Hawkins' results had to be due to a combination of chance and his own wishful thinking. It took several years for the astronomical theory to win a measure of acceptance within the academic community. By that time Hawkins had corrected earlier mistakes and refined his measurements. Today few doubt his basic case that the builders of Stonehenge were aware of the major cycles of the sun and moon. Even so, we have little idea how important their astronomy was in relation to the other religious and social purposes undoubtedly served by the monument. In addition, there is no real agreement about how advanced the skywatching skills of the Stonehenge people became, nor exactly how precise they were to begin with; these important matters of detail remain open to conjecture. Indeed, the evidence of a single site is inevitably limited, particularly one as complex and as heavily vandalized as Stonehenge.

During the years of the Stonehenge debate, Maria Reiche continued her labors at Nazca in relative obscurity. Her lack of interest in publishing her work widely meant that there was virtually no controversy or recognition surrounding it. Nevertheless, when a British filmmaker who had traveled throughout the Andes, Tony Morrison, told Hawkins about Reiche's theories, Hawkins was immediately intrigued. Here was another challenge similar to that of Stonehenge.

Faced with thousands of possible sight lines at Nazca, Hawkins decided against launching a full-scale survey. Instead, he chose to concentrate on one particular area at the edge of the Ingenio Valley, where there was the greatest concentration of markings. As a result, his study represented only a tentative exploration of the problem, rather than an exhaustive analysis.

Besides taking measurements on the ground, Hawkins arranged for an aerial survey based on photogrammetry, a photographic mapping technique. Hawkins was attracted to this method because of the success of a similar survey he had supervised at Stonehenge three years earlier. On that occasion, the new measurements provided by the survey showed that many of the Stonehenge alignments were more accurate than he had previously thought.

Now Hawkins applied the same technique to Nazca: at his request, on August 1, 1968, the crew of a Peruvian air force plane flew over the pampa and took a series of high-resolution black-and-white photographs with a stereo camera. The resulting overlapping prints were carefully pieced together to form a continuous three-dimensional record of a large strip about 1½ miles long by 1 mile wide. Then cartographers at the Peruvian Geophysical Institute used the photo mosaic to plot a highly accurate map. Besides showing the natural relief of the pampa with the aid of contours, this map recorded every man-made marking visible on the photographs: there were nearly a hundred such markings in all.

After measuring the directions of all the lines plotted on the chart, Hawkins was ready to run the same computer program

has anyone ever worked the sites with crystals... as they were supposed to.??

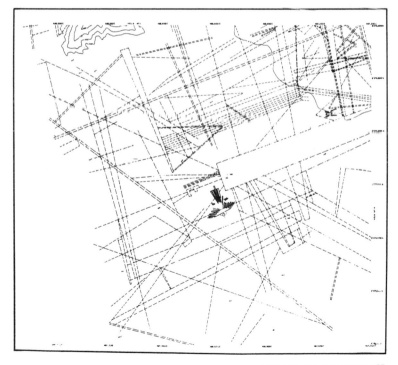

Detail of the air survey organized by Gerald S. Hawkins in 1968 and conducted by the Peruvian Air Force.

he had applied to Stonehenge. It was designed to compare individual alignments against the movements of the sun, moon and stars along the horizon. The program took into account the slight changes in sky motions that had accumulated since the Nazca period. Another correction was also added for the height of the local horizon around the pampa; since the foothills of the Andes lay to the east, this height factor was in some cases considerable. With these adjustments complete, Hawkins fed a total of 186 line directions to the computer.

In weighing the results, he adopted a stringent "all-or-nothing" policy. For the astronomical theory to be convincing, Hawkins argued that the lines *had* to point to one particular pattern of celestial events (such as the solstices or the major moonrises or moonsets). If the sky objects they indicated were an inconsistent mixed bag (including, say, faint stars along with planets), then Hawkins was prepared to discount the entire theory.

Furthermore, it was essential that an overwhelming majority of the lines should successfully match up with astronomical events. If only a few lines were involved, then the possibility was strong that even the alignments that *did* work might be due purely to coincidence. In Hawkins' view, the astronomical theory was acceptable only if it provided a *total* explanation for the lines.

However, single, all-embracing solutions to the Nazca mystery have always proved elusive. Of the 186 directions Hawkins selected, 39 fitted the major angles of the sun and moon to within a margin of 1 degree on either side. At first glance, this might seem like an impressive result. Nevertheless, there were actually many sky "targets" to choose from: no fewer than eighteen different solar and lunar positions. By chance alone, we would expect about 10 percent (or nineteen) of the lines to match these crucial positions.

Even though the computer found thirty-nine potential sun-moon lines (twenty more than we would expect by chance), Hawkins was still doubtful. The results were not very consistent: some cleared triangles, for instance, scored successful "hits" against the sun or moon, while other triangles did not.

Moreover, Hawkins suggested that even the total of thirty-nine might be exaggerated because it included eight "duplicates," cases where a single line matched a winter solstice event in one direction and a summer solstice event in the other. Hawkins argued that these cases might be suspect, simply because the sun's swing through the sky during the year creates a symmetrical pattern of rising and setting points. Thus, winter positions on the horizon naturally fall opposite summer ones.

These eight double-ended alignments might therefore be due to the harmony of celestial motions, rather than to the deliberate intentions of the Nazca builders.

All these arguments convinced Hawkins that the theory of sun and moon alignments he had applied so successfully to Stonehenge could not possibly account for the layout of the Nazca lines. Nor were star alignments any more promising, as further computer tests showed. Turning to the planets, Hawkins knew that they are always visible inside a fairly narrow band of the sky (within 30 degrees on either side of the east-west line). Since fewer than half of the Nazca lines pointed toward this band, there was little reason to pursue the possibility further.

Another plausible theory might have been that the lines commemorated an unusual, short-term event in the sky—a comet or a supernova (a brilliant exploding star). Yet, here again, Hawkins showed that his lines did not tend to cluster toward any particular single direction. Concluding an account of the negative results in his popular book *Beyond Stonehenge*, Hawkins declared confidently that "the star-sun-moon calendar theory had been killed by the computer."

Though Hawkins had pronounced the astronomical theory dead, a few critics still thought a postmortem of his methods was necessary. One area of concern was the way in which he had selected alignments for the study. Like Maria Reiche, Hawkins treated the different types of markings alike, so that triangles and trapezoids as well as individual straight lines were included in the analysis. This was a reasonable enough decision. But there was one curious procedure among the details of his study: he measured the imaginary center lines of triangles rather than their actual sides. In fact, the center lines of several cleared areas were marked by heaps of stone located at their extreme

Air view of the Great Rectangle, showing one of the stone mounds located at either end. Many lines converge on the mounds, which seem to have been used for offerings involving pottery vessels.

ends (the most obvious example being the Great Rectangle). However, there were many cleared figures without these mounds, and it would surely have been more consistent to measure just the sides of each feature.

A more serious problem was the completeness of the aerial survey. Though the chart Hawkins worked from was remarkably precise (accurate to within a fifth of a degree, as he convincingly demonstrated), nevertheless it omitted many lines visible on the pampa. During one of his field sessions, Hawkins compared the chart with an actual group of markings on the ground, and claimed that any line wider than about a foot across had been recorded. Yet even a casual glance at an aerial photograph reveals that a large number of quite distinct lines are missing from the survey map.

This is not really surprising, since the visibility of particular lines from the air varies enormously from day to day and from hour to hour. In fact, the color contrast between the lines and the surrounding pampa is so slight that good aerial photographs can be taken only in the early morning or evening, when slanting sunlight emphasizes the slightly raised borders belonging to each line. Even under these conditions, the variation in detail between one set of Nacza photographs and another is striking.

Moreover, similar difficulties are encountered by surveyors

British explorer and filmmaker Tony Morrison, right, taking notes from an informant during one of his many expeditions to remote regions of highland Bolivia.

on the ground: some lines are virtually invisible, again depending on the time of day. The problem of defining a particular sample of lines is not, therefore, just confined to the case of Hawkins' air survey. No matter how exhaustively any program of fieldwork is pursued on the pampa, some lines are always bound to elude researchers.

For this reason, a purely statistical approach to the question of astronomy at Nazca will always be somewhat unsatisfactory. Nevertheless, as a preliminary, pioneering investigation of a complex problem, Hawkins' research certainly deserves credit. It was the first systematic attempt to grapple with the problem of the astronomy of the lines. In addition, his discussions of the geology of the pampa and of the pottery he found there were more thorough than any previous accounts.

The Problem of Star Lines

HAWKINS HIMSELF was well aware of the limitations of relying too heavily on statistics. In fact, a decade after his original Nazca survey, he reconsidered the possibility that a few significant lines *could* be astronomical. His fresh involvement was again prompted by Tony Morrison, the British explorer and filmmaker who had originally engaged his interest in the lines. Morrison himself has visited Nazca regularly since 1961; in fact, he has produced several BBC documentaries on the lines, together with one of the best popular books written about the subject. This book, *Pathways to the Gods*, published in 1978, includes many striking photos and anecdotes of Morrison's adventures in the Andes.

As he was preparing the book, Morrison approached Hawkins with the idea of featuring in it some of the thirty-nine possible alignments that had been found by the computer. Though Hawkins had based his original report strictly on the "all-or-nothing" logic of statistics, he now decided to single out particular alignments that *might* be significant.

There were some obvious candidates: the sides of the Great Rectangle, for instance, and the grid of parallel lines beside it. (These could have indicated the rise of the Pleiades around

A.D. 600 to 700.) Other possibilities included a solstice alignment that cut across the outstretched wings of the giant bird beside the Rectangle and another solstice line that formed the stem of the flower design. In addition, Morrison briefly discussed a few similar associations between animals and star lines.

But were these alignments intended by the builders? Hawkins himself was noncommittal when it came to this question; he had merely raised the possibility that they were. Nevertheless, Morrison reproduced the original aerial survey in *Pathways to the Gods* with a number of the possible sight lines boldly emphasized. He gave them labels such as "Plaza of the Pleiades," "Grid of the Pleiades," "Grid of the Sun" and so on. A casual browser, glancing at such titles, might be forgiven for assuming that the astronomical identity of these markings had been firmly proven.

The significance of individual figures associated with astronomical lines had, of course, been pondered for many years by Maria Reiche. Not surprisingly, most of the examples discussed by Morrison were already known to her and had been described in her previous writings (as Morrison acknowledged in his text). In fact, Reiche had suggested several further possibilities, such as the solstice lines that seemed to be connected to the beaks of two separate bird designs. Altogether, she proposed about a half-dozen cases where astronomical alignments were apparently linked to animal figures. (This was out of a total of perhaps thirty or so animal designs.)

One of Maria's most interesting cases concerns the spider beside the Great Rectangle. This figure has always excited attention because of its giant scale (nearly 150 feet long) and highly realistic proportions. As early as 1947, Kosok and Reiche suggested that a straight line crossing over the figure marked an astronomical orientation, though at first they did not specify which.

The line in question runs between two "radiating centers," one located close to the spider at a gap in the border of the Great Rectangle, and the other at one corner of another large rectangle nearly a mile away. Though many lines converge on both these centers from all directions of the pampa, Maria insisted that the one line crossing the spider was special. The Nazca people built this line, she thinks, to indicate the setting of the constellation Orion in the evening sky.

Reiche's basic idea is quite plausible. The people of Nazca may have needed to observe constellations such as Orion in order to set up a calendar. This calendar would operate differently from one based either on the moon's phases or on the swing of the sun along the horizon from midwinter to midsummer. In fact, a single star rises and sets at roughly the same points on the skyline from one night to the next, but the *time* at which this happens changes slowly as the seasons pass. (The "star clock" actually gains about four minutes a day.)

During part of the year, the star will rise in daylight and so be invisible. As the timing of the event slips back earlier and earlier, however, there will come a day when the star just begins to be visible in the early morning for the first time. Before the sun gathers strength, the star will gleam for a few minutes in the dawn sky.

The dates on which these so-called heliacal star risings occur are almost exactly the same each year, so they were naturally useful to calendar keepers in the ancient world. For example, the heliacal rising of Sirius around midsummer was the most vital event in the ancient Egyptian calendar, since it coincided with the annual flooding of the Nile on which all agriculture depended.

In an exactly similar way, Maria Reiche supposed that observers at Nazca watched for heliacal risings and settings to help correct their calendar. The only example she has discussed in any detail concerns the figure of the monkey with the spiral tail. If her interpretation is correct, star lines associated with the monkey would have helped predict the arrival of underground water in the Nazca Valley in late November.

Plausible as this speculation may seem, *all* theories involving star alignments pose unique problems for the investigator. Taken by itself, a single star indicator is highly questionable because there are so many potential star targets available. (There are about a dozen of the brightest, or first magnitude, stars, while more than a hundred others can be seen rising over the Andes on a clear evening.)

Then there is the problem of dating, particularly acute in a case like Nazca, where the precise age of the markings is unknown. Dating the star lines is critical because of a steady, subtle shift in the rising and setting positions of the stars from one century to the next. While sun and moon alignments would still function today with only slight corrections necessary, any star line would be useless after just two or three generations.

The shifting positions of the stars occur because the earth wobbles slightly as it rotates around its axis; each wobble takes about 26,000 years to complete. Astronomers refer to this cycle as the "precession of the equinoxes." Despite the immense time period involved in the entire wobble, the gradual drift of star positions along the horizon might have been noticed during the lifetime of a single attentive observer: over about fifty years, the observer would see a shift roughly equal to the diameter of the full moon. If we suppose that a Nazca line was built to indicate the setting of a star in Orion, after three centuries the line would be more than 1 degree off target.

For many years, Maria Reiche has suggested that the Nazcans were aware of this precession effect. Indeed, she thinks their knowledge of it accounts for some of the distinctive patterns on the pampa, such as the grids of multiple lines all roughly parallel to each other. These would represent successive alignments to a single star, each one replaced as the star gradually shifted its position over the centuries. She has also speculated about the long cleared triangles, suggesting that they started off as single, narrow observation lines, and later grew wider and wider to accommodate the angle between old and new sightings of the same star.

Her ideas would be much more convincing if wider evidence could be found linking the lines to the stars. But virtually *any* line can be made to fit a star at one time or another, given the fact that there are so many stars, and that they all "drifted" considerably across the horizon during the thousand or so years covered by the Nazca culture.

To drive the point home, consider again the example of the Great Rectangle. Maria has claimed that its borders were directed toward the rising of the Pleiades around A.D. 500 to 700. In his original report, Hawkins confirmed the accuracy of her calculations: the borders of the Great Rectangle would indeed have indicated the brightest star in the Pleiades in A.D. 610. But there was a problem: the same alignment, he pointed out, also coincided with many other stars at different dates, such as the rise of Regulus in A.D. 410, and the setting of Antares in A.D. 210. Since there is so much uncertainty about the actual dating of the figures, it is impossible to choose between one potential star alignment and another.

In fact, even if the choices are narrowed down to just the dozen brightest stars in the sky over a period of five hundred years, there is still a one-in-three chance that *any line* will pick up a star target.

All this suggests that most claims involving the stars are highly suspect as long as the precise age of the lines remains unknown. As for the sun and moon, few alignments have been documented beyond the barest mention, never mind in the kind of detail that might ultimately prove convincing. At present, only about a sixth of all the animal figures appear to be linked to possible solar lines (and in several cases, the connection seems tenuous).

The possibility that *all* the individual examples described by Reiche and by Morrison might be due purely to chance means that it is essential to pursue some kind of overall statistical as-

the lines or the triangles accurately mark the precession but we will not be able to see them in time...

sessment such as Hawkins attempted. Even though his survey can be faulted for incompleteness, its negative result strongly implies that astronomy cannot provide a total, all-embracing explanation for the Nazca lines.

At the same time, this type of test still leaves open the possibility that *some* lines were, indeed, astronomical. Skywatching may well have figured as just one minor aspect of a whole range of activities that originally inspired their construction.

In other words, if we seek a reasonable approach to the complexities posed by the astronomical theory, it seems necessary to strike a careful balance. Too much reliance on statistics, on the one hand, or on studies of particular individual lines, on the other, clearly leads to trouble. By 1980 it was clear that the verdict on the astronomy of the lines was likely to remain inconclusive unless a more thorough, well-rounded program of investigations was launched. The following chapters describe the results of just such a comprehensive new approach to the mystery of the lines.

CHAPTER 6

WATCHERS OF THE DARK CLOUDS

Creatures of the Celestial River

UNTIL 1980, MOST RESEARCHERS involved in the astronomical theory overlooked one important area of evidence: the living traditions of skywatching still practiced in the Andes today.

For instance, despite decades of contact with the people of Nazca, Maria Reiche apparently has little interest in their ideas about the sky. She once remarked to me that local people "know their stars" and mentioned, as one example, their constellation of the pelican, yet it was obvious that she attached little importance to this type of information.

Only later did I discover that the local people actually identify the pelican with parts of the constellation we call Orion. This was intriguing, for either Maria's theory that the spider figure was associated with Orion was wrong, or else local beliefs had changed drastically since the time of the line builders. Was it possible that folklore of this kind might contain clues about the astronomy of the ancient Nazcans, despite the catastrophic impact of the Spanish Conquest?

There is a long history of neglect and condescension toward native Peruvian skywatching. Though several early Spanish chroniclers were sufficiently interested to compile lists of constellations and calendar festivals, they frequently introduced this material with apologetic remarks. For example, the Jesuit Father Bernabé Cobo, writing in 1653, recognized the central importance of the Milky Way in the cosmology of the Incas. He avoided further discussion, however, by asserting that their beliefs about it were "a world of nonsense which it would take too long to tell about."

While the prejudice of the conquering Spanish is understandable, it is less easy to explain why modern scholars almost totally ignored the heritage of Andean astronomy until recently. It was only in the 1970s that anthropologists began systematic efforts to record the cosmology of the Quechua-speaking inhabitants of remote villages in the mountains. Even so, they often assumed that the constellations described by local informants corresponded to the same star patterns as our own constellations. Some anthropologists actually dismissed the importance of Quechua astronomy in terms that echoed those of Spanish chroniclers centuries before.

During the past decade, however, attitudes changed rapidly as a new generation of students emerged, determined to understand the communities and traditions of the high Andes more deeply. One such scholar, Gary Urton, spent a year and a half living in an isolated village about 30 miles from the city of Cuzco. At this village, called Misminay, located among 10,000-foot-high mountains, local farmers gradually revealed to him their remarkably complex vision of the universe. Urton found that their constellations and their beliefs about the Milky Way corresponded in many details to those noted among the Incas by the Spanish chroniclers.

At the Crossroads of the Earth and the Sky, Urton's book about his fieldwork in Misminay, came as a revelation when it appeared in 1981. Together with research by other scholars carried out in several different communities, it opened a new perspective on the outlook of the Quechua.

It is now clear that native Andeans have managed to preserve the essentials of their religious beliefs and calendrical system over at least four centuries. Widely scattered villages observe the same identifications of the stars and the same major fiesta days, and show similar patterns of village layout and orientation. Considering the long record of Spanish influence and cruel repression, the survival of this unified core of belief is astonishing. Moreover, much of the astronomical lore that Urton recorded is utterly foreign to European conceptions of the sky.

Today, when our night vision is overpowered by city lights, we can scarcely imagine the awareness of the stars our ancestors had even a century ago. Among high-altitude communities in the Andes, located far from any source of electricity, the night sky still exerts an overwhelming presence. Though I knew this

An astronomer of the Inca period as depicted by Poma around 1600.

A typical house interior in Misminay, a village in the high Andes about thirty miles northwest of Cuzco, photographed in 1977.

from reading Urton's book, my first glimpse of it came almost as a shock. Even before my eyes had adjusted to the darkness, I was aware of the intense glow of the Milky Way arching over my head. It completely dominated the sky and seemed brighter than moonlight. For the first time I began to appreciate its importance to the Quechua and why they picture it as "the River," the source of all moisture on earth. Though I looked for individual star patterns, most of them seemed submerged under one immensely long, luminous stream.

Indeed, the Milky Way was so radiant that it was the *gaps* along its course that first drew my eye. Dark patches, where no stars shone, were actually more conspicuous than the ordinary constellation patterns I was familiar with from studying charts of the night sky. These distinctive silhouettes are created by clouds of interstellar dust that shut off the light from distant stars. Urton describes the patches as "dark cloud constellations," and has shown how vital they are to Quechua beliefs about the cosmos.

Perhaps the most impressive of these patches is the llama, a

Diagram of the "dark cloud" animals of the Milky Way traditionally identified by Andean skywatchers.

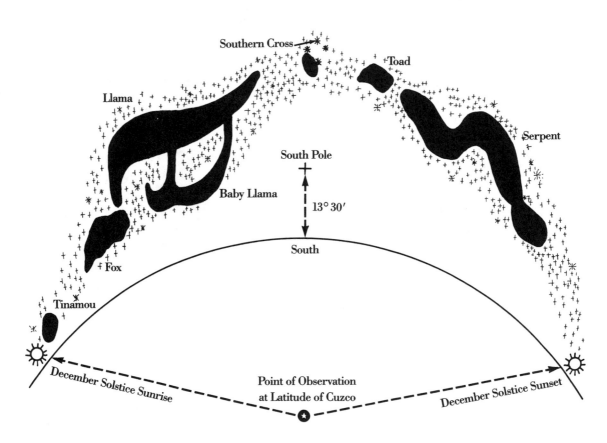

dark shape that almost fills the entire sky on cloudless nights during the rainy season. It is said to be suckling its baby, a smaller dark patch connected to its lower edge. Described as "blacker than the night sky" by Francisco de Avila in 1608, the llama was obviously well known to the chroniclers and their Inca informants.

After recovering from my initial shock at the Milky Way's brilliance, I recognized the llama and its baby almost immediately. As my vision adjusted, I found the "eyes of the llama" (two bright stars, Alpha and Beta, in Centaurus), and suddenly the entire outline seemed to spring into shape above me. For a moment I had the illusion of a huge living black creature in the sky. The more abstract patterns of our own constellations had never seized my imagination like this.

Other less immediately obvious animals are scattered along the central course of the Milky Way. These consist of a long zigzag streak, the serpent, together with a fox located close to the llama; also several dark blobs, variously identified as a toad and a pair of partridgelike birds known as tinamous.

The Quechua sometimes weave fables around these figures, as a woman informant once explained to Urton. She was exasperated by the difficulty she experienced in picking out the animals, but her husband saw them well and used to talk about the nightly race between the toad and the tinamou. Unexpectedly, the creeping toad always wins. (In reality, the toad cloud reaches the horizon each night before either of the two tinamou clouds.) Thus her husband likes to characterize himself as a toad in comparison to others who are timid tinamous.

However, the shapes seen in the Milky Way signify far more than mere pretexts for storytelling. The Quechua envision the Milky Way as the celestial river flowing through the sky, and for them it is a reflection of the waters that circulate through the streams and rivers on earth. Moreover, it plays an active part in this circulation of water. As it sets below the horizon, the River is believed to take in water from the cosmic sea before passing into the underworld. On rising in the east, the Milky Way transports moisture up into the atmosphere and is responsible for rain, thus completing the cycle of flowing water. This association of stars with moisture has a practical aspect, since the Quechua often watch the relative brightness and clarity of the stars from one evening to the next in order to forecast rain.

The Quechua are also convinced that the dark cloud animals actively contribute to this life-sustaining cycle. Four centuries ago, Avila recorded this belief about the *yacana* (llama) in the sky: "They say that this *Yacana* comes down to earth at midnight when it cannot be noticed or seen and drinks all the water from the sea. They say that if she did not drink this water, the entire world would be drowned."

Again, this was not merely a fanciful image, but almost certainly reflected actual observation. During the dry weather of the Andean summer season, the llama and most of the other dark cloud creatures stay below the horizon. (Thus they are "unseen," drinking in the cosmic sea.) As each animal gradually reappears in the sky throughout the various stages of planting and harvesting, so the Andean observers have naturally endowed each one with its own special significance.

The serpent, for instance, has a connection with moisture through images of rainbows and springs. The legendary "Rainbow Serpent," or *amaru*, is thought of as a double-headed monster who rises up out of a spring following a rain shower. The *amaru* then arches its multicolored body through the sky and buries one of its heads in another spring. Urton believes some of the *amaru*'s supernatural qualities were inspired by stories of the giant boas and anacondas of the Amazon, since as far back as Inca times there have always been contacts between the mountains and the jungle.

Though the actual name of the dark cloud serpent, Mach'acuay, refers to less spectacular local snakes common in the Cuzco region, there is little doubt of the cloud's association with moisture. Like the Rainbow Serpent, the dark serpent shape rises from a water source (the cosmic sea), arches its body through the sky, and eventually buries its head in the opposite horizon. The time period during which this occurs exactly spans the rainy season: the head first appears over the skyline as planting begins in August, and by the start of February (the most intense period of rain), its body looms vertically overhead at midnight.

Like most Quechua beliefs, these mythical animal images are rooted in everyday observation. The dry months, when the serpent and the other dark clouds are concealed beneath the earth, is also the time when actual serpents around Cuzco are in hibernation. The arrival of the celestial serpent's head corresponds not only to the onset of rain but also to the emergence of terrestrial serpents from their long sleep. (In fact, the most common snake of the Cuzco area gives birth to its young at this time.) Furthermore, rainbows—the *amarus*—can also only appear in the sky during the rainy season.

Far from indulging in irrational or fanciful folktales for mere amusement, the Quechua have developed myths that are grounded in logical observations of the natural world. Their beliefs about serpents clearly represent a consistent set of ideas linking astronomy to the cycles of climate and animal behavior.

Urton has demonstrated equally intricate relationships between events on earth and each one of the dark cloud animals. The celestial toad, for instance, follows after the serpent, first appearing toward dawn around the beginning of October. This is the time when toads emerge from their burrows in the earth and begin mating.

Two common local names for toads, "Earth Child" and "Turning of the Earth," emphasize how important their burrowing activity is to the Quechua. They associate the image of emerging toads with the crops that must also eventually sprout from the life-giving earth. If they encounter many toads in their fields during October, they take it as a sign of an abundant harvest to come. Similarly, if they hear particularly loud and insistent croaking during the mating season, they believe abundant rain and crops will follow. Once again, the arrival of one of the dark animal shapes in the sky reflects the timing of important down-to-earth events.

Clearly, then, the Quechua custom of recognizing animals among clouds in the Milky Way is no mere idle pastime, based simply on coincidental shapes. Instead, they carefully observe many natural cycles associated with a particular animal, and link these cycles accurately to the complex motions of the night sky.

Furthermore, according to the Spanish chronicler Polo de Ondegardo, the Incas conceived of the dark clouds as exerting a direct effect on the fertility of beasts on earth. In his 1571 treatise on the "errors and superstitions of the Indians," Polo claims the Incas "believed that all the animals and birds on the earth had their likeness in the sky, in whose responsibility was their procreation and augmentation."

Like the Quechua today, the Incas obviously projected their daily concerns and observations onto patterns in the sky. Polo's remark suggests, however, that this was not just a one-way connection: they also believed that these same patterns could actively influence the course of events around them.

Dialogue with the Stars

BESIDES THE DARK SHAPES in the Milky Way, the Quechua also recognize star-to-star constellations, most of them located along the fringes of the Milky Way. These constellations are

A street scene in Pacariqtambo, about forty miles south of Cuzco. Though the villagers lack electricity, running water and most other material comforts, they engage in a complex cycle of ceremonial and social activities.

generally identified with inanimate objects: for example, there are several crosses, a plow, a storehouse and a llama corral. Unlike the dark clouds, which the Quechua link to the cycles of nature, they connect the star-to-star constellations to the destiny of humans.

With his artist wife, Julia, Gary Urton lived during 1981 and 1982 in Pacariqtambo, a remote Quechua village located about five hours' drive south of Cuzco along a dirt road through the mountains. Here he established that the villagers recognize at least thirty-five separate stars or constellations. Besides the dark cloud animals, they identify several star-to-star patterns that differ from our own familiar ones. For example, they view the belt and sword of Orion as a self-contained group and speak of it as "the Plow."

In the mind of the Pacariqtambo farmer, the Plow is associated with the harvest because it first appears above the eastern horizon in the early morning at harvest time. (The Pleiades, appropriately named "the Storehouse," have a similar association and are also visible during the harvest.)

This all-important period from late April to late June is marked not only by the presence of the Plow and the Storehouse in the sky, but also by changes in the elaborate religious festivals sponsored by different sections of the community. In Urton's view, there is a kind of "dialogue" between the cycle of ceremonies conducted by the villagers and the cycle of the stars overhead.

To understand this point more fully, we might take the case of the Southern Cross, one of the most distinctive constellations in the Andean sky. The villagers of Pacariqtambo identify it as "the Small Cross." In addition, they refer to another star group,

Scenes from the farming year at Pacariqtambo during 1982–83: (opposite, below) *breaking the soil with foot plows in May*; (left) *threshing grain crops in January*; (below left) *hoeing maize in February*; (below right) *planting with oxen, also in February.*

consisting of parts of our constellation of Scorpio, as "the Large Cross."

Once again, the arrival in the sky of both these star groups corresponds closely to the agricultural cycle: the Small Cross becomes visible in early September as the crops are being planted, and the Large Cross appears for the first time on November 30, which marks the fiesta day of San Andrés and the official end of planting.

As part of the celebration of San Andrés, wooden crosses are carried to the hilltops by each of the groups within the community. These crosses stand overlooking the fields and are thought to protect the crops from hail throughout the growing season. After about five months they are finally removed during a festival known as Cruz Velakuy staged on May 3. This date also corresponds to the time when both celestial crosses begin to disappear in the early morning twilight. It is a moment of high anticipation within the village, since the harvest is about to begin.

So the religious activity of the villagers as they carry their crosses up to the mountains clearly reflects the appearances of the stars above them. They view both the celestial and man-made crosses as essential aspects of the life-giving cycle that sustains the community.

To put it simply, the people of Pacariqtambo blend human, agricultural and astronomical rhythms into one intricate pattern. This is not a rigid framework that constricts their lives, since there is considerable flexibility in the timing of all their activities. For instance, in deciding on the most favorable moment to begin planting a farmer does not necessarily depend on the appearance of a particular star on a specific date, but will rely on his own judgment. Nevertheless, if he then recognizes a particular constellation associated with planting, it lends an extra sense of security to his actions.

Today the Quechua use the printed almanacs of the Catholic church to determine most of their festival dates; before the advent of such aids, they must have relied much more heavily on astronomical events to set their calendar straight. All the same, Urton's work suggests that the purpose of stargazing was probably always more than the mere fixing of a practical agricultural timetable. By recognizing a particular star event, the Quechua confirm and reinforce the decisions habitually taken by both the individual and the community.

The Sky Lore
of Modern Nazca

THE FARM OF JUAN ELIAS lies beside an ancient Nazca cemetery. To visit the farm, I walked along a sandy river terrace strewn with bleached human bones and broken pottery. Then I descended through a grove of twisted carob trees, catching a glimpse of rows of neatly planted green cornstalks beyond. As I reached the fence, I recognized Gary Urton, his face weatherbeaten from weeks of laboring in the fields around Pacariqtambo.

For several years, Urton had combined his long stays in the highland village with occasional visits to Nazca, in the hope of discovering similar traces of the traditional pattern of life there. Now he was strolling among the corn rows, conversing in Spanish with Juan Elias, a broad-shouldered man whose powerfully built body and taut, darkly complexioned face made him look far younger than his sixty-nine years. Elias was gesturing at the crops around him, evidently describing some of the techniques he had acquired in tending his fields over the past fifty or so years. While they talked, I retired to the shelter of a carob tree, grateful to be out of the sun.

Later, Urton joined me at the foot of the tree and told me what he had learned from Elias. Like all the other farmers Urton has spoken to around Nazca, Elias was mainly concerned with water. ("The primordial struggle is the lack of water," he

Irrigated fields beside the farm of Juan Elias in the Nazca Valley.

had told Urton.) Conditions have definitely deteriorated over the past twenty years, partly because more wells have been dug farther up the valley, causing the water table to shrink. As a result, it is no longer possible to grow a second crop of corn, melons and sweet potatoes without irrigation, as was once common practice. Nevertheless, Elias thinks that since the advent of chemical fertilizers and herbicides, local farmers can now afford to be more casual about picking a date for planting their crops.

Anticipating water resources is another matter. Here is an issue of constant concern, for the amount of water present in the underground irrigation canals directly affects both the type of cultivation and the size of the area that can be planted. For instance, every November Elias has to decide whether there will be sufficient water to irrigate a fresh planting of cotton, or whether he will be forced to prune back the previous year's crop instead. (This results in a less productive yield.)

How can he judge what the future will bring? The answer is his skillful knowledge of the cloud cover over the distant Andes. According to Elias, if the clouds are heavy and black around the end of July and August, then he expects a good season. The amount of snow on the high peaks is another clue. When Urton asked him if he ever looked at the stars to judge the weather or the timing of agriculture, he merely shrugged; he only knew about "practical things," he said.

Anthropologist Gary Urton discussing irrigation with farmers in the Nazca Valley in 1984.

Other Nazca farmers whom Urton interviewed were less pragmatic and did express an awareness of astronomy. Since his time was always limited because of the demands of his major project in Pacariqtambo, Urton was unable to build up a truly thorough picture of local sky lore. Nevertheless, in 1982 he established that people in Nazca do indeed recognize many of the same major constellations as do people in the high Andes: for instance, they identify the dark cloud Llama and the Storehouse (the Pleiades). To predict rain, they watch the shimmering of the stars and Venus from one evening to the next, a practice also common at Pacariqtambo.

The appearance of unusual birds over the valley (pelicans or herons from the coast, or condors from the mountains) is another signal of rain. To confirm their predictions, the farmers look at the horns of the moon during its first crescent phase; if the horns are at a right angle to the horizon it is a good omen, but if they are at a slanting angle it is thought that drought will follow.

The first crescent is also considered the best moon phase for planting maize, castrating animals or cutting down carob trees; it is unwise to attempt such operations during the new moon, since disease or insect blight will result.

Perhaps the most interesting item of local knowledge is the identification of the place on the skyline where the sun rises around the time of the December solstice. This place is a giant sand dune perched high on the mountains overlooking the Nazca Valley. Known as Cerro Blanco, it forms a striking landmark, since it is composed of brilliant white beach sand blown some 30 miles from the coast. Local farmers also refer to it as the "Volcano of Water," believing it to be the source of the underground streams and canals that sustain the valley. Since these subterranean waters do, in fact, begin flowing around the time of the December solstice, it is not surprising that people in Nazca relate the arrival of water to the rising of the sun over Cerro Blanco.

They also anticipate the December solstice by watching the movement of the pelican constellation (made up of parts of Orion). At midnight around the solstice, the pelican passes vertically overhead (or through the zenith, as astronomers term this point directly over the observer). If we recall that the appearance of pelicans from the coast in the daytime sky over Nazca is considered an omen of rain, then once again this folklore implies a link between celestial motions and the arrival of water.

Urton found that similar ideas were visualized in great detail among the highland villages of Misminay and Pacariqtambo. To begin with, he discovered that the Quechua have developed a scheme of directions quite unlike our own. Since there is no star located anywhere close to the South Pole, north-south lines are much less obvious or important to observers in the southern hemisphere.

Once again, the Milky Way provides the most natural frame of reference. Its rising and setting positions on the horizon provide the Quechua with the equivalent of our cardinal directions. Thus, the Milky Way influences the layout of villages, since major streets are laid out toward these same Milky Way directions, and these streets in turn separate the different social groups that make up the community. Furthermore, all local streams and irrigation canals are thought to originate from the same directions as the Milky Way, since it is visualized as the celestial river.

The sun is also drawn into the pattern, for the Quechua apparently observe the fact that the sun rises into the central course of the Milky Way at only two times during the year, around the December and June solstices.

In other words, the Quechua have developed a unified model for their universe based on the Milky Way. In this model, the calendar provided by the sun is part of the same scheme that determines the flowing of water and the organization of villages.

Moreover, as we have seen, the dark cloud animals in the Milky Way are connected to the cycles of agriculture and to the natural behavior of creatures on earth. In the Quechua mind, then, the Milky Way not only unifies space and time, but also regulates the cycles of moisture and fertility that sustain life itself.

While no explicit lore about the Milky Way seems to have survived in the Nazca Valley, the association of water with the direction of the December solstice is significant. Perhaps, at one time, people in the valley conceived of their world in the same highly integrated way that the Quechua of the high Andes do today.

Of course, it would be unwise to project exact details of Quechua cosmology back over many centuries. If we bear in mind Peru's long succession of natural disasters and social upheavals, we can expect that a great deal of uncertainty will always surround any attempt to reconstruct Nazca sky lore. However, the *general* way in which the Quechua identify water with celestial motions does have implications for the astronomical theory of the lines.

Consider Maria Reiche's basic concept of the animal figures depicted on the pampa, for instance. Her idea that they may represent constellations associated with agricultural cycles and with the flowing of underground water seems entirely plausible. The importance of the dark cloud animals in Quechua cosmology suggests that similar beliefs about animal constellations could well have strongly influenced the thinking of the ancient Nazcans.

* Such a different system than that found among Western "people/thinkers"

On the other hand, the material collected by Urton casts doubt on other aspects of the Kosok-Reiche theory. An astronomical calendar is evidently *not* essential to survival in the Nazca Valley as they originally claimed: today, farmers in the valley ultimately rely on practical observations such as the shapes of clouds over the distant mountains. If the animal figures *did*, in fact, represent constellations, their significance in Nazca eyes was probably far more complex than the mere requirements of an agricultural calendar.

Furthermore, though Maria Reiche has spent many years attempting to link the animal figures with modern constellations, it seems highly improbable that Nazca star patterns would correspond to our own. This can only add to the many problems of actually *proving* the reality of star lines associated with the figures.

As for the existence of other astonomical alignments, most investigators have limited their testing efforts to positions of the sun and moon that are important in European traditions of astronomy. By contrast, the new research among the Quechua has drawn attention to quite different observations of long-established importance in the Andean world. (These include the boundaries of the Milky Way on the horizon, for example, or events associated with the overhead passages of the sun or stars.) If these unfamiliar alignments are ignored, then investigators simply commit the same error of cultural blindness made by the Spanish chroniclers centuries ago when they denigrated the profound and intricate outlook of the Andean skywatchers.

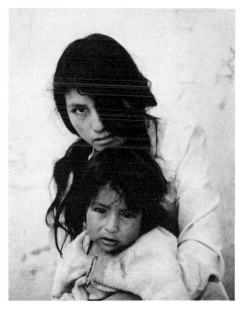

Two modern inhabitants of the Ingenio Valley.

CHAPTER 7	# THE RIDDLE OF THE RAY CENTERS

A New Approach to Nazca

BY 1980, when so much information had emerged about traditional Andean astronomy, an entirely fresh approach to the Nazca lines seemed possible. This was a prospect that particularly excited Gary Urton and his colleague, Anthony Aveni. An enthusiastic and ebullient lecturer, Aveni, like Urton, teaches at Colgate University in New York state. He was originally trained as an astronomer, but became enthralled by the ruins of the ancient Maya civilization of Central America. During field expeditions to the jungles of Mexico and Guatemala throughout the 1970s, Aveni pioneered the study of the astronomical alignments that Maya architects incorporated in the layouts of their temples and pyramids. His surveys provided important new clues about Maya skywatching skills.

Aveni never became a stuffy academic, however. His endless flow of comic anecdotes is legendary at Colgate: as a volunteer on two of his Mexico expeditions, I remember mainly his prodigious energy and good humor as he propelled his large frame along jungle trails that left me and his teenage Colgate students breathless.

Aveni's interests eventually led him to survey in Cuzco in 1978, where he collaborated with an anthropologist of Dutch origin, Tom Zuidema. From Cuzco it was natural to turn to Nazca, because Zuidema's studies of the Incas and Urton's discoveries among the Quechua raised so many possibilities for the purposes of the lines.

Together Urton and Aveni devised a novel and ambitious Nazca research program. Rather than picking out an arbitrary selection of lines and then subjecting them to astronomical tests, they began with a more fundamental question: was there any kind of orderly system underlying the layout of the lines? If some basic principle of organization could be detected behind the apparent chaos, this would set the inquiry on a much more secure footing. Such a consistent pattern would help to make the daunting task of surveying the pampa more manageable.

It was not long before Aveni and Urton decided to concentrate on Kosok's "radiating centers," for which they adopted the more convenient term "ray centers." The importance of these centers was obvious even before they set foot on the pampa. If one even casually examines aerial photos of Maria Reiche's charts, it soon becomes apparent how many straight lines converge on the starlike centers.

Persis Clarkson and Anthony Aveni, who have made important contributions to recent studies of the Nazca lines, here seen during fieldwork on the pampa in 1984.

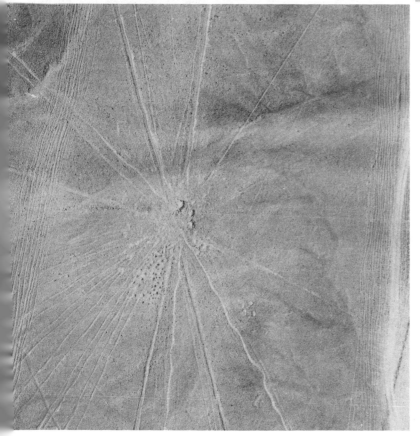

Air view of a major ray center on the Nazca pampa. Most lines begin and end at such centers, which are often situated on top of rocky hillocks at the edge of the pampa.

As these flow
where to go ? ....

Actually, Maria's sketch map of the pampa shows only about a dozen ray centers, but as soon as Aveni and Urton took to the field they discovered many more. Though they were excluded from surveying inside the specially protected zone where the markings are clustered most thickly, they found ray centers even on the remotest fringes of the pampa. In fact, whenever they began to follow the course of a straight line, it almost invariably led, sooner or later, to a pile of stones, a low hill, or a promontory. From these points, new lines always fanned out across the desert.

In 1984, I joined the field team for a few days as they pursued their exacting work of plotting one ray center after another. Aveni had trained his volunteers to measure the direction of

View from the ray center described in the text, showing a narrow line that runs directly down the steep slope and out across the distant expanse of the pampa.

each line with a surveying instrument or "transit." They also
had to make sketch-plans of the cleared triangles and trapezoids
that they frequently encountered beside the ray centers. Their
final task was to walk along as many lines as possible to establish
which centers were connected to which. At the same time, they
had to take great care not to damage the markings with their
footprints.

With no shade anywhere and temperatures frequently nearing
100 degrees, great perseverance was necessary to accomplish
these tasks, but Aveni had an unusually dedicated field crew at
his disposal. Recruited by the American organization Earthwatch, the volunteers included two foresters from Oregon, an
IBM executive, a hardware salesman and a fiber artist. For several of them, the pursuit of seemingly endless lines across the
monotonous pampa was their first taste of academic research.

In the grueling heat, one line began to look very much like
another. Several of the ray centers, however, were impressive ← these were not
places to visit. One consisted of a row of steep hillocks eroded meant to be walked
long ago by the drainage of the Nazca River. To reach the crest
that connected the miniature peaks, I had to scramble on all
fours up a sheer slope of loose, brittle volcanic pebbles. At the
top, there was an uninterrupted view of the immense, flat
pampa spread out in the haze some 200 feet below.

Climbing to one of the higher peaks, I noticed a narrow line
that seemed to cut across the landscape with knifelike precision; its absolutely straight path was aimed toward the peak on
which I stood. As my eye followed the line, I was disconcerted
to see that the line actually continued directly up the steep slope ← laser?
I had climbed. However, unlike the route I had taken, which
wove from side to side to allow me to negotiate the gradient, the
line's path shot straight up the hill without the slightest deviation, ending just a few yards from where I stood at the top. This
was such an astonishing fact that I sat down breathlessly to take
stock of possible explanations.

Whatever had motivated the builders of the line, absolute
straightness had obviously been one of their most important
requirements. It seemed absurd to think of anyone following
this vertical route up the slope as a practical pathway. Nor did
it seem likely that the line was an astronomical direction
pointer, since it grew progressively fainter and disappeared
from view long before it reached the horizon; its visibility in
the twilight would be even worse.

However unsatisfactory it was from the point of view of practical theories, the line's visual impact was an overwhelming success. It was remarkable the way it captured and focused my
attention so precisely in the void of the pampa below.

I began to wonder if this was not exactly the effect for which the builders had been striving. Could the line have been intended for a solitary, stationary viewer like myself, perhaps to aid some kind of spiritual exercise such as meditation? Certainly the narrow summit where I sat could have accommodated no more than two or three others, a fact that encouraged my speculation that some ray centers might be "spiritual retreats." It was obvious that previous visitors *had* climbed to this spot, since a few dull brown scraps of pottery lay near my feet.

Like all simple explanations of the lines, my newly formed meditation theory soon proved inadequate. As I turned to face a different direction, I noticed two or three other lines, less conspicuous than the first. Each one climbed the slopes beneath me at a slightly different angle, aimed toward separate parts of

Lines and figures were sometimes executed in apparent disregard for the rugged terrain of the pampa. Here a broad line marches straight up a hillside; the surface is so steep and rocky that it is difficult to climb or stand upright on it.

they had to be.

A cleared rectangle with a pattern of stone heaps in the middle. Such heaps probably represent construction debris left over from incomplete figures.

the ridge. At this ray center, like many others, there was no single point of focus for the lines; their beginnings (or were they endings?) were widely distributed around the group of hillocks.

Then I noticed another extraordinary fact: one of these lines broadened out as it climbed upward and turned into an avenue, perhaps a meter or two wide, ending just below the summit where I sat. This narrow parallel-sided figure had been executed neatly on a slope so steep that it was difficult to stand upright on it. Previously, I had thought such avenues might have been built for processions: I had imagined Nazca priests solemnly making their way to ceremonies held on the giant cleared triangles and trapezoids. In reality, they couldn't have retained much dignity if they had tried to march up this precipitous rectangle. If, on the other hand, the builders were simply indulging in geometric exercises, why should they have chosen a dangerously steep hillside for their activities?

← is dignity necessary for this?

Besides the avenue and the narrow lines, a third feature, again typical of many ray centers, caught my eye. Beneath me, where the level expanse of the pampa began, I spotted a quadrilateral several hundred meters long, surrounded on three sides by the steep hill slopes. The location of this rectangle in the bowl of the valley made it oddly reminiscent of a farmer's cultivated field; along its length there were regular bumps that even reminded me a little of furrows. This, I knew, was ridiculous, since the central area of the pampa is so arid it could never have been farmed. But could this be a symbolic or magic "field," laid out to implore the gods to send moisture to other areas, such as the fertile valleys bordering the pampa?

Actually, the "furrows" consisted of rows of small stone heaps, apparently abandoned by the builders in the midst of their unfinished operation of clearing the figure. When I later climbed down to the pampa and examined the interior of this figure, there was nothing else to be seen among the low stone heaps: no smashed pottery or other refuse, such as I would have expected had a ceremony with many participants taken place there.

Pulling together my impressions of this ray center, I knew I had recognized three characteristic features: numerous narrow lines, less common broad avenues, and the occasional trapezoid or cleared figure situated nearby. All these markings seemed to be focused around the group of low hills I had climbed. It was almost as if the peaks had been visualized as a source of some sort of power radiating out into the landscape.

Recalling the local Nazca legend of the "Volcano of Water," the mountain that Nazca farmers still believe sends the underground water to their fields, I wondered if some such belief might once have attached itself to *all* of the foothills, promontories and mounds in the Nazca area. Could the lines have been intended to exert supernatural control over the flow of invisible, underground moisture?

The Age of the Markings

As THE SUN GREW FIERCER, my head began to reel with too much speculation. My overactive imagination seemed very different from the attitude of caution and open-mindedness adopted by Aveni and Urton. As their field crew discovered one ray center after another, their attention was increasingly focused on accurate sketching and surveying. The more information they compiled, the more precisely could they hope to define the characteristics of a ray center and what its purpose might be.

During just one of the days that I traveled with the crew we discovered five or six new centers. All we had to do was set off along a fresh line until we arrived at the next mound or hillock. In fact, during their 1984 season, the team systematically worked its way along the plateau overlooking the Nazca Valley, locating a starburst of lines on virtually *every* major promontory or headland.

Once out of sight of the valley, it was easy to become lost in the featureless open pampa. Nevertheless, the recollection of how a particular ray center was laid out sometimes helped us to reestablish our bearings. Did the ray centers in fact form some kind of continuous grid or network, allowing those who ventured on to the pampa to travel from one place to another without becoming disoriented?

Far from the heat of the pampa, I took up this question with Gary Urton in the comfort of his office at Colgate University. "Our conclusions aren't all in yet," he emphasized, "but my own impression is that most lines do seem to have been used for travel at one time or another. Practically every line of the hundreds I've walked has a footpath along it. You don't see individual footprints, but in the middle of a line there's usually a meandering, sunken trail. In fact, along a broad avenue a couple of pathways often run side by side. Some of them appear to be old, because there's desert varnish over the sunken surface of the pathway.

"The curious thing is that the lines were obviously set out perfectly straight to begin with, yet the pathways do wander from side to side quite a bit. This can make a narrow line look quite irregular at close range. Only when you look in the distance do you realize it was very straight at one stage."

If evidence of foot traffic along the lines is still visible, what of other activities? Astonishingly, nobody made any systematic effort to tackle this question until 1982, when Persis Clarkson, a young graduate student from Calgary University, set off to walk along as many of the straight lines as possible outside the protected zone. Her aim was different from that of the Aveni team, with which she collaborated: instead of mapping and measuring the ray centers, she concentrated on recording all the man-made remains visible on the surface.

During three seasons Clarkson trekked over 1,000 kilometers of the pampa and the surrounding foothills. Despite the endurance tests many of these walks must have presented, I found her remarkably good-humored about the sparseness of her finds.

"Not much!" was her cheerful response when I queried her about what was visible along the lines. In fact, she did confirm the existence of numerous stone cairns, often located at ray centers or at junctions between lines and cleared triangles and trapezoids. She also noted other stone features, such as low walls running in a straight line, and upright stones laid out in a circle or semicircle. These walls and circles were usually situated beside a ray center, or at places where a line crossed an old dry stream bed. Few finds accompanied these features, suggesting they could hardly be the product of everyday activities.

Though most Nazca lines are remarkably straight, meandering footpaths often follow their course and sometimes create the ragged appearance visible here.

During many weeks of walking the Nazca lines, anthropologist Persis Clarkson discovered many peculiar stone features, often located where lines cross dry streambeds. While the age and purpose of the structures are uncertain, one possibility it that they represent remnants of shrines erected by the line builders or later visitors.

It's all around them. Why can't they see?!

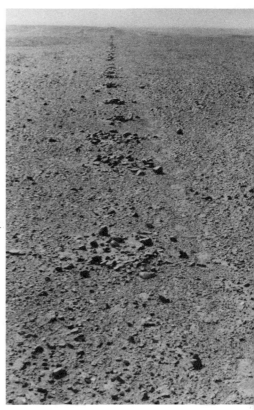

"Pottery of all kinds is pretty scarce along the lines," she explained to me. "And what little you see is mostly unspectacular, ordinary domestic ware. It's mostly late—Middle Horizon or Late Intermediate." (This corresponds roughly to A.D. 1000 onward, right up to Inca times.)

As if to confirm Persis Clarkson's preliminary conclusions, I saw nothing at all on the ground among the few lines and cleared figures I explored under her guidance. Apart from the meager scraps of pottery I had spotted on top of the high ray center I had climbed, the pampa seemed absolutely barren.

This struck me as curious, since I knew that early visitors to the pampa had reported just the opposite: masses of pottery lying everywhere, particularly near the animal figures and the large quadrilaterals. Most of these researchers had walked among the thickest concentration of designs, in the zone now protected by Maria's guards.

In 1968, for instance, Gerald S. Hawkins had surveyed inside this zone and found the desert littered with broken pots in every direction. He still recalls how easy it was to locate and photograph the smashed fragments. He found them among the stones of the open pampa as well as on the lines themselves, though the heaviest concentrations lay clustered around the low stone mounds. Beside the mound at the west end of the Great Rectangle, for example, he photographed pieces that belonged to ten different vessels. Elsewhere, he managed to reconstruct entire pots from remnants grouped together in a small area. This suggested to him that the pots had originally been placed there undamaged, presumably as offerings. (In fact, during an early visit to the pampa, Maria Reiche found a pair of intact pots placed upside down at the junction of two cleared areas.)

Hawkins speculated about why the pots were eventually smashed. The possibilities included high winds and perhaps even deliberate vandalism by the *huaqueros*, or local artifact collectors. One local informant told Hawkins that treasure hunters had removed the best pieces from the pampa and smashed the inferior ones to keep the market prices for Nazca pots high.

Hawkins' field crew even discovered ceramic fragments on top of a steep hill overlooking the end of a line, just as I had. Hawkins commented on his discovery: "These foothills were most difficult to climb because they consisted of loose screes and crumbling rock faces. Two members of the expedition fell, one gave up the climb. Yet despite the difficulty, at least five of the ancient pottery vessels had been carried to the top of this peak, which is clearly not the best route for travelers."

His observation again suggests that the summits of the ray center mounds and hillocks were particularly significant to the builders.

In an attempt to study the pottery more systematically, Hawkins picked out a narrow strip across the main area of drawings and sampled the pot fragments that lay there. They were so densely concentrated that originally, he concluded, thousands of complete vessels must have been placed on the pampa.

Though nearly every ancient local ceramic style was represented among the fragments he recorded, by far the largest number of fragments belonged to a specific time period. This was the period of the so-called Classic style, when the craft skills of the ancient Nazcans reached their peak.

Of course, it was always possible that the pots had been offered up long after the original construction and use of the lines, as Hawkins himself recognized. Nevertheless, he thought it reasonable to assume that most of the markings dated to the same Classic Nazca era as the pots. Though archaeologists cannot provide hard-and-fast dates, even with laboratory techniques such as the radiocarbon method, their tentative dating of this period places it at a century or two around the birth of Christ.

Some fifteen years after Hawkins' survey, Persis Clarkson began her treks outside the protected zone, and a dramatic contrast to his results soon became obvious. After preliminary study of the sparse pot fragments typically found at ray centers and their connecting lines, she believes they date to a much later time. In fact, the pottery mostly belongs to periods well after the distinctive Nazca style had run its course—a full thousand years or more after the sample recorded by Hawkins.

This discrepancy is no mere academic quibble; it has vital

implications for discovering the purposes served by the lines. What could be the explanation for the apparent differences between the protected zone and the rest of the pampa?

The most obvious distinction between the two areas is the absence of animal figures outside the zone. Indeed, if all the animals are plotted on a map, it is clear that these special designs were mostly confined to a small area south of the Ingenio Valley.

Were they limited in time as well? Since Hawkins found the relatively early Classic pottery concentrated in the same area, it is tempting to assume that the animals must be early, too. There is further evidence to support this possibility, notably the distinct resemblance in style between several of the figures drawn on the pampa and depictions of similar creatures painted on Nazca pots.

Another clue emerged when Persis Clarkson and I visited one of the few isolated animal figures lying outside the protected zone. To reach it, we followed an old trail of tire tracks along the edge of the Nazca Valley, the wheels of our Volkswagen bus churning up a thick gray cloud behind us. Only after we had parked did I look back and realize that the well-worn dirt road actually snaked right across the surface of two huge trapezoids. The fresh white tracks we had left behind were a glaring intrusion beside the dignified straightness of the ancient clearings.

Here, just a few yards away across the pampa, Clarkson led me to the giant design of a killer whale. Not that it was easy to spot the identity of the creature: the only truly recognizable parts were the long dorsal fin and the huge concentric rings that formed its eye. Once I had stepped gingerly onto the outline itself, setting one foot directly in front of the other to stay on the narrow line, the entire pattern was even harder to make out.

It was a curious experience to follow the contours of the whale through all its twists and bends. By the time I completed the circuit, I had faced every direction of the compass and felt slightly disoriented, almost as if I had been inside a maze. Finally, Persis interrupted my thoughts to draw attention to the area beside the mouth of the whale.

There, on the ground within the creature's open jaws, lay a scattering of pottery fragments. I knew at once from the bright orange finish of the decorated pieces that these must be Classic Nazca, quite different from the drab-looking later ceramics. Were these fragments all that remained of an offering to the "whale spirit"?

Only a carefully organized archaeological survey within the protected zone will show if similar Classic Nazca pots were, indeed, deposited alongside other animal drawings. If this

There are at least three major depictions of whales on the Nazca pampa. The one described in the text, top, is nearly two hundred feet long. Ground view, right, looks toward the whale's open jaw. The upper jaw is visible at the left, while archaeologists stand beside the lower jaw. Fragments of Classic Nazca pottery, bottom, were scattered around the area enclosed by the jaws.

could be proved, then it would imply that the animal designs belong to a particular period of a century or two around the birth of Christ.

At this stage, the function of the drawings apparently involved the participation of many people from the surrounding valleys, who left thousands of beautifully decorated pottery vessels behind them in the desert as offerings to the spiritual forces represented by the drawings of the animals. It also seems likely that, at this early date, most of the elaborate networks of narrow lines did not yet exist.

It was, perhaps, only many centuries later that the network of ray centers developed, covering the pampa with its dense spiderweb of connecting lines. By then (around A.D. 1000?) the Nazca culture was dead, and the creation of the lines reflected a different society with different ceremonial needs. Though it is difficult to guess precisely how the ray centers satisfied those needs, it appears that there was no large-scale participation in religious activities as there had been during the earlier period. The scarcity of finds suggests a more solitary or exclusive use of the pampa.

Of course, much of this argument is pure speculation, but it does seem likely that the majority of straight lines have little or no connection with the animal figures. This presents yet another stumbling block for the astronomical theory. For example, consider Maria Reiche's efforts to demonstrate the astronomical identity of a few of the animals by surveying the lines that cross them. It is quite clear that certain of these lines are, in reality, connectors running between different ray centers. Since such lines could well have been created as much as a thousand years later than the animal figures they cross, this kind of approach sseems highly dubious.

What of the ray centers themselves? By identifying them as the organizing principle behind the lines, Aveni and Urton simplified the task of resolving the astronomical issue. The ray centers presented a well-defined unit of analysis, so their major problem was simply to survey enough of them to make their verdict comprehensive and convincing.

In fact, after a total of nearly six months spent on the pampa during the years 1980 to 1984, they had compiled data on no fewer than five hundred lines; of these, about one hundred can be traced to sixty-two separate ray centers. They estimate that this represents perhaps 80 percent of the ray centers that exist on the pampa.

"We are still busy analyzing the data from our survey," Aveni told me as this book was going to press, "but at this stage an overall astronomical solution doesn't look promising. We think

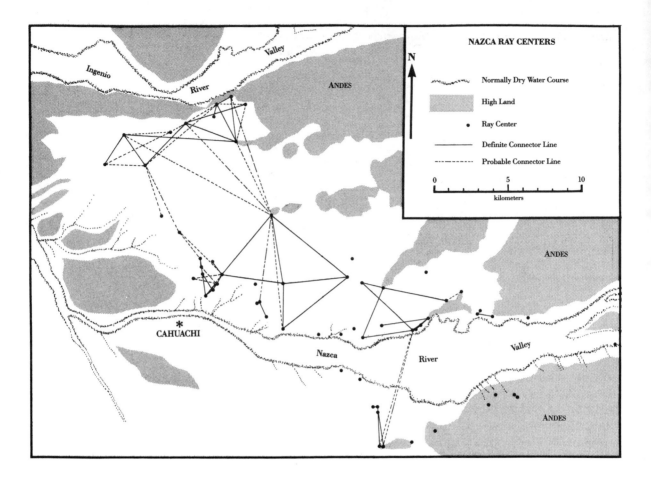

N

Normally Dry Water Course

High Land

Ray Center

Definite Connector Line

Probable Connector Line

0   5   10

kilometers

Ingenio

River

ANDES

Valley

ANDES

ANDES

* CAHUACHI

Nazca   River   Valley

Plan of the ray centers investigated by Anthony Aveni and his team during 1980–84.

that a small proportion of the lines may well have possessed some sort of astronomical function, but it's clear that the ray centers were not exclusively dedicated to astronomy. In fact, our overall conclusions point toward a broad range of explanations for the lines, not any one single theory."

This did not surprise me, since my own subjective impressions from visiting the ray centers left me in little doubt of the inadequacy of any single theory I could think of to explain them.

Indeed, the assumption that the Nazca lines were built for purposes we would define as "useful" or "practical" has obviously led nowhere. Before Aveni and Urton's work, many researchers brought their own narrow, twentieth-century vision to the pampa, without even stopping to consider the distinctive social and religious traditions of the Andean peoples. Further clues will surely come only from broadening the inquiry into the lives of the ancient Nazca people and their descendants.

Since the lines were evidently an important expression of their complex outlook, it is scarcely surprising that they fail to correspond to the narrow technical preoccupations of our own world.

Nazca Geometry: The Problem of Precision

ON MY LAST DAY IN NAZCA, I participated in an attempt by the Earthwatch team to create its own desert drawing. This was staged for the benefit of the visiting British television crew, who needed an "action sequence" to liven up its documentary. At first Aveni was reluctant, since the experiment formed no part of his original research program and was a distraction from the ray center survey. However, once the volunteers began to debate the best way of making a line, assigning each other joking titles such as "slave," "foreman" and "chief priest," Aveni plunged into the effort with characteristic enthusiasm. After all, in assessing the magnitude of the task involved in creating the lines, there could be no substitute for firsthand experience.

We selected a remote corner of the Nazca Valley for our experiment, far from any genuine ancient markings. Though the surface here was rougher than that of most parts of the pampa I had seen, consisting of coarse volcanic stones, it was easy to create the color contrast required for our line. All we had to do was peel away the crust of dark brown surface rocks to reveal the dusty yellow-white clay immediately beneath.

Our reconstruction began with a simple surveying procedure: we lined up two tall poles to coincide with a cleft in the distant horizon and then stretched string between them. This formed one border of our line. To set out the other border, we measured off another pair of poles side by side with the first.

Within the avenue of string thus created, we spread ourselves out at arm's length, one behind another. The idea was that each volunteer would squat on the ground and gather up all the stones within arm's reach into a single pile. This seemed an efficient way to collaborate on removing the surface. Moreover, it reproduced the small, regularly spaced stone heaps still visible inside many (presumably unfinished) cleared figures.

The final phase was to get rid of the piles by spreading the stones out along the borders of the line. At this stage it was useful to have "Chief Priest Aveni" standing by to point out where the edges of the line still appeared ragged or crooked. Eventually the strings were removed, and the result looked remarkably like the perfectly straight avenues we were emulating.

As "entry-level line builders" we had no previous experience to draw on, yet the working procedure was so simple that everyone adapted to it quickly and enjoyed the communal effort. The only drawback was the bruised fingers and knuckles that resulted from the constant manhandling of the stones. Quite possibly, as Maria Reiche has suggested, a rakelike tool might have made this operation more convenient. However, no examples of such implements exist, and only our careful tidying of the borders by hand could have produced the exact straightness so characteristic of the original lines themselves.

As we grew more confident in our efforts, Aveni decided to extend the line in a spiral pattern. This time the borders were set out with the aid of a string swung in an arc like a giant compass. As the spiral curved around, so we progressively shortened the radius of the string by folding it in half each time. At regular intervals we planted little stakes in the ground to mark the edges of the tightened curve. By stretching strings between these stakes, the spiral took shape on the ground as a series of straight segments. At this stage it was a "kinky" spiral, but satisfactory enough for us to renew our operation of clearing off the surface.

Once each straight border segment was complete, we simply pushed out the stones a few inches to create the final shape of the curve. To my astonishment, this crude "eyeballing" technique resulted in an almost perfectly smooth outline. Viewed from the top of a nearby hill, the spiral appeared absolutely regular, as if it had been set out with a sophisticated knowledge of geometry. In reality, all we had done was fold over lengths of string and push straight lines out into curves entirely by eye. This experience naturally left me wondering about the degree of skill exercised by the Nazcans when they set out their giant spirals and animal designs.

During her earliest years on the pampa, Maria Reiche, too, had been surprised by the precision that could be achieved by the unaided eye, in this case by her local Nazca assistant. With his "telescopic vision" (as she put it), he proved invaluable during her early surveying efforts. "It may seem incredible," she wrote in 1949, "but it was an everyday experience that this In-

Volunteers from the Earthwatch organization experiment with drawing techniques in an area of the Nazca Valley far from any ancient drawings. They created an impressive, smooth-sided spiral with surprisingly simple improvised techniques.

dian helper could see a stake at two-thirds of a mile's distance and was able to indicate the exact place where it would coincide with a nearer one. After setting up the theodolite at that spot, a look through the telescope showed that indeed the two stakes coincided. This man was a skilled 'furrow tracer' (*rayador*)."

"Furrow tracers," Maria goes on to explain, were hired by the large cotton plantations to mark out parallel rows for planting. They did this simply by scraping along with their feet. (The wear and tear on the soles of their shoes was included in the price negotiated for their services.) Maria believed that the skill of these men was a trait handed down directly from their ancient ancestors who had created the lines on the pampa.

The furrow tracers seemed to demonstrate that long, straight lines could be set out with a minimum of equipment or knowledge. However, Maria was convinced from the start that the more elaborate figures involved considerable technical refinement. The perfect proportions of the spider or of the hummingbirds, for instance, could not have been achieved by eye alone. Somehow they must have been scaled up from a small model.

Once again, Maria's 1949 account provides an interesting discussion of how this might have been done. She suggested that a string was laid across the original pattern to measure each corner or bend in the design; these distances were then transferred to a rope, at a scale perhaps a hundred times larger. As for establishing the correct angles for the rope, she imagined that the Nazca designers sighted along the string they had laid across the original model. (This technique would have been quite similar to the use of a plane table in modern surveying.)

An equally interesting alternative was her idea that "auxiliary lines"—presumably a grid pattern of some kind—were involved in scaling up a figure from a model. To support this, she published a photograph that shows inconspicuous straight rows of pebbles lying across the surface of a huge fish design. Perhaps these were the remains of just such a grid.

Throughout her work, Maria was also convinced that the line builders had worked with precise and consistent units of length. Here her arguments are particularly difficult to evaluate. Just as in the case of her astronomical claims, she has supplied little detailed evidence, so it is impossible for other researchers to test her theories.

However, in virtually every one of her major publications, she proposes a *different* value for the Nazca unit of length. Between 1949 and 1984, she offered no fewer than *nine* distinct suggestions for this "Nazca Yard" (ranging from 84 meters all the way down to 32.5 centimeters). Nowhere does she explain why previous values for the unit proved unsatisfactory.

In recent years, Maria has at least been consistent in stressing the importance of body measurements to the Nazca designers. Her idea that arm spans were the basis of the unit is entirely plausible, but again it is impossible to rely on such suggestions when she fails to supply the supporting evidence. While the work of the line builders must surely have entailed numbers and lengths of some kind, we have no way of knowing at present whether one or several such "Nazca Yards" were in use.

Another of Maria's strongly held convictions is that the designers worked with great precision. Though some of the curves incorporated into animal figures look rather sloppy and irregular, she believes that *every* part of the design was composed of precisely calculated arcs, each one related to the Nazca unit of length.

But were the designers really such fastidious mathematicians? To bolster her contentions, Maria has published drawings of these detailed curves and outlines overlain with a complicated mass of separate arcs. They all conform to the "Nazca Yard," but hardly represent either an elegant or straightforward method of construction.

The possibility that such designs were laid out by simpler techniques seemed highly probable to me after our experiments with the spiral. Perhaps a combination of different methods was involved, including the use of grids and pebbles, arcs of string and eyeballing. In any case, a one-track approach to the problem of Nazca geometry seems as fraught with difficulty as a one-track approach to their astronomy.

While our reconstruction effort left many questions unanswered about the design methods of the builders, it was at least clear that the creation of a line did not demand immense labor. It took us a little over an hour to complete our figure. (And less than a minute to kick over the stones and destroy it, to avoid confusing a future generation of archaeologists!) Weighing up the experiment, Aveni calculated that each one of us could remove an average of about two square meters of pampa per hour. Admittedly, this was not a terribly impressive rate. On the other hand, we were all amateur line builders, and the calculation included the time taken to survey our line and improve its final appearance. Based on this probably overgenerous figure, the Great Rectangle would have involved one hundred people in something like two months of continuous effort.

To coordinate activity on this scale would obviously require good organization, yet clearing the largest trapezoids would not have demanded anything even close to the manpower devoted to other monuments of the ancient world. (For example, the Greek historian Herodotus claimed that the Great Pyramid of

0 1 2 3 4 5
meters

Maria Reiche's survey of the spider's body. The straight lines belong to a construction of multiple arcs that she hypothesizes was used by the original builders of the figure. The lengths of the radii correspond to whole units of one of the "Nazca yards" proposed by Maria (in this case, 38 cm). However, she has never investigated the possibility that other, simpler geometrical methods were used to produce such outlines.

It was so much closer than they think!

Egypt involved four teams of one hundred thousand men for twenty years. In the case of Stonehenge, the single task of transporting stones for the final stage of the monument from their origin 20 miles away is estimated to have occupied five hundred men for nearly six years.)

There seems no real necessity to imagine hordes of unwilling Nazca slaves hauling piles of stone under the fierce sun of the pampa. But if quite small numbers of Nazcans collaborated on the designs, who exactly were they? Could anyone in the community join in the line-building task, or was this a sacred activity reserved for a few? To extend the inquiry beyond the narrow boundaries of astronomy and geometry, it is first necessary to establish what kind of society could have given birth to the lines.

IN SEARCH OF THE LINE BUILDERS

CHAPTER 8

Cahuachi, City of Bones

A VISIT TO THE "CAPITAL CITY" of the ancient Nazcans is an unsettling experience. The site of Cahuachi is located about ten miles from the modern town of Nazca on the desolate floodplain of the river. Strong evening winds have buried much of the area under sand dunes, transforming it into rows of identical gray hillocks. My guide was an archaeologist who had spent many months in the area; nevertheless, we drove around in circles among the dreary dunes for half an hour, completely

View across the plaza at Cahuachi, major center of the Classic Nazca culture. In the background is a seventy-foot-high stepped pyramid, together with remains of other man-made structures partially covered and eroded by windblown sand.

unable to spot the main ruined pyramid of the city, even though it rises about 70 feet above the floodplain. Except in the slanting rays of evening light, the man-made remnants of walls and plazas are difficult to distinguish from the natural undulations of the sand.

What *is* obvious, everywhere, is the presence of human bones. Between the city and the river lie an estimated five thousand looted graves, gaping like shell holes on a devastated battlefield. In their hunt for artifacts, the diggers, or *huaqueros*, have tossed aside bones and skulls, and sometimes even entire mummies, which they have stripped of their wrappings and then abandoned, naked and shriveled, among the sand heaps.

One of the thousands of looted ancient graves at Cahuachi.

As the wind whirls among the fragments of cloth and bone scattered across the ground, one is soon overtaken by the melancholy atmosphere of Cahuachi. There is so little respect for the dead Nazcans here that any attempt to recover their two-thousand-year-old lives and beliefs seems hopeless.

In fact, the mental world of the Nazcans is not entirely lost, since their textiles and pottery present us with richly informative images. These are not simple scenes of everyday life, but instead depict a distinctive array of animal figures, plants and humans. The style is often realistic, yet bizarre and sinister imaginary creatures are equally common.

The particular combinations of images are repeated so faithfully, century after century, that we can safely assume such designs were never merely decorative; surely, they must illustrate particular stories or beliefs, forming, in fact, a kind of code, one that we can use to unlock the sacred dimension of Nazca thought.

Mummies in the Sand

ONE OF THE FOLKTALES of the Peruvian coast concerns a rose-colored granite hill overlooking the Bay of Paracas, about 100 miles north of Nazca. During the night of the waning moon, a spectral woman descends from her dwelling place among the rocks. She is clad in such brilliantly colored clothing that she will blind even the bravest man who glimpses her on the beach. With her animal helpers—the fox, the owl and the condor—she watches over the fields, protecting them against any danger.

According to another story, the enchanted hill contains a great treasure: sometimes, at new moon, a ball of gold guarded by two condors appears on the summit and rolls down the hill to disappear in the breakers.

Unaware of these legends, the Peruvian archaeologist Julio C. Tello was nevertheless intrigued by a local *huaquero's* report about an archaeological site at Paracas. At first Tello was concerned that his antiquated car, its wheels scarcely wider than a bicycle's, would not make the journey across the sand dunes. However, a freak rainstorm intervened (one of many that devastated Peru during the great El Niño of 1925) and, during the afternoon of July 26, the track became passable. Setting out with his American colleague Samuel K. Lothrop, Tello finally arrived at the foot of the hill, where they spotted the unmistakable craters and dumps left by the *huaqueros*.

At that exact moment, Lothrop later recalled, the sun shone through the clouds and illuminated shreds of vividly colored textiles half buried in the sand. (It was perhaps such shreds that had given rise to the local legend of a brilliantly clad woman.) Strewn around in all directions were sun-bleached or yellowing skulls, the outlines of each cranium deformed to an extraordinary, elongated shape. (These deformities were deliberately produced by binding the heads of infants between a pair of wooden boards; later, Tello was to find babies' skulls with the boards still attached.) Even more remarkable, many skulls had a large circular or square opening cut into them, the results of a risky surgical operation known as trepanning. Its purpose, one might guess, was to relieve strokes, migraines or psychological disturbances. New growths of bone along the edges of the holes in many skulls showed that it was actually possible to survive the operation.

Still scarcely grasping the importance of their discovery of the Paracas culture, Tello and Lothrop managed to load their

Elaborate masks and ornaments were buried among the mummy bundles from Paracas. A partially unwrapped mummy reveals a feather fan, right. From another bundle came the ceremonial fox mask, below. *Skull*, below right, *shows deformations and a surgical opening typical of the burials at Paracas.*

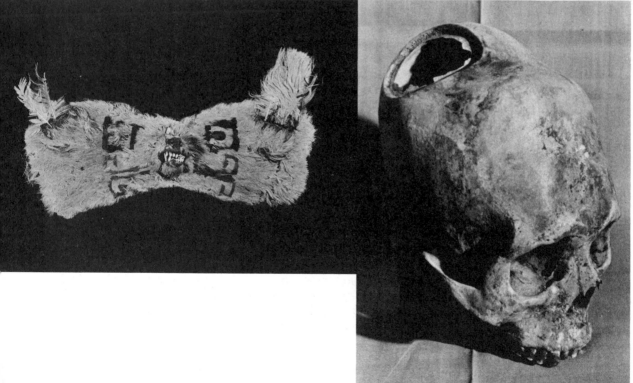

car with forty-five skulls, and then set out in torrential rain for Lima, where they arrived, cold and muddy, two days later.

This experience hardly dampened Tello's enthusiasm, for within a month he was back at Paracas for the start of a two-year campaign of excavations. His dig soon revealed the spectacular burial practices that had taken place from about 600 to 150 B.C. among the red peaks of the hill, known locally as Cerro Colorado.

Here, on the summit, the excavators found shafts dug deep into the clay and granite, widened at the base into chambers where the mummies of the dead were placed. The mummies (of both children and adults, especially women) were bundled together inside coarse cotton wrappings, their bones and flesh poorly preserved; these subterranean chambers with their burials were named the "Cavernas" by Tello.

The climax of Tello's work occurred farther down the hill in October 1927, when his team unearthed a substantial mass burial place, or "Necropolis," as he called it. Here the bodies (apparently mostly male) were much better preserved, because they had been covered by dry sand within the foundations of ancient buildings. Eventually, a total of 429 mummy bundles were removed from the Necropolis and shipped back to Lima, where they were stored in the National Museum of Anthropology. When Tello resigned from the museum in 1930, only about 50 of the bundles had been examined, leaving the remainder still unopened to this day. But those that were unwrapped consisted of layer after layer of superb textiles, embroidered with such skill that their quality has rarely been matched by the weavers of any other civilization. It is these startling embroidered images that aid our understanding of Nazca, since the sacred designs adopted by Nazca potters and weavers were strongly influenced by the ideas of their predecessors, the craftsmen of Paracas.

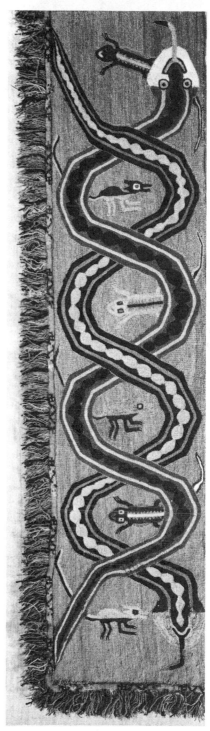

Details from Paracas textiles.

Visions of Monster Beings

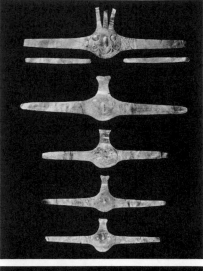

Ornaments of beaten sheet-gold retrieved from Paracas mummy bundles. These were probably "badges" of supernatural authority, since Nazca pottery designs show both humans and deities displaying them prominently on their foreheads and faces.

THE STRANGENESS OF THESE IDEAS is obvious from a close look at any single embroidered design, such as the elaborate example illustrated here. The motif is stitched in wool and shows an ornately clad being apparently flying through the air. This being has clawed feet and a face that seems part human and part animal. From its chin a snakelike streamer leads to a small winged creature with a similar face. Both these beings have a kind of winged badge on their foreheads, as well as exaggerated whiskers resembling masks. (These no doubt represent the actual ornaments and masks of sheet gold that have been discovered in some of the bundles.) The tail of the large being ends in an unadorned feline face with a protruding tongue.

Perhaps the most striking feature of the design is the profusion of disembodied heads that appear everywhere on parts of the large being's birdlike costume. Tiny heads are even worked into the corners of the whisker mask. The being holds the clearest of all these head designs in its right hand: the head is obviously human, and the being is grasping it by the hair.

This image is typical of the Paracas "monsters," which usually combine an endless variety of human, bird and feline characteristics in a single body. In practically every case they are shown wearing or carrying heads; on several textiles, the beings are actually shown devouring heads or tiny human bodies.

Besides these rather sinister imaginary creatures, the Paracas weavers often selected a realistic animal or an abstract geometric pattern as a major decorative theme. The most common animal depictions are of predators such as falcons and condors, sharks and killer whales, foxes, snakes, and seabirds feeding on fish. Masked human warriors or dancers also appear, most obviously distinguishable from the "monster beings" by their fully human feet. In general, however, the Paracas weavers were not preoccupied with representing details of the natural world around them. For example, there are scarcely any vegetable or flower motifs, except for a few beanlike sprouting plants carried by humans or "monsters."

What *all* the designs share is a sense of action: winged beings are shown in full flight, while warriors brandish spears, arrows, clubs and knives. Vigor and movement are conveyed by such details as the unbound, swirling hair of humans, or by the flailing "snakes" that sprout from the tongues and tails of the "monster beings." It is this suggestion of action that perhaps more

than anything suggests a magical, transformative meaning for the designs.

Yet no matter how extravagant or freakish any single image might appear at close range, its impact is carefully controlled by the overall design of the textile. The Paracas weavers accomplished this by varying the color scheme chosen for each detailed part of the repeating figure. Their harmonious, rhythmic balancing of color is hard to appreciate from photographs. However, in the example illustrated on page 148, the ranks of winged beings clasping severed heads would obviously look monotonous without a subtle, variable color scheme for their shirts, wings, masks, legs and so on. (In fact, the weavers used no fewer than sixteen different shades of dyed alpaca yarn to embroider these particular images.)

The secret of the Paracas weavers was not technical refinement, since most of the embroidery was done with a simple stem stitch. It was their unsurpassed skill in manipulating color and pattern that makes such a strong impact on the viewer today.

The embroidered "monster being" described in the text.

← not unlike the dragons of China

Who Were the Weavers?

BUT WHAT WAS THE EFFECT originally intended by the weavers? Many of the finest textiles were designed as garments such as ponchos, tunics, cloaks, shirts, headbands, turbans and loincloths. In general, most of the clothing shows little or no signs

The magnificent textile described in the text, *right, and in detail, below, features winged warriors devouring human heads; it is now preserved in the Textile Museum in Washington, D.C.*

those who came from the sky?

The weavers of Paracas may have associated their "monster beings" with beliefs in fertility, since they frequently depicted them bearing sprouting beans or branches.

of any wear, though repairs on a few items suggest that they were not simply offered up for the exclusive use of the dead. The most likely explanation is that they were worn only on special ceremonial occasions. Exactly who wore them and where these people came from is unknown, however. The mystery is heightened by the contrast between the richness of the textiles and the barren setting of Paracas itself.

With so many trepanned heads present at the Cavernas site (though they are scarce at the later Necropolis), Tello speculated that Paracas was a sanatorium for the convalescence of privileged patients from all over Peru. The people of Paracas certainly did enjoy wide-ranging trade connections, to judge from exotic offerings, such as shell ornaments acquired from Ecuador, wrapped up with the mummies. Another clue is the dishes propped up against the knees of the mummies containing foods such as peppers, beans, peanuts, maize and yucca. These crops could scarcely have grown in the exposed pink sand dunes around Cerro Colorado, but were staples in the nearby cultivated coastal valleys such as Pisco and Ica.

If the sanatorium theory seems a little fanciful, a more plausible explanation may be that Paracas was a sacred center, the site of burial ceremonies for privileged families from an extensive area of southern Peru. (In fact, Paracas-style pottery has been identified at locations from the Cañete Valley in the north down to Ica in the south.) Perhaps the site itself was only temporarily occupied whenever ritual events demanded. We might assume the presence of priests or ceremonial dancers from the many finds of musical instruments, including a variety of reed pipes, whistles, ceramic bells, drums, rattles and panpipes.

Some burials were unquestionably more important than others; over thirty of the Necropolis mummies were wrapped and wrapped until the bundles grew to be about 5 feet in diameter, two or three times larger than average. Such oversize bundles presumably reflected the exceptional status of certain individuals in Paracas society. The variety of styles and techniques present in each large bundle indicates that many individual weavers contributed to them.

Despite all the variations in status and style, however, the power of certain Paracas images was so great that they were repeated faithfully from bundle to bundle, century after century. The central importance of the masked, partly human "monsters" remained constant throughout. Other subtle groupings of particular themes also recur, as if illustrating a special legend or referring to the emblem of an individual family or tribe. (Examples of such linked motifs are: felines, beans and severed heads; winged killer whales and condors; feline birds

Ceramic figure of a Paracas flute player.

A wooden drum from Paracas, with the original leather skin preserved intact.

Two traditional Andean loom designs: the backstrap loom, strapped to the weaver's body (here seen in Poma's woodcut from around 1600), and the ground loom, supported on a horizontal framework and still widely used in the southern highlands.

and falling humans, and so on.) Perhaps in these clusters of designs we can recognize the "signature" of particular social groups who shared the responsibility for the stitching of the textiles.

They invested prodigious energy in this task. One relatively simple Necropolis embroidery, consisting of a geometric pattern of crossbars, is thought to consist of *at least* 1,200,000 stitches in the center panel and an additional 800,000 stitches along the borders. What the most elaborate mantles must represent in terms of months or years of patient stitching one can only guess, but the time and effort involved must have been as demanding, in its own way, as a pyramid-building project on the north coast. Weaving clearly played a more significant and sacred role than the mere act of providing fancy robes for chiefs or priests.

Even some of the plain, undecorated wrappings that enveloped the dead were spectacular productions, since from time to time they were woven on an enormous scale. Lothrop reported plain-weave fabrics over 80 feet long and nearly 20 feet wide, containing 100 miles or more of two-ply yarn.

A simple backstrap loom, the traditional weaving instrument of the Andes, would be quite impractical for turning out such a huge textile. In fact, recent examination of a pair of large mummy blankets has indicated that teams of weavers must have worked side by side, passing a number of separate wefts to each other in a regular sequence.

Curiously, no weaving equipment of any kind other than bobbins and needles has ever been found at a Paracas or Nazca site, despite the excellent preservation of most wooden items there. One possibility is that the weaving was done on horizontal "ground looms," which are still used in the southern highlands of Peru: these looms consist of a simple framework of beams resting on supports close to the ground. If such a device was used by the Paracas and Nazca weavers, it would help to explain how they managed to handle very large areas of cloth, while its rudimentary construction would probably leave few traces for archaeologists to discover.

Even so, the production of some textiles must have been an extraordinary feat. Perhaps the most remarkable of all was discovered at Cahuachi, the Nazca "capital." The first serious attempt to excavate there was made in 1952 and 1953, when William Duncan Strong and a team from Columbia University sank several test trenches into man-made mounds at the site. The purpose of these trenches was to aid the archaeologists in defining ordered sequences of pottery. However, when the team probed an area near the part of the ruins they had named "the

Great Temple," they discovered something much more remarkable than potsherds. In the lowest layers was a single giant piece of plain cotton. Its edges had been tucked in from side to side like the pleats of an accordion and the whole piece had then been folded over end to end at least three times. The cloth was over 20 feet wide and Strong's conservative estimate of its length was a staggering 160 to 200 feet. Its appearance reminded the archaeologists of the plain mummy bundle wrappings of Paracas. Nearby, the team found a number of deep empty tombs that had never been looted but instead were carefully sealed off with bundles of canes. Throughout this area of the site, the soil had been extensively scorched by very hot fires, while here and there fragments of deformed skulls typical of the Cavernas type were unearthed.

Putting all these clues together, Strong concluded that either there must be Paracas mummies at Cahuachi that neither his team nor the *huaqueros* had managed to find, or else that Cahuachi was a place where the privileged dead of the Nazca Valley were smoked, wrapped in bundles and then transported north to their final resting place under the rose-colored dunes of Paracas.

The Rise of Nazca Religion

THESE EARLIEST INHABITANTS of Cahuachi—perhaps some five centuries before the birth of Christ—lived not in splendid palaces, but in rows of simple, sturdy huts overlooking the Nazca river. Strong found traces of upright posts made from the enduring algarroba tree; the wall spaces in between were joined by wattles woven from cane and reed and plastered over with mud.

While the rites and symbols of the early Nazcans seem at first to have been dominated by Paracas beliefs, this was to change gradually over the following centuries, or so the evidence of pottery and cloth fragments suggests.

In fact, no textiles as elaborate as those from Paracas have ever been discovered in the Nazca Valley. But if we pursue the comparison further, we find that a freer, more natural Nazca

Air view of the ruins at Cahuachi beside the Nazca River, showing complexes of rooms, pyramids and plazas. The masses of small craters are actually thousands of looted graves.

style was emerging. There was a new emphasis on realistic depictions of animals such as killer whales, fish and birds, together with images of sprouting plants and fruit. It was as if the early Nazca potters and weavers were expressing their own special preoccupations with the natural world and with agricultural fertility.

Eventually, these notions of fertility and growth merged with the all-important symbolism of the severed head, and it was this strange, paradoxical mixture of images that came to dominate the bold ceramics of Cahuachi.

Meanwhile, the skill of the Nazca potters steadily improved, stimulated by a vital technological innovation. In the era before about 400 B.C., they decorated their pots by engraving and painting them *after* the vessel had been fired. The breakthrough came when the Nazca artisans learned how to grind up bright mineral pigments into special paints or "slips" that they applied *before* the vessel reached the kiln. This technique of "baking in" the colors added a new intensity and vividness to the designs. Eventually, up to fourteen or fifteen different shades were used by the Nazca potters. They chose the most difficult method possible of painting the designs: the background colors were applied first, and only at the last stage were the black outlines that marked the borders and details of the figures added. This ensured a superb finish to the painted motifs and indicates how familiar the potters must have been with each image that they set out to portray.

A masked dancer or supernatural being in Early Nazca style; a detail from a painted textile, perhaps intended as a wall hanging for a dwelling or temple.

This swimming deity casting a net typifies the boldness and naturalism of the Early Nazca art style. Maritime themes are common in Nazca art and indicate the economic and religious importance of the sea.

The vigorous outlines and brilliant, burnished colors of the Nazca pots have made them some of the most sought-after art objects of the ancient world—a fact sadly reflected in the wholesale looting of Cahuachi and other sites.

By about 150 B.C., no more embroidered mantles were buried

IN SEARCH OF THE LINE BUILDERS • 153

at Paracas, and Cahuachi gradually became the most important ceremonial site in southern Peru. At the same time, pottery grew to be the most valued means of expressing sacred and symbolic ideas, so much so that weaving standards slipped: Nazca embroidery was now simpler and less refined.

Still, there was no revolutionary break with the Paracas past. Strong's dig at Cahuachi demonstrated how smoothly the ceramic arts of Nazca developed, without a break from their roots in the Paracas culture. And the painted Nazca images clearly preserve many of the same peculiar preoccupations that figured on the great Necropolis textiles.

Typically, Nazca pots were dominated by complicated "monster beings," just as the textiles had been. A characteristic image, like the one traced from a pot and illustrated at left, shows a creature with many details recognizable from Paracas: a winged forehead badge, a whisker mask, a trailing appendage ending in a cat or other feline, and severed human heads and bodies.

Here, surely, must be the selfsame demon or deity depicted at Paracas. Yet several other details are new: the unmistakably human legs and feet, for instance, and the emphasis on plants that run along the creature's coat and sprout from the severed heads. It is clear from this and many other Nazca vessels that the "monster" had become established as a god of fields and gardens, as well as of war.

A second type of mythical animal also haunts the surfaces of Nazca pots (see below). This is a striped cat creature, usually identified as an ocelot or pampas cat, a small, docile feline whose habitat is normally the jungles of eastern Peru. The cat creature is always shown wearing a mask of upswept whiskers, which once again may well represent an actual type of mask worn by priests or ritual dancers. Like the "monster beings," the cat creature was obviously associated with fertility, since it is often shown clasping a fruit or vegetable between its paws.

The most common type of "monster being" has partly human features, disguised by feline whisker masks and forehead ornaments. The designs often incorporate severed heads and sprouting plants.

Less frequently, a more docile-looking cat-like creature is depicted, wearing a mask of upswept whiskers like those of an otter.

Indeed, images of beans, peppers or guavas sometimes make up the entire decoration of early Nazca pots. In other cases, the theme is a single bold design of an animal such as a killer whale or a hummingbird. These fresh, vivacious animal depictions are perhaps the most appealing aspect of Nazca art, and also represent the closest parallel to the great animal figures that were traced on the surface of the pampa.

Was There a Nazca Empire?

As THE POTTERS mastered and refined their technique, this playful realism gradually disappeared. By about 150 B.C., flowing outlines had given way to a more abstract, angular style. Instead of recognizable individual creatures, mythical beings became more and more prominent. Parts of real animals, such as falcon wings and killer whale jaws, were combined within the increasingly complicated bodies of the beings. While the charming spontaneity of the Early Nazca style was lost, these later pots are extraordinary for their brilliantly polished surfaces and startling symbols, precisely rendered in rich shades of dark red, orange, cream and black.

The Nazca potters developed their remarkable skills over a wide area of southern Peru. Despite local variations in the shapes and details of pot design, the basic Nazca symbols were repeated consistently from one valley to the next, from the Pisco Valley in the north all the way down to the Acari in the south.

To account for this far-reaching influence, Strong assumed that Cahuachi was the capital of a unified Nazca culture. Other researchers soon began to speak of it as an urban site, the center of an empire imposed by military force over the people of the coastal valleys. Since severed heads are so insistently painted on the pots, and had actually been dug up at Cahuachi and other sites, it seemed obvious that Nazca society was, indeed, aggressive and militaristic.

Moreover, some sites had traces of fortifications. Strong believed that much of Cahuachi had been enclosed by massive adobe walls. At another smaller site in the far south, the occu-

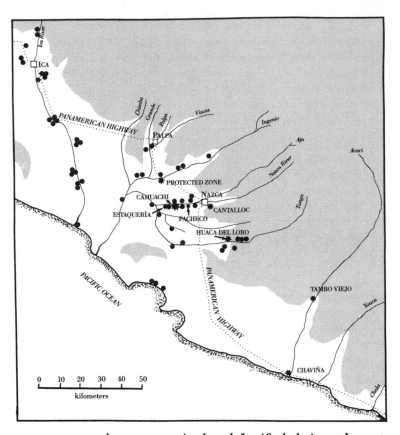

Map of some of the key archaeological sites in the Nazca region.

pants seem to have reorganized and fortified their settlement when they adopted Nazca ware. This site, known as Tambo Viejo, now stretched for nearly a mile with its shrines, plazas and rectangular, stone-footed houses, all protected by a defensive wall. Was this site a military outpost of the Nazca empire? Or were the walls merely a sign of general unrest and insecurity?

Despite his belief that Cahuachi was the Nazca capital, Strong found little evidence of dense human occupation there during the period when Nazca power was at its peak. What he did find were the remains of ritual activity. Beautifully painted pottery vessels had been smashed everywhere, perhaps deliberately in the course of ceremonial drinking.

The most imposing structure of all, which Strong named "the Great Temple," was a pyramid about 70 feet high, built of mud-bricks around a natural hill. Below it, a series of walled courts and buildings covered the broad terrace that sloped down to the Nazca River. At the Great Temple itself, Strong unearthed the remains of ceremonial or sacrificial offerings, including bird plumage, llama remains and an unusual number of broken ceramic panpipes.

Such panpipes are among the most interesting of Nazca artifacts. A researcher in ancient music, Jorge Haeberli, has recently demonstrated that the tuning does not correspond to a Western pentatonic scale. Instead, panpipes found in different valleys and probably dating to different periods all share a deliberate, consistent pattern of tuning. (In technical musical terms, Haeberli describes this special tuning as an arithmetic scale corresponding to equal-frequency stops.) Haeberli concludes that only a standard, centralized system of music could explain the tuning of the pipes.

Just as a consistent set of images was painted by Nazca potters, so, it seems, a unified form of music was practiced by the pipe players. The presence of instruments at the Great Temple suggests the importance of this music in religious activities and reinforces the idea that Cahuachi was the center of a highly organized ceremonial cult.

But was it necessarily a city, or the capital of a military empire? The assumptions based on Strong's digs of 1952 and 1953 remained unchallenged until 1984, when a new investigation began at Cahuachi. The project's director, Helaine Silverman, emphasizes that her work is still in progress, yet already her findings suggest a radically different picture of Nazca society.

It now seems unlikely that Cahuachi was ever a bustling population center. The newly excavated areas of the site have none of the refuse normally associated with everyday occupation. Instead, raised platforms and pyramid mounds, all built of mud bricks, were arranged so as to enclose an impressive series of plazas and patios. Much of this formal layout of structures was kept scrupulously clean; clearly, it was not intended for ordinary activities.

Nor does the evidence found at other sites besides Cahuachi appear to support the "military empire" theory. The results of Silverman's new survey of some of the major river valleys in the Nazca region point to a very different picture. Though still incomplete, the survey suggests that Nazca populations were scattered evenly across the agricultural valleys. There are no unusually large or complex ruins such as we might expect if the Nazca leaders had been called upon to govern a kingdom. Indeed, there are no traces of the storage rooms, administrative facilities and military barracks that are all clearly visible at Inca sites dated some thousand years later. Evidently the requirements of an imperial state simply did not exist in the Nazca epoch.

The conclusion seems obvious: it was the prestige of Nazca religion, and the sanctity of the cult centered at Cahuachi, that briefly united the peoples of the south coast. Nazca priests and

A clay panpipe, decorated with the figure of a dancer.

chiefs must have relied more on their spiritual authority than on the control of material goods or armies.

Of course, the fact that Nazca beliefs were widely shared does not necessarily mean that the people of the south coast lived together in peace and harmony. But the violence implicit in the painted scenes of warriors and severed heads is more likely to have arisen from small-scale feuding than from wholesale campaigns of conquest.

The End of the Cult

THE HEYDAY OF CAHUACHI was short-lived. Based on her latest investigations, Helaine Silverman estimates that the period of most intense activity at the site may have lasted for as little as two centuries. Then, perhaps around A.D. 200, Cahuachi was abandoned along with several other important sites, including Tambo Viejo.

Whatever had happened, it did not spell the end of Nazca culture. On the contrary, the distinctive later styles of Nazca pottery are distributed even more widely, spanning 300 miles of the Peruvian coastal strip from the Cañete Valley to the Yauca. It is difficult to know whether this new pattern corresponds to an actual spread of Nazca people, or whether a more subtle shift had occurred in the relationships of trade and exchange that linked one valley to the next.

At first glance, the designs on Late Nazca pottery suggest a radical break with the past. The surfaces of the vessels are supercharged with restless patterns, mainly in the form of unpleasant-looking creatures intertwined with each other's bristling tongues and curling hair. The potters seem to have hated blank spaces; they filled each corner with curling scrolls and jagged rays. Nothing could be more remote from the pure lines of the early, realistic animal images than this late, baroque style. Yet a careful look at the details of these energetic patterns suggests that the essential themes had in fact changed very little.

Consider, for instance, the exaggerated whiskers, protruding tongues and winged forehead badges displayed by the creatures:

In the Late Nazca period, potters decorated their wares in an increasingly abstract, frenetic style, though they continued to draw on earlier traditional designs, such as masked semi-human "beings" and killer whales.

these were symbols of supernatural authority that had originated in the period of the Paracas mummies nearly a thousand years before. The basic identity of the "monster being" had obviously persisted from one generation to the next, although the Nazca art style itself grew less and less realistic. Even the details added on to the monster's body must have kept their meaning: the face ornaments, severed heads and animal emblems are still recognizable, though reduced to abbreviated, "shorthand" forms.

Perhaps the most notable aspect of these frenetic late designs is the abundance of killer whale jaws and severed heads, which may indicate a deepening preoccupation with death and killing. Had Nazca society actually become more violent or militaristic, as some researchers have argued?

The current work at Cahuachi confirms that the basic beliefs of Nazca religion persisted even after the desertion of the site. For several centuries after the last pyramid mound was raised, the faithful still visited the site to make solitary offerings among the sand dunes. They left behind tokens such as a richly decorated pot, a stone knife wrapped in layers of wool and maize leaves, and even a mummified human head.

The continuing importance of the Cahuachi area is further suggested by the remarkable site known as La Estaquería. ("Estaquería" means "place of the stakes.") As late as the 1920s, a strange, unnatural "forest" of algarroba trunks was to be seen here, commanding a terrace above the Nazca River, about two miles downstream from Cahuachi. The six-foot-high posts had been arranged in twelve rows of twenty posts each. They were set up on top of a rectangular adobe platform that was oriented roughly east-west. An extension of the platform to the west supported at least one row of tall trunks about twelve feet high.

A view of La Estaquería taken in 1985, showing remnants of over two hundred posts originally erected in the Late Nazca period. Below, the striking wooden carved face discovered at the site by Strong in 1952.

Today fewer than a couple of dozen posts remain at La Estaquería, and some of these are now reduced to pathetic stumps. All the rest have long since been hauled away by local farmers, who prize the algarroba wood for its exceptional durability; the surviving posts are still iron-hard after more than a thousand years.

Old photographs show that nearly all the posts were forked at the top, as if to support some kind of roof or canopy. Isolated single posts with forked tops also seem to have been used as grave markers in the surrounding cemetery. If the forked shape had some intrinsic meaning, it may be that La Estaquería was an unroofed colonnade, rather than an actual building.

Whatever its precise nature, we know that visitors left pottery and refuse there for at least a century (probably around A.D. 600 to 700). This was a time when the Nazca world had begun to change, slowly but profoundly, as the first of a series of "waves of influence" from the Andes spread down to the coast. These influences flowed from two major highland sites, the citadel of Huari near present-day Ayacucho, and Tiahuanaco, famous for its monolithic stone temples, situated on the desolate Bolivian altiplano. For a time, these two sites may have functioned as rival or joint administrative centers that exerted power over an immense area of Peru. Archaeologists have still not agreed whether this happened as the result of aggressive military conquest or because of a profoundly influential religious and cultural movement.

In the Nazca region, there were certainly fundamental changes in the old way of life, though none of them happened overnight. Among the first signs of the highland impact are three unusual circular structures, each located at a strategic point

William Duncan Strong, a pioneer investigator of Nazca sites, seen standing on the excavated circular stone wall of the temple at Huaca del Loro. Map of the site, right, is based on Strong's excavation plan.

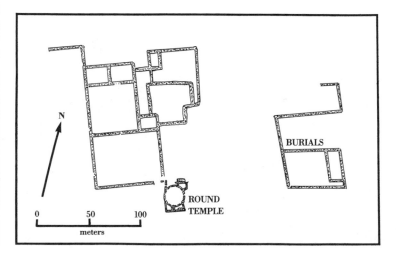

along major tributaries of the Nazca basin. They were not defensive towers, however.

When Strong excavated one of them, at a site he named Huaca del Loro (Parrot Mound) on the Tunga River, he came across unmistakable signs of ritual activity. The circular structure had been built sturdily of stone, plastered over with adobe and painted red. In the complex of rooms that adjoined it, Strong unearthed a curious fossilized whalebone leaning against a wall. Nearby there were other unexpected objects including llama bones and mummified macaws: presumably these were remnants of sacrifices or offerings. Similar finds of llama bones were also reported at another circular structure at Pacheco, a site located close to Cahuachi. It seems clear that the round towers were actually temples rather than fortifications.

Similar round towers are known from the highlands around Huari, and they certainly represent a new development in the Nazca region. For the first time, a religious structure was built compactly out of stone, rather than in the form of a sprawling earth mound or pyramid. Even more significantly, the extensive room complexes adjoining the temples suggest that the population of the valleys was now drawn together around the new sites.

Around A.D. 600–700, Nazca art finally waned as new traditions developed under influence from the highlands. A major center for the new styles was Pacheco, not far from Cahuachi on the Nazca River, where this magnificent vessel was found. Though retaining elements of Late Nazca craftsmanship, the images on the vessel are in a much stiffer style, and probably depict a "storm god" of highland origin.

R. Apache!?

... think of the kachina dolls

Meanwhile, highland influences were registered in local weaving and pottery designs. A few of the age-old Nazca images persisted (notably the head of the mythical "monster," so abbreviated as to be almost unrecognizable), but new symbols were now painted just as prominently, such as broad bands filled with triangles.

There is an obvious danger of reading too much into such changes in artistic taste. However, it does look as if the fundamental identity of the Nazca people was being reshaped by outsiders. According to one theory, the new religious influences represented by the round towers were later followed by a full-fledged colony of Huari settlers established at Pacheco, not far from the old deserted "capital" of Cahuachi.

Another theory suggests that the pressure of a prolonged drought during the seventh and eighth centuries may have stirred the territorial ambitions of the highlanders. The impact of such a drought could equally well have affected the Nazca population, prompting them to congregate in the first real towns of the region. In any case, the result was a gradual shifting of political relationships with their highland neighbors. The old way of life was not crushed by sudden invasion; indeed, it may have been transformed from within as much as from the influence of outsiders.

One thing is clear: the ancient achievements of Nazca were not totally lost. Nazca contributions to Huari art, for example, were substantial. Through the same channels, aspects of Nazca beliefs are likely to have survived, and may well have become part of the complex mixture of traditions celebrated by the Incas.

But what exactly *was* the Nazca belief system? Is it possible to make any sense of such a strange collection of creatures—the whiskered winged cats, the whale-jawed flying monsters, the sprouting severed heads? Were the ideas behind these images as fantastic as their appearance might lead us to think?

HEADHUNTERS AND HALLUCINOGENS

CHAPTER 9

Revolt of the Head-Shrinkers

Oが

ONE OF THE MOST HORRIFIC INCIDENTS in the history of Spanish colonialism occurred in 1599 in the eastern foothills of the Ecuadorean Andes. Here the Paute, Zamora and Upano rivers tumble in a long series of steep rapids and waterfalls toward the Amazon.

Early Spanish settlers were attracted to this rugged, inhospitable jungle because of its rich placer gold deposits. For a time, local Indian tribes were compelled to work the deposits for their Spanish masters. However, when the local governor decided to levy a large tax to pay for the celebration of King Philip III's coronation, a plot was hatched among the most aggressive of these tribes, the Jívaro.

The conspiracy was so well organized that a Jívaro army of twenty thousand men entered the town of Logroño at midnight and caught the Spaniards completely by surprise. The naked governor was forced out of bed; the gold intended for his tax was heated in a crucible and poured down his throat. The Jívaro massacred everyone except for the "eligible" women, and then turned their attention to another major settlement at Sevilla del Oro. After a day-long pitched battle, a second massacre began; altogether it was rumored that twenty thousand or more Spaniards died in the two cities.

Though the Spanish made several subsequent attempts to reconquer the region, all their expeditions met disastrous ends, their forces decimated by the spears and blowguns of the Jívaro. In fact, the Jívaro are the *only* Native American people who ever revolted against Spain and then successfully maintained their freedom.

Status symbols, past and present, among the Jívaro of eastern Ecuador: a warrior displaying the shrunken head of his victim at a victory feast, photographed in the late 1920s, and (right), a man in the late 1970s with a radio for picking up broadcasts from the Jívaro's own educational network.

Even in recent decades, they have preserved a remarkable independence in adapting to the pressures of modern civilization. Since 1964, a group known as the Shuar Federation, backed by missionaries and governed by Catholicized Jívaro, has established legal landholding rights and promoted Jívaro culture through its education program and radio broadcasts. Nevertheless, in the process some highly distinctive features of Jívaro society have been lost. During the 1960s and 1970s, the missionaries collaborated with the Ecuadorean military to suppress the ferocious blood feuds that had made the Jívaro notorious. This campaign apparently stamped out their most infamous practice of all, the shrinking of human heads.

When miniature heads reached European curio markets in the mid-nineteenth century, the Jívaro quickly became synonymous with primitive savagery and cunning. Not surprisingly, few scientists ventured near them until the late 1950s, when University of California anthropologist Michael J. Harner spent a total of fourteen months among the widely dispersed communities of the interior. These families had no regular contacts with white people, and, as Harner soon discovered, lived in constant fear of violent death. At night, house doors were always barred against the possibility of attack. Men slept with guns at their sides and rarely ventured more than a few hundred feet from their houses unarmed. When they visited another family, it was customary for their hostess to sample her manioc beer before serving it, to demonstrate that it had not been poisoned. Children grew up with few friends outside the close-knit family household, partly because neighbors were usually half a mile or more away, and partly because of the need for constant vigilance.

The Jívaro loathed the territory of other tribes, so wars of conquest were avoided. Violence sprang almost entirely from interpersonal feuds and quarrels, the grievances nursed until revenge was taken. Small assassination groups, recruited from the most reknowned killers as well as from immediate male family members, always worked with extreme stealth and secrecy, usually at night. Shooting a victim in the back involved no dishonor; the only shame was failure to avenge a death.

What was it that compelled the Jívaro to accept as normal an atmosphere of perpetual terror? Since they practiced shifting cultivation and there was no shortage of jungle, the drive behind their conflicts was obviously not territorial. Bloodshed often followed quarrels over women, but the real motivation was an extraordinary belief system.

The very word *shuara* ("Jívaro Indian") was synonymous with the word "enemy." A male Jívaro's identity and virility rested on his ability to eliminate other Jívaros. Prestige in life was inseparable from skill in delivering death; the collecting of trophy heads was the most dramatic symbol of this fact.

The Jívaro believed that the ordinary, waking world was an illusion. Access to the hidden world of spiritual forces was obtained by vigils, fasting and particularly by ingesting plant hallucinogens. These substances were such an important part of Jívaro life that mild hallucinogens were even administered to newborn infants to awaken their powers of insight.

At about six years of age, the most important quest of a Jívaro man's life began—his mission to acquire ancestor ghost souls, known as *arutam* souls. Over the course of several days, the boy would seek a vision of an *arutam* at a sacred waterfall. The vision would come to him either while he strode back and forth under the cold spray of the waterfall, or as a result of ingesting datura, a powerful, dangerous hallucinogenic plant. When the *arutam* came, it often took the shape of menacing jaguars or anacondas, or a human head. If he dared to rush forward and

A Jívaro shrunken head.

touch the frightening vision, the boy established contact with the *arutam*. Later, at nightfall, the same ancestral spirit would come to him in a dream and enter his body, where it lodged in his chest.

Once acquired, an *arutam* soul made a man invulnerable to murder or sorcery. Moreover, it also aroused in him a powerful homicidal urge, an urge that was essential to his survival, since the protection provided by the *arutam* was only temporary. After about two weeks, the *arutam's* power would ebb away completely unless renewed by an act of murder. By joining in a successful killing expedition, he would then be entitled to a new *arutam* soul that would "lock in" the power of the previous one. If the intended victim escaped, however, some other enemy or victim was invariably picked, since the assassins would be expected to die within weeks if they did not kill someone. Those Jívaros who survived long enough to acquire many *arutam* souls through multiple killngs acquired genuine security and prestige, since they were considered invulnerable to attack.

Revenge played as important a part in the supernatural world as in the human. When a man who had acquired an *arutam* was killed, he formed another soul known as a *muisak*, or avenging soul. If no attempt was made to control it, the *muisak* would turn itself into a venomous snake and stage an "accident" that would kill the murderer or one of his relatives. The most secure means of controlling the *muisak* was to cut off the victim's head and shrink it with hot sand. This process was done as quickly as possible, to force the avenging soul to enter the head. Later, the Jívaro held a series of feasts, not only to ensure that the *muisak* remained trapped in the head but also to exploit its power.

Besides its avenging aspect, the specter inside the trophy head was a source of regenerative, fertile forces. Women in Jívaro society were relatively powerless, since they could rarely acquire *arutam* souls; nevertheless, they could absorb the influences of the *muisak*. To do so, they held on to the body of their killer kinsman in the midst of the feast. As he raised the shrunken head aloft, its power was believed to pass through his body and into the women. This act enabled the women to work harder and be more successful in cultivating crops (their major responsibility besides cooking and housekeeping).

In the Jívaro mind, these paradoxical notions of fertility and vengeance, life and death, were drawn together in a delicate state of balance. The trophy head was a potent symbol of this balance of opposites.

Sex, Death and Severed Heads

T HOUGH SUCH A BELIEF SYSTEM seems extraordinary to us, we know that it was by no means confined to the eastern Andes. Miguel de Estete, who accompanied Pizarro on his third voyage of exploration in 1527, encountered head-shrinking natives on an island off the coast of Ecuador. He described their practices in detail:

> So many are the baths that they give it, so as to cure and preserve it, that they make the face of a man to be wasted and shrunken and become quite small, much more so even than that of a newborn child. After having reduced it to a small size, they guard it in some small chests that they have in the temple, and it lasts so many years without rotting that the Indians say it lasts two or three ages. Certainly it is a thing to admire, and one never seen before. And so it seemed to us when we first saw it, holding it to be certain that they were faces of a race of dwarfs that had lived in the country, until we learned the truth of the matter.

Furthermore, warfare and fertility are still linked together in the Andean mind. In certain remote areas of highland Peru and Bolivia, ritualized battles are held each year between different communities (or sections of communities). These may involve considerable bloodshed. According to informants, the blood spilled in combat serves to feed the female earth mother, Pachamama, and so restore fertility to the crops. Traditions like these suggest that Jívaro beliefs were not simply the freak products of an isolated jungle existence, but were actually concepts that had once been widespread in the Andes.

The strongest evidence for head-hunting beliefs in ancient Peru comes from the cultures of Paracas and Nazca. We have seen how the severed head dominates the imagery of Paracas textiles and Nazca pottery. A popular type of Nazca drinking mug was decorated entirely with almost life-size features of a trophy head. Other painted or embroidered scenes show both human warriors and "monster beings" who grasp trophy heads by the hair, carry them in baskets or slung from belts, or display them emblazoned on their bodies or costumes.

Many of these depictions convey an impression of power pouring out of the head, perhaps similar to the concept of the *muisak* soul. Indeed, the humans and "monsters" usually seem

Human heads were popular subjects for Nazca potters. Details of decoration suggest that most were meant to represent mummified heads rather than living portraits.

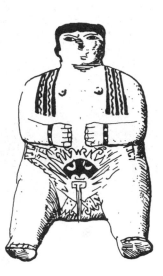

Nazca artists seem to have connected sexuality or menstruation with images of bloodshed and aggression. Pottery effigy, above, *shows a woman with the killer whale symbol over her vagina. A more abstract vessel,* below, *shows a row of female faces beneath the killer whale; red streaks resembling blood flow from the killer whale jaws.*

to be caught in the midst of a supernatural transformation. Their tongues (or blood?) are almost always shown flowing out of their mouths, sometimes as a long streamer that joins with otherworldly creatures. Severed heads, too, often seem to be emitting power through their tongues or hair. To Nazca artists, this power may have carried an aggressive meaning, perhaps signifying vengeance, since they constantly painted trophy heads alongside predator symbols such as the jaws of the killer whale and the wings of the falcon.

Yet the Nazca artisans were not obsessed merely by images of death. Occasionally they depicted realistic, carefully observed scenes of pregnancy and childbirth. In one case, a woman is shown in labor in a crouching position, so that the presence of a midwife may be inferred. Several other Nazca vessels feature women's sexual organs painted with remarkable anatomic accuracy, including details of the clitoris. In two examples, Nazca potters even represented the hymenal membrane, centuries before European anatomists of the sixteenth century recognized its connection with virginity.

Surprisingly, the trophy head, too, is associated with sexual and fertility themes. A number of fully modeled ceramic vessels in the form of fat naked women with clear sexual markings show the trophy head on the woman's body. (In one case, the woman is actually in the process of giving birth.) Furthermore, the killer whale mouth (a death symbol) is also shown on these women, in some instances right over the vagina.

The trophy head was also associated with plant fertility. On some Paracas embroideries, the flying "monsters" carry sprouting beans as well as severed heads. In fact, occasionally beans *are* trophy heads: the two designs alternate and seem to be interchangeable, as if they amount to the same thing. Furthermore, Nazca pottery frequently shows peppers, beans or fruit sprouting from the mouth of a disembodied head.

These extreme "life" and "death" oppositions in Nazca art hint at the presence of beliefs similar to those of the Jívaro. Of course, it is difficult to know whether life in ancient Nazca really was as fraught with violence as it was until the 1970s in the jungles of Ecuador. Nevertheless, the Jívaro example does help us to imagine how an ideology of human trophy heads could have functioned as a spiritual driving force and as the vital inspiration for the religious art of Nazca. The key question, clearly, is whether there really *is* evidence of Nazca head-hunting, or whether their beliefs were grounded only in myths and legends.

A shrunken head presented during the last century to Prince Albert, Queen Victoria's Consort, was said to have come from a tomb at Pisco, near Paracas. (Unfortunately, the Prince's reaction was never recorded!) However, other than this one example, there have been no indisputable finds of miniature heads at ancient Peruvian sites.

Full-sized trophy heads, on the other hand, are well-documented in many different parts of the Andean world. The practice of burying carefully mummified heads seems to have been common in southern Peru; headless bodies are often reported from the same cemeteries. A typical Nazca trophy head is perforated with a hole in the forehead through which a rope was passed; often, fragments of this rope survive. In its original state, the rope would be threaded through the skull and tied to the base of it. Portability of the head, it seems, was an important factor.

The process of mummifying heads must have been a skillful, gruesome operation. Studies of the Nazca heads suggest that the skin was removed first, the skull was then boiled to clean it, and finally the skin was stretched back into place and painted with an unidentified red preservative. Intriguingly, certain details of this process were identical to Jívaro practice, such as the binding of the upper and lower lips with thorns. Did these Nazca heads, then, represent "enemies" in the Jívaro sense?

Unfortunately, only one discovery of trophy heads has ever been documented carefully. This investigation was conducted in 1967 and 1969 by archaeologists Maximo Neira and Vera Coelho at an ancient cemetery known as Chaviña, located near the sea at the southern limits of Nazca territory. Though the site had been heavily looted, they found a total of eleven mummified heads, most of them still undisturbed from their original resting places. The heads had been deposited in a line running along the base of a mud-brick wall about a meter and a half thick, far too solid and substantial to belong to an ordinary domestic structure. Neira and Coelho suggested that it was the remains of some kind of ceremonial building.

Most of the heads had been carefully wrapped in cotton cloth (two in fine multicolored gauze), and then set in shallow holes dug in the bedrock. One head had been placed for protection inside a large domestic cooking pot with a broken base. Two others were covered by coarse pot fragments and a stone respectively. The mummified body of a yellow-haired puppy was also discovered. It was wrapped in the same kind of cloth and had been deposited at the same level, perhaps as a sacrificial offering. No weapons or other objects came to light, but most of the heads were buried with food offerings such as maize, peanuts and guinea pig meat.

A careful examination of each head revealed some intriguing

Carefully buried, mummified heads are common at Nazca sites. The example here, above, has the original carrying rope still intact. Effigy head, below, probably buried with a headless corpse, is decorated with copper eyes and scarlet parrot feathers.

facts. At least one belonged to a woman, another to a child between the ages of about nine and twelve. All eleven skulls displayed the deliberately deformed, elongated shape typical of the Nazca culture, and all were pierced with a hole for a carrying rope.

Signs of violent death emerged from the study of one skull heavily stained by a black substance, subsequently identified in a chemical analysis as blood. The jaw had been struck so severely that the lower right part of it was missing, even though the entire head had been carefully wrapped up inside a cloth. The investigators concluded that this individual had been violently beheaded.

Can we explain all this evidence by supposing that mummified heads were prepared as a special kind of burial rite or as a magical act of sacrifice, rather than as a direct consequence of war? That is what the discovery of the heads of a female and a child at Chaviña seems to indicate.

In any case, the practice obviously represents more than just a crude habit of displaying heads of vanquished foes. While feuding or head-hunting between Nazca communities could still be involved, the most likely purpose of the trophies was not so much to celebrate aggression as to control a potent source of supernatural power. Even today, Andean folktales speak of ominous "flying heads" that leave the body of a sorcerer to work mischief while he sleeps. In ancient times, the beliefs surrounding trophy heads were clearly a central ingredient in a complicated ritual system. The heads themselves survive as macabre museum relics of a distinctive religious outlook in which thoughts of death and fertility were intertwined.

Nazca warriors, some human and some evidently supernatural; images drawn from a variety of decorated pots.

Flights Out of the Body

THE GLOWING COLORS and contorted figures of Nazca and Paracas art have a visionary, dreamlike quality. Some are so peculiar and disturbing that it is natural to wonder if they could be the products of something else besides mere imagination.

In fact, many natural mind-altering substances have been known and exploited in Peru for thousands of years. The most widely used is coca, a bush whose leaves are chewed by native Andeans to suppress hunger and fatigue at high altitude. (Cocaine is artificially refined and concentrated from the same plant, in a process unknown among traditional societies in Peru.) In addition, coca leaves are an excellent source of vitamins and have a soothing effect on the digestion. Normally their stimulating effects are mild (so mild that tourists arriving at Cuzco are advised to drink tea brewed from coca to counteract altitude sickness). But in excessive quantities, coca can bring on trancelike states in which traditional healers are able to diagnose sickness or forecast the future.

Although today coca is grown mainly in the eastern Andes, a smaller-leafed variety is also known on the coast. The leaves were certainly circulating among coastal peoples by at least 2500 B.C. Traces of the plant were discovered at Huaca Prieta, a site dating to that period located in the central coast region. Moreover, Nazca pottery designs sometimes depict men with bulging cheeks who are probably chewing coca.

This activity is likely to have been highly sacred, to judge from the Incas' veneration of the bush. The fields where coca was cultivated were considered sanctuaries, while the ritual burning or scattering of the leaves was an essential preliminary for any kind of ceremony. The Inca reserved coca exclusively for the elite classes; its use spread to farmers and laborers throughout the Andes only after the Conquest.

A coca branch, most revered of the traditional sacred plants of the Andes.

The Nazca elite probably had access to much more powerful stimulants than coca. For example, Nazca pottery designs depict a graceful, curling plant motif resembling the tendrils of datura, the potent plant hallucinogen used by the Jívaro. In more recent times, Peruvians drank infusions made from the leaves and black seeds of datura to contact ancestors, to work love magic, and even to discipline naughty children. Another hallucinogenic plant known as *wilka* may have been important because it was traditionally grown in the highland area closest to Nazca, around the present-day city of Ayacucho. *Wilka* was usually taken as a snuff, or its seeds were mixed with tea or maize beer. Apparently, it granted either visions of the gods or communications with the devil. In the case of yet another plant, a coastal fruit known as *espingo*, the seeds added to maize beer "made people go crazy," according to Spanish chroniclers.

Ancient Peruvians made a potent hallucinogenic snuff known as wilka *from the seeds of a tree* (Anadenathera colubrina). *On Moche pots from the north coast, this tree is often depicted alongside deer designs. Contemporary healers such as Eduardo Calderón associate deer with swiftness and elusiveness—desirable qualities for the soul in the midst of its hallucinogenic trance.*

It is unlikely that any of these substances were taken in a casual, recreational setting, the way most drugs are consumed today. Instead, hallucinogens provided a gateway to spiritual realms that were dangerous to enter without extensive ritual preparation. Even today, only Peruvian folk healers who have undergone years of training can master the forces that they may encounter in the trance state.

Such folk traditions underline the essentially religious nature of the drug experience in Andean culture. Could the sanctity of the plants be connected with some of the sacred symbols depicted by Nazca and Paracas artists?

In fact, one plant in particular offers remarkable insight into the meaning of their designs, and perhaps also the significance of the Nazca desert drawings.

I first became acquainted with the San Pedro cactus at a remarkable institution near the main square of Lima. Here, at the Museum of Health Sciences, a distinguished neurologist and botanical scholar, Dr. Fernando Cabieses, has established a center for the study of traditional Peruvian medical practices. Among the exhibits is a roof garden where Cabieses' assistants

A San Pedro cactus sliced in half, and right, comparison of the star-shaped section with a motif common on Nazca pottery.

cultivate a wide range of living herbs, flowers and cacti still used by folk healers of the present day.

On this roof garden, under the perpetual gloomy smog of the Lima sky, Dr. Cabieses led me to a bowl where a thick, green, elongated cactus with a star-shaped cross section was growing. This, he explained, was the San Pedro, one of the hallucinogenic plants most venerated and sought after by Peruvian healers today.

Cabieses believes that it was also highly regarded by the people of Nazca. To demonstrate this, his assistant chopped the cactus neatly in half, revealing a pale white interior with a faint green ring around the center. He then produced a rather plain Nazca bowl painted with a simple repetitive pattern. This pattern was almost identical to the cross section of the San Pedro, complete with its starlike outline and the ring at the center. Cabieses thinks that this supposedly abstract design, quite common on Nazca pottery, was actually a symbol standing for the cactus and signifying its sacred importance to the Nazca culture.

At one point Dr. Cabieses was called away to attend to business and I was left alone on the roof garden, faced with the glistening white end of the San Pedro still exposed to my view. The temptation grew too much, and on an impulse that I quickly came to regret, I brushed my finger lightly against the moist flesh of the cactus and dabbed it on my tongue. Moments later, I started to sweat, my heart pounded, and I began to experience an alarming feeling of disorientation. Fortunately, this lasted only for a few minutes, but I was left in no doubt of both the risks of casually experimenting with the sacred plants and the power of the San Pedro itself.

Chemical analysis has shown that a dried extract of the cactus contains no less than 2 percent mescaline, the highest concentration of this hallucinogenic agent known in any plant. Traditionally, Peruvian folk healers boil up pieces of San Pedro for several hours, often stirring in other ingredients such as datura. In addition to drinking this mixture, those present at a ceremony often inhale a potion of tobacco, perfumes, lime juice and cane alcohol through the nostrils. What does a participant experience in such a formidably altered frame of mind?

Most of our knowledge comes from the study of one gifted man, Eduardo Calderón, an artist, fisherman and healer living on the north coast of Peru. Since 1970, anthropologist Douglas Sharon has apprenticed himself to Calderón and has also studied the practices of other healers in the same region. Their collaboration led to the making of a memorable film, *Eduardo the Healer*, which includes highly dramatic sequences shot in the midst of Eduardo's night-long curing sessions.

Calderón himself classifies his clients' sicknesses either as natural illnesses or as ailments brought on by potions added to food or drink or by the mental action of witchcraft. The manner of his healing is as much psychological as physical, since it addresses the self-image and spiritual condition of his clients. The San Pedro cactus is essential to his healing, allowing him to "see" into his patients' illnesses and remove the causes of them. Eduardo explains it like this:

> What do we look at? The color of the aura, which is a reflection of the person's personality. Everything that he has done before and after to contribute to alienation, to sickness, to fear, to apprehension, to anxiety leaps forth at that moment. Why? Because the San Pedro and all the other herbs help us. They make one vibrate. They make one light up. Each person has a special vibration jointly with the master and with the elements that envelop him. In a curing session this "vision" develops by means of the potion of San Pedro and the other herbs.

The rituals are held at night because the patient is then in a dreamlike state, in touch with both past and present emotions.

To help effect cures, Eduardo has collected dozens of special objects or talismans that he arranges on a rectangular piece of linen placed on the ground in front of him. This is his "table," or *mesa*, and on it are assembled seashells, fragments of ancient pottery, distinctive natural stones and crystals, herbs, images of saints, and various scents and perfumes. Planted upright in front of the *mesa* is a row of carved wooden staffs, together with a pair of swords, just in case they should be needed to combat malevolent spirits in the trance.

The tops of several of the wooden staffs are carved in the forms of individual animals, such as a greyhound, an eagle, a

hummingbird, a swordfish and a serpent. Each of these animals represents a spirit helper that assists in the cure; the hummingbird, for instance, "gathers together" or sucks out pains and sickness.

All these *mesa* objects are arranged in a careful sequence; those associated with "the Field of Evil" are grouped on the left. The remainder (mostly statues of Christ and his saints) represent "the Field of Justice" and are placed on the right. Eduardo relies on the central portion of the *mesa* to balance out these two opposite "fields," or contrary forces, and it is this mediation between good and evil that leads to a successful cure.

The objects themselves are merely tools through which Eduardo perceives and interprets the flow of supernatural energy. Depending on his patient's condition, the staffs vibrate or an object on the *mesa* "jumps," guiding Eduardo in his diagnosis. All this takes place in an atmosphere far removed from clinical modern medicine, for Eduardo performs lengthy chants and invocations to the spirits while shaking his rattle.

Curing sessions like these almost certainly go back centuries, if not thousands of years, on the Peruvian coast. Wooden staffs and rattles almost identical with Eduardo's "tools" have been unearthed in Moche tombs just a short distance from his home town. Moche pots often show realistically painted or modeled healing scenes. Eduardo is not only able to interpret these

Eduardo Calderón's mesa, *showing the "power objects" he calls upon to aid him in his trance, and* right, *Eduardo in action. The large can in front of the staffs contains the infusion of hallucinogenic San Pedro cactus.*

scenes in detail but actually studied them as guides during his own apprenticeship.

One of the most common ways in which healing is represented on a Moche pot is by the form of an old woman wearing an owl mask and holding a piece of San Pedro cactus in her outstretched hand. Eduardo has a staff carved with this woman's image, and he identifies her as a supernatural guardian of the highland lagoons where sacred herbs and plants grow. The Moche figure indicates that the central role of the San Pedro in north coast rituals goes back over a thousand years.

Painted Moche scenes also depict warriors wearing eagle wings as if poised in "magical flight." For Eduardo, the eagle is an important creature; his eagle staff, carved of black wood with the dried head and claws of an eagle fixed to its top, stands for the attributes of personal intelligence and vision. These are qualities necessary to improve the morale of the patient.

During his curing chants, Eduardo associates the eagle with the high mountain peaks of Peru and with the soul's magical ability to leave the body and soar through the air. Eduardo himself performs these flights in the San Pedro trance, visiting the far peaks of the Andes and entering the passageways of caves and ancient tombs. As he explains, there is no question of his body's actually leaving the ground during these flights. What flies is:

A Moche pot from northern Peru depicting an owl-headed supernatural folk healer. Though the pot was probably made at least a thousand years ago, many of the owl-woman's power objects are identical to those still used by curers on the north coast today.

a person's mental force, nothing more, as well as the element of the herb (the potions that I drink) working united with it, that activates the "third eye," the "sixth sense." What works is the mind. . . . The mind is what makes one fly.

Out-of-the-body experiences are apparently one of the most common effects of ingesting San Pedro. At the Museum of Health Sciences, Dr. Cabieses explained to me that he, too, had felt the sensation of flying after taking the cactus.

Then he showed me Nazca pots on which faithful depictions of the San Pedro appeared side by side with animals such as spiders, lizards, foxes and, above all, birds. Falcons and hummingbirds were particularly common. The most impressive vessel I saw was in the shape of a finely sculptured falcon on top of a spherical cactus.

Cabieses and other researchers suggest that such themes are not just examples of decoration, but convey a message: the soul can "fly" under the influence of the cactus. Since many of the best Nazca pots were almost certainly made specifically to accompany the burial of the dead, it was only appropriate that the designs painted on them should symbolize the ability of the soul

Eduardo Calderón now regularly initiates westerners into his healing practices. This recent photograph shows him with a stone spiral specially constructed for these activities. Eduardo believes that many of the Nazca figures were similarly used as mazelike pathways to initiate healers in the midst of hallucinogenic trances.

to leave the body. Falcons were a natural choice for such designs, since their keen eyesight may have been likened to the far-reaching "vision" of the Nazca priest as he "flew" during the San Pedro trance.

The phenomenon of magical flight was obviously important on the Peruvian coast at least as far back as the 1630s, when Antonio de la Calancha, an Augustinian cleric, reported that native healers had experiences of flying while divining the future. If, as seems likely, Nazca religious leaders really did have out-of-the-body experiences, could this help to explain why animals were traced on the pampa on such a large scale that they could only be seen properly from above?

Although some of the Nazca animals may well have represented "star gods" actually visible in the night sky, it seems just as likely that they stood for the hidden supernatural energies still invoked by healers on the Peruvian coast today. Perhaps the animal drawings on the pampa were talismans on a giant scale—intended, like the animal staffs of Eduardo's *mesa*, to contact the power of spirit helpers encountered in the hallucinatory trance. The fact that birds (including two hummingbirds) predominate among the creatures traced on the pampa may be significant. The *belief* that Nazca priests flew as they communicated with supernatural animals may have been one of the crucial motives in setting out the gigantic designs.

Few scenes in Nazca art appear to relate to healing (severed heads, we recall, were a more popular theme!). On the other hand, nearly all the unreal "monsters" painted on Nazca vessels and embroidered on Paracas textiles are shown as if they were flying through the air. Falcon wings and tails are frequently joined to their bodies. Do these fearsome beings represent the spiritual power released by the hallucinogenic experience? Are they, in fact, images of the priest or healer himself, transformed in full flight into a master of supernatural energy?

Furthermore, if animals represent important spiritual forces summoned up during the trance, as they do in Eduardo's practice, then the whisker masks that appear so persistently carry a special meaning. One clue to this meaning may be the belief, widely reported among South American tribes in recent times, that a shaman can transform himself into a jaguar or another feline by taking hallucinogenic substances. Some such belief was probably established in Peru at least three thousand years ago, since sculptures of half-human, half-feline beings grasping the San Pedro cactus can be dated back that far. If this concept was indeed in the minds of the Paracas or Nazca artists, then the catlike mask may be an emblem of transformation. It may, perhaps, signify the release of magical animal power as the soaring voyage of the soul begins.

Even if we take speculations such as these seriously, there are nevertheless some important differences between Eduardo's healing and Nazca religion. The images on pots and textiles do not refer simply to a system of folk medicine, but to a complex series of religious ideas that were followed with remarkable consistency from one valley to the next in southern Peru. As we have seen, the substance of these ideas seems to have been connected with agricultural fertility, death, and perhaps war and aggression. While the specific meaning of trophy heads and killer whale jaws will probably always elude us, the method of contacting and controlling the supernatural may well have resembled the practices of Eduardo Calderón and other modern healers, or even those of the Jívaro shamans.

When a Jívaro seeks to bewitch another, he first drinks a hallucinogenic brew in order to enter the "hidden" world. Once in the trance, he calls up a *wakani*, a soul or spirit bird. Blowing on the bird, he dispatches it to the house of the victim. It flies round and round the man in circles, terrifying him and leading to fever, insanity and, eventually, death. Can we imagine the priests of Cahuachi "flying" in their San Pedro trances, calling up the forces of ancestral heads and of the animals figured on the pampa, to do their supernatural bidding, for good or ill?

Supernatural being holding a San Pedro cactus; a carved stone relief from the site of Chavín, which may date to around 1,000 B.C.

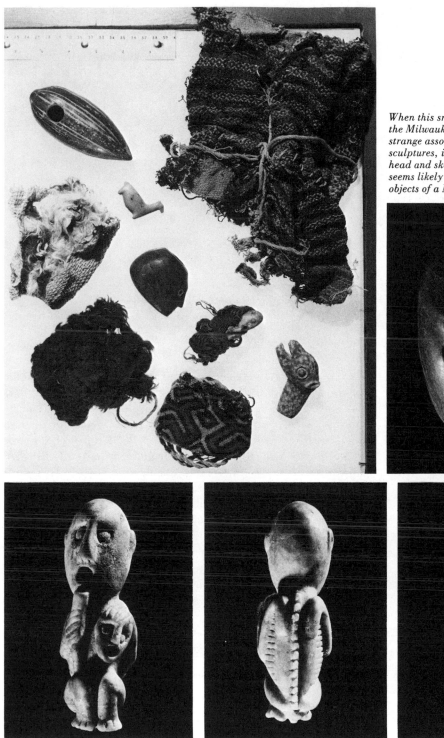

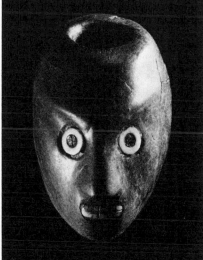

When this small bundle was unwrapped in the Milwaukee Museum, it yielded up a strange assortment of miniature sculptures, including those of a trophy head and skeletal flute player, bottom. It seems likely that these represent the power objects of a Nazca healer or shaman.

CHAPTER 10	# ORDER AND ENMITY: THE SOCIAL WORLD OF THE ANDES

The Festival of Saint Peter

The act of clearing ceremonial strips of ground is still important in the high Andes. Here Baltazar Quispe Herrera sweeps a rectangular section of the plaza at the village of Pacariqtambo, in preparation for the festival of Saint Peter on June 29, 1984.

BALTAZAR QUISPE HERRERA grasped the bundle of *chachakoma* bushes in both hands and began sweeping the village plaza with slow, even strokes. The festival day of Saint Peter, June 29, had just dawned with a heavy overcast and bone-chilling dampness. Shuffling awkwardly because of the leg injury he once suffered after a fall from his horse, Baltazar patiently brushed his way across the plaza, each stroke sending up a puff of dust. Here, at Pacariqtambo, the constant human and animal traffic crossing from one side of the community to the other had left behind a litter of clay, stones and dung, and this debris had to be swept aside before the festival could begin.

Baltazar performed his task with solemn concentration, as if it represented more than a mere practical chore. In fact, it was soon clear that he was not sweeping at random; all of his work was confined to a narrow strip that ran across the plaza. This was the ritual cleared area (or *chuta*, as the people of Pacariqtambo call it) that belonged to his own particular section of the community. It was Baltazar's special responsibility to clean this rectangular area before any dances or processions could begin.

To watch him work was thought-provoking, even though I was shivering and exhausted from a night-long drive through the mountains. My mind naturally jumped from the *chuta*, evidently an important ingredient in the fiestas of Pacariqtambo, to the cleared triangles and trapezoids of Nazca. Could I be watching a reenactment of the same kind of practices that had taken place centuries ago on the Nazca pampa and that still thrived here among the villages of the high Andes?

In fact, Pacariqtambo's links to the remote past are the subject of legend, for it was in a cave near the village that the first Incas are supposed to have emerged from the underworld. According to the myth, Manco Capac, founder of the Inca dynasty, led his brothers and sisters out of the cave and across the mountains, eventually reaching the sacred hill that now overlooks the city of Cuzco. Here Manco is said to have staked his claim to the Cuzco Valley by hurling slingstones toward the four corners of the earth. Even today, the inhabitants of Pacariqtambo (or Tambo, as it is usually nicknamed) are proud of their connection with the Inca origin myth.

← how interesting

The villagers are also aware of present-day realities. Despite their isolation from obvious sources of news (for instance, most have watched television only in store windows during rare visits to Cuzco), I discovered some of them to be sharply conscious of political events. On learning that I was British, several farmers immediately began to tease me about the war against Argentina over the Falkland Islands. Their good-humored jokes came as a great surprise, since their mountain village seemed so utterly remote from the world outside.

Men of Pacariqtambo build a temporary ceremonial altar at the start of the festival of Saint Peter.

But on that day, the festival of Saint Peter, the villagers were preoccupied by the seemingly timeless traditions of the Andes. As Baltazar swept the *chuta* clean, other members of his particular landholding and ceremonial group (or *ayllu*) appeared in the plaza. Together they began to erect a temporary altar at one end of the strip Baltazar was sweeping. They wedged tall upright timbers into the ground, then lashed wooden cross beams to the uprights to form a lattice-shaped framework. Into the middle of this scaffolding they hoisted a shrine containing an image of Christ, surrounded by a boldly patterned mosaic of red and silver foil. Meanwhile, a second work party drawn from a different *ayllu* began raising another, almost identical, altar alongside the first. These twin structures seemed to symbolize the joint effort of the two *ayllu* groups that were sponsoring the festival. In addition, the altars were the focus of strong religious feelings that were to reach their climax later in the morning.

As the clouds gave way to the brilliant clarity of high-altitude sunshine, so the music and dances began. There was a four-piece band from Cuzco, consisting of a fiddle, a flute, an accordion and a magnificent, wide-bodied Andean harp. Tuned to the old five-note (pentatonic) scale of the Incas, these instru-

Is this tuning, significant w/ regard to old healing practices/tones?

ments struck up a melody based on an old colonial *contra-danza;* the unfamiliar harmonies made it sound almost like a parody of the original Spanish tune. Its heavy, insistent rhythm was matched by the formal and stately steps of the dancers, who were clad in brightly embroidered scarlet tunics. They split up into pairs, then joined together again in carefully balanced, wheeling patterns. (These formations reminded me of the Morris dances I had seen performed on English pub lawns and village greens.) Their leader wore a grinning, white-complexioned mask, again suggesting an element of humor at Spanish expense.

Contradancers at the festival of Saint Peter. Their costumes, music and dance steps reflect Spanish traditions, but the masked figure suggests an element of satire, too.

The interweaving of the contradancers presented a pleasing image of balance and order, yet encircling them was a very different group of figures. This was a troupe of bear dancers, or *ukukus,* who had been invited from a neighboring village. Their function seemed to be to take every opportunity to disrupt and ridicule both the dancers and spectators. Their bodies were clad in full-length shaggy brown tunics resembling bearskins, while the stocking masks concealing their faces made them appear sinister and threatening. Nevertheless, most of the time they acted like clowns, playing pranks on the dancers and communicating only in ridiculous, falsetto squeaks.

This mingling of formal and disorderly behavior seemed to characterize the spirit of the Tambo festival as a whole. Even though a mood of reverence and sobriety accompanied most of the day's events, a bowl of the local *chicha*, or maize beer, circulated among the men almost continuously.

The beer's effects were not really noticeable until late afternoon, when a group of men gathered in a field outside the village for their traditional "bear dance." In an everyday setting, Quechua men are characterized by extreme modesty and propriety, but this event (staged well away from the community as

Left, the festival of Saint Peter comes to a climax as the saint's image is carried into the plaza at Pacariqtambo and blessed in front of the temporary altars erected there.

a whole) apparently functioned as a safety valve for the men of Tambo. It quickly degenerated into a bacchanal, as the rhythm of the *contradanza* band became increasingly wilder and more erratic. Some men became too drunk to continue dancing or even to stand up, while others indulged in obscene playacting. Such conduct was not only unheard of during normal daily life, but formed a striking contrast to the behavior of everyone in the village just a few hours before at the climax of the festival.

This climax took the form of a grand procession, as a life-sized effigy of Saint Peter was carried down from the church to the plaza below. Led by the priest from Cuzco, the procession consisted of almost the entire population of Tambo. As they paced slowly down to the plaza, hundreds of voices rose in the solemn chanting of a hymn; even the mischievous *ukukus* sang in earnest with the rest. Finally, the saint's image was positioned in front of one of the temporary altars in the plaza. The crowd sank to its knees as the priest blessed the image. I noticed that green cornstalks had been fastened around the figure of the saint, perhaps to signify the harvest that had just ended. I wondered if the cornstalks might represent an ancient, pre-Christian aspect of the ceremony.

As Gary Urton discovered during his stay of over a year at Tambo, a series of saint's day festivals such as the one I had

Drinking chicha, *or homemade maize beer, is an important focus of both social life and ceremonial activities in the Andes. Here artist-anthropologist Julia Meyerson shares a beaker of* chicha *with men from the village of Colque Urqu near Pacariqtambo.*

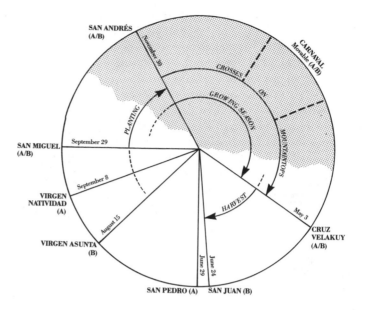

SAN ANDRÉS
(A/B)

November 30

CROSSES

CARNAVAL
Movable (A/B)

ON

GROWING SEASON

PLANTING

MOUNTAINTOPS

SAN MIGUEL
(A/B)

September 29

VIRGEN
NATIVIDAD
(A)

September 8

HARVEST

May 3

VIRGEN ASUNTA
(B)

August 15

CRUZ
VELAKUY
(A/B)

June 24

June 29

SAN PEDRO (A)   SAN JUAN (B)

The major festivals at Pacariqtambo, showing how the responsibility for planning them follows a regular pattern; it is both shared and alternated between the two major divisions of the community.

witnessed occurs every year in a regular sequence. Each social group within the community takes its turn to contribute to a particular festival.

In fact, the village as a whole is organized according to a carefully balanced pattern. The total of ten *ayllus*, or landholding groups, is divided into two halves (or moieties, as anthropologists describe this type of division). The task of sponsoring the major festivals of the dry season passes alternately from the upper to the lower moieties. For example, the expense of the Saint Peter event I had attended was borne by one of the village's upper *ayllus*, but the next, on August 15 (dedicated to the Virgin), was due to be subsidized by one of the lower ones.

So the cycle of ceremonies continues until the arrival of the planting season in late November. From this point onward the pattern changes, for then each festival becomes the joint responsibility of groups drawn from both moieties of the community. In other words, duties are now shared rather than alternated.

Looking at the overall pattern, we see that social life in Tambo is marked by a balanced rhythm of sharing and alternating duties that divides the year in two. This rhythm not only influences ceremonial events, but also affects the organizing of major community projects such as cleaning irrigation canals or repairing the road to Cuzco. Such tasks are invariably split up between the lower and upper moieties.

Perhaps the most striking symbols of the interdependence of

the moieties are the *chutas*, the rectangular strips crossing the plaza that must be swept clean in advance of any ceremony. Urton's plan of the plaza shows that the sequence of different *chutas* falls in a mirrorlike pattern, balancing upper against lower. Apparently, in present-day Tambo the act of clearing a rectangular area signifies how one section of the community relates to, and depends on, all the others.

Though the *chutas* seem to emphasize how power is dispersed throughout many different sectors of the village, nevertheless, the landholding groups are not exactly equal in number or size. In fact, membership in an *ayllu* is based on family ties, so its size naturally fluctuates. Historical documents researched by Urton reveal that two centuries ago one of the Tambo *ayllus* consisted of just one married couple, while other groups had died out altogether. At the present day, the largest *ayllu* in the village consists of about sixty members.

In the Andean world, the greater power one accumulates, the heavier one's obligations grow to the community as a whole. Thus, the task of providing for the most elaborate and costly ceremony of all, the week-long celebration of the Nativity of the Virgin in early September, naturally falls to the largest of the upper *ayllus*, referred to by the villagers as the "first" or "supreme" *ayllu*.

In a similar fashion, powerful *ayllus* are expected to contribute more to major construction projects than smaller, weaker ones. A striking example of this was recorded by Urton during the most exciting event in the festival calendar, the bullfight staged on the eve of the Nativity of the Virgin. Apparently, the bulls selected for this event are usually too tame to inflict much damage on the mounted matadors of the village. Nevertheless, a heavy wooden fence must be built to protect the spectators.

As well as the planning of religious festivals, practical tasks are also assigned to different sections of the community at Pacariqtambo. Baltazar Quispe Herrera is here seen planting barley with men of his particular ayllu *in 1982. During their lunch break,* right, *the men sit down in order of seniority and social status.*

All ten *ayllus* share the job of assembling tools, ropes and eucalyptus logs, as well as the actual construction of the bull-ring. Interestingly enough, the *ayllu* representatives once again use the term *chuta* to refer to each individaul section of the fence assigned to a particular group. The relative length of each *chuta* is debated by the representatives; there are no standard units of length, but they manipulate a long measuring string by folding it over and doubling it. This operation involves considerable haggling, since there are no fixed rules for how long a *chuta* should be; it is all a matter of active negotiation between the different groups within the community. On the occasion that Urton watched, the measuring operation turned into a shouting match before the *ayllu* representatives grudgingly settled on an agreed length.

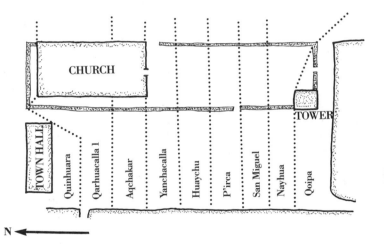

Gary Urton's plan of the chutas, *or ceremonial strips at Pacariqtambo, showing the names of the* ayllus *responsible for clearing each one.*

Exactly the same process occurs when the *chutas* of the plaza are swept clean in advance of a ceremony. The lines that form the borders of each strip are not marked on the ground in any permanent way. Instead, Baltazar judged where the edge of his strip should lie by looking at changes in the appearance of the main wall overlooking the plaza. Since the maintenance of this wall is another community effort, it, too, is divided up into distinct sections, each one the responsibility of a particular *ayllu*. The divisions of the wall are obvious because every few yards there are pronounced changes in the shapes of its archways, in its roofing materials or in the condition of its coat of whitewash. It is as if each of the *ayllus* has adopted a trademark to advertise its participation in the upkeep of the wall.

So the task of setting out the *chuta* was simple: all Baltazar had to do was line himself up with the appropriate point along the wall where the architecture changed its appearance, and this marked the edge of his strip. Not surprisingly, such an informal method of defining a *chuta* often leads to arguments over exactly where one strip ends and another begins.

As in many Andean communities, the inhabitants of Tambo share a concern for carefully ordered space. Such devices as the *chutas* apparently help them to express and reconcile the different interests of the community. The interdependence of the *ayllus* is emphasized as each one participates in a carefully arranged pattern of ritual activity. Hence the mirrorlike sequence of the festivals, as first the upper groups in the village take their turn, then the lower, until finally both collaborate.

Despite such a strong emphasis on social order, most of the customs observed by the villagers are, in practice, fluid and flexible. Just as the *chuta* boundaries are never marked permanently on the ground, so there are no fixed rules about how powerful a particular social group should be. In fact, Urton's research has shown that the sizes of particular *ayllus* and their respective *chutas* have, indeed, changed over the centuries. Though the villagers often engage in ordered patterns of activity, these are not rigid schemes that constrict their lives and dictate their behavior. On the contrary, the ceremonies offer frequent opportunities for conflicts to be aired and resolved.

Why should such elaborate means of diminishing tensions be necessary in an Andean village? There is one obvious source of problems: even though farming resources are abundant and varied, they are not spread equally across the landscape. Since Tambo is perched above the plunging slopes of the Molle Molle Valley, many Tambo farmers must hike for two or three hours every day to reach their fields; along the way, they may pass through several diverse growing zones. At 8,000 feet, on the valley floor, for instance, farmers cultivate citrus fruits, bananas and cotton, while 7,000 feet higher up they raise high-altitude tuber and grain crops such as barley, quinoa and potatoes.

Since particular crops can be grown only at certain specific levels within this "vertical" environment, it is in everyone's interest that the communally owned lands should be evenly distributed. In theory, if any one *ayllu* and its landholdings grew to be too great, it could easily monopolize a particular crop resource, and hence deny or limit access to it for the other groups within the community.

The possibility of real enmity among the people of Tambo is vividly enacted each year at Carnaval. During this festival, held in February or early March, a mock battle is staged between the heads of the various *ayllus*. (They catapult stones and unripened peaches at each other with woolen slings.) Once again,

View of Pacariqtambo overlooking the Molle Molle Valley.

Orlando, a young inhabitant of Pacariqtambo.

it seems that ritual behavior presents both an outlet for frustrations and an opportunity for dramatizing potentially serious disputes. This important function of ceremonies—to defuse conflicts and tensions—may explain puzzling aspects of the behavior I witnessed at the festival of Saint Peter, such as the disruption of the formal contradancers by the anarchic *ukukus*.

To put it simply, relationships within Andean communities are characterized by a unique blend of freedom and formality. The rituals help to maintain a fine balance between the traditional patterns fixed in the villagers' minds and the ever-changing demands of their daily world.

Of course, their beliefs have developed over many centuries and have acquired a momentum of their own; it would be foolish to explain them away entirely by the pressures of their "vertical" environment. Nevertheless, as we have seen, several important ingredients of these spectacular Quechua festivals begin to make more sense if we consider the unusual demands and stresses of their mountain setting.

Nazca's
Astonishing Aqueducts

O N THE SOUTH COAST, the most serious problem facing human communities is the lack of water. As we have seen, this problem constantly preoccupies the Nazca farmers, who expect the river to flow for only a few months during a good year, and more often must rely totally on underground moisture. Without a system of rights and obligations for the use of water, a settled existence here would surely be impossible.

At some point in their history, the inhabitants of Nazca devised an impressive system for channeling the flow of subterranean water. About forty underground aqueducts, some as much as 2 or 3 miles long, crisscross the Nazca River valley and its tributaries. While their dimensions vary a good deal, most are large enough for a person to crawl or walk through. (Indeed, locals told Gary Urton that it is possible to pass underground from one side of the Nazca Valley to the other.)

Even during years when the riverbed is completely dry, water usually begins to run in the aqueducts around the end of November. In many areas, farmers are still completely dependent on the aqueducts to irrigate their cotton and corn. In addition, the underground streams supply them with drinking water and catfish. These systems work so well that in 1955 an extension of one of the old aqueducts was built to improve the supply of drinking water in the town of Nazca.

The ambitious scale of the aqueducts indicates a remarkable grasp of engineering and hydrology. Most of them are designed to take advantage of the sloping water table of the valleys; this means that their starting points are generally situated close to the hillsides, while their courses follow the east-west direction of the rivers. The range of any single canal depends mainly on its depth: the longest systems lie no less than 15 or 20 yards beneath the surface. (And in some places, according to informants, separate aqueducts actually cross over one another at different levels.)

About every hundred yards or so, inspection pits, resembling shallow, stone-lined wells, provide access to the aqueduct below. These pits (or "eyes," as they are called locally), enable the Nazca farmers to climb down into the aqueducts each year at the end of the dry season and scoop them free of mud and debris.

A modern aqueduct in the Ingenio Valley. Unlike the Nazca Valley immediately to the south with its subterranean canals, the Ingenio has enough water to make aboveground canal systems possible.

The underground canals in the Nazca Valley involved remarkable engineering skills. Above, massive stone terraces surround the junction of two subterranean systems at Ocungalla. Right, view of a typical "eye," or inspection pit, essential for the cleaning and maintenance of the channels.

After scrambling down the side of one of these pits, I was surprised at how cool and clean the water seemed to be as it flowed against my hand. By peering through the opening in the roof, I could see that the sides of the channel were lined with rounded pebbles laid neatly together like a drystone wall. The roof was bridged over with horizontal posts of acacia wood. These posts felt completely firm to the touch and were obviously resistant to rotting; apparently they also allow moisture to seep down into the channel below. On top of the posts, the builders had placed substantial stone roof slabs. The final stage of construction must have involved filling in the remainder of the original excavation trench with earth and rubble.

Who was responsible for such carefully surveyed and solidly built waterworks? The principles underlying the Nazca aqueducts are by no means unique. Underground channels, originating from wells and punctuated by ventilation holes, are widespread in many arid regions of the Mediterranean and the Near East. Their obvious advantage is that they conserve the moisture normally lost by evaporation from a surface canal; also, less of a gradient is necessary for them to work successfully.

The idea of tapping groundwater in this way seems to have begun in Persia over two thousand years ago. However, some of the most elaborate systems were introduced much later into North Africa and southeast Spain by the Arabs. Many of these underground channels, or *qanats*, are functioning today. One medieval aqueduct located under the streets of Madrid still directs drinking water to the city from an outlying spring.

Since exactly similar aqueducts exist in southern Spain, could the Nazca system have been planned by early Spanish settlers following the Conquest? This seems highly unlikely, for it is difficult to believe that they would have conceived of waterworks on this scale. From the Spanish point of view, there would surely have been little incentive for such an enterprise in what by then were relatively obscure south coast valleys, depopulated by disease and warfare.

Instead, an ancient, pre-Conquest origin for the aqueducts seems far more probable. Perhaps the most important clue to their date is the remarkable proficiency in handling stone that is evident in their structure. They must surely have been built at a time when the inhabitants of the Nazca Valley had grown accustomed to working in stone. Since there is no trace of stone architecture at Cahuachi or other sites belonging to the period of Classic Nazca culture, the aqueducts probably date much later.

As we saw in Chapter 8, the round temple of Huaca del Loro

seems to have been one of the earliest stone structures in the region. This new style of building was apparently introduced from outside as part of the first wave of influence from the highlands, in around A.D. 600 to 700. Conceivably, then, the aqueduct system may have been the idea of the highlanders of the Huari empire, who perhaps imposed it on the local Nazca population. If this guess is correct, the aqueducts would belong to roughly the same time frame as the straight lines and ray centers that crisscross the pampa.

The Myth of Despotism

WHILE THIS DEBATE over the age of the aqueducts may seem like an academic quibble, it has important implications for any effort to reconstruct the society of the line builders. Paul Kosok, it may be remembered, was convinced that wherever the remains of irrigation appeared in ancient Peru, a hierarchy of chiefs, priests and bureaucrats must originally have been present to supervise their construction and maintenance. This idea was nothing new. At the time when Kosok was writing, in the 1940s and 1950s, many anthropologists would have agreed with the link he drew between irrigation and the rise of the state. In particular, most scholars thought that irrigation had played a central role in the emergence of bureaucracies in ancient Egypt and Mesopotamia.

This association of improved technology with the growth of privilege and power derived ultimately from the writings of Marx and Engels. Their concept of "oriental despotism" was only an incidental part of their major theories, yet it influenced a generation of scholars. It referred to a key stage in social evolution during which, for the first time, local communities surrendered their independence to the state in return for the organization of large-scale public works. Many prehistorians (notably V. Gordon Childe) thought that this stage of development in the Near East had a crucial impact on the rest of the prehistoric Old World. "Oriental despotism," they thought, transformed Europe in ancient times as profoundly as capitalistic enterprise in the nineteenth century. The spread of irrigation technology from the east was believed to be one of the major factors that introduced inequalities of wealth and power to ancient societies everywhere.

Though the immense canal networks of the Peruvian coast must have arisen separately from those of the Old World, it was natural to assume that they, too, were evidence of a repressive state bureaucracy. The existence of towering mud-brick mounds on the north coast, superficially resembling the Egyptian pyramids or the Babylonian ziggurats, seemed to justify the comparison further. It appeared as if Andean states had developed exactly as had their Old World counterparts, even though many of the north coast sites did not appear to be cities in the conventional sense. (More often than not, the mounds seemed to be grouped together in ceremonial centers, while the ordinary farming population was widely dispersed in the surrounding valleys.)

In any case, many believed that irrigation was the key that enabled despotic regimes to come to power along the Peruvian coast. The appearance of the first major canal systems in valleys

An intricate pattern of abandoned irrigation ditches in the Pisco Valley.

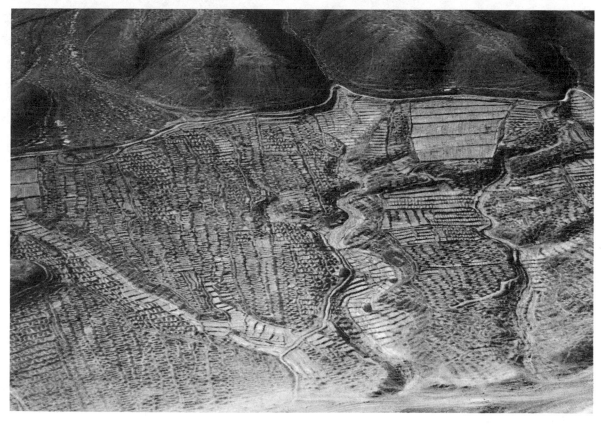

such as the Chancay and Virú around the time of Christ was viewed as a critical turning point. Most scholars, like Columbia University anthropologist Edward Lanning, supposed that these canals inevitably brought with them a centralized, autocratic power structure in each valley. In 1967, Lanning made the following assertion:

> although it might have been possible to dig the irrigation ditches through a system of intercommunity cooperation, the annual cleaning of the ditches and the equitable distribution of water could only have been accomplished by an over-all authority capable of dictating the destinies of all the dwellers in a valley.

However, more recently scholars have become increasingly dissatisfied with the oversimplified notion that improved technology gave birth to tyranny. Indeed, when we begin to examine the management of irrigation more closely, we find many ex-

amples of canal networks that were constructed and maintained entirely at the level of the local community. Even in ancient Egypt, the distribution of the Nile's water was organized among the farmers themselves, not by the upper levels of society; the pharaoh exerted a purely ceremonial role in these proceedings.

Another good example is the underground canals of southeast Spain, which resemble the aqueducts of Nazca so closely. The medieval cultivators of Valencia traditionally controlled all aspects of the maintenance of these canals. Their independence was respected by the local authorities and was enshrined in common law. During the fifteenth century, for instance, any farmer owning land served by a canal was automatically a member of the "commons," or local organizing body, which was usually convened in a local monastery at regular intervals. These meetings were licensed by the king's governor, and enabled the local farmer to elect administrators for the irrigation network. This case shows us that a canal system exactly like that

In the early centuries A.D., the Moche of the north coast built vast mud-brick mounds as foundations for royal residences and temples. Though Kosok and others assumed they were built by slaves or peasants under an oppressive regime, recent evidence suggests that cooperative labor practices were important in their construction. Running across the foreground of this panorama is the eroded summit of the gigantic mound at Pampa Grande in the Lambayeque Valley, one of the largest ancient man-made structures in South America.

of Nazca need not *necessarily* have been managed by a strong central authority.

Just as the richness of Quechua sky lore remained unknown until recently, so researchers have only now begun to appreciate the full measure of Andean social practices. One of the most remarkable breakthroughs has emerged from the study of legal documents compiled shortly after the Spanish Conquest. Unspectacular records of taxes, land titles and lawsuits now present a picture of a coastal society that was dramatically different from the one suggested by the conventional, "despotic" theory.

POWER IN ANCIENT PERU: A REAPPRAISAL

CHAPTER 11

New Light on the Canal Builders

IN THE DECADES FOLLOWING THE CONQUEST, Spanish administrators faced the task of reorganizing Peruvian coastal communities that had been decimated by warfare and disease. Even though the old way of life had been disrupted so much, the Spanish still encountered strong native traditions concerning the rights and duties of the individual. Evidence of these traditions, newly discovered in Spanish legal and administrative documents, has overturned many previous assumptions about how native society was organized in Peru—in particular, how the Peruvians managed the labor involved in their remarkable canal- and monument-building projects.

An important step in this reappraisal came in 1984, when University of Massachusetts anthropologist Patricia Netherly published far-reaching conclusions from sixteenth-century documents relating to the north coast. These refer constantly to *parcialidades*, a rather unenlightening Spanish word meaning simply "a part of the whole." Netherly was able to show that a *parcialidad* was actually the basic unit of society, a fundamental grouping that defined the ethnic identity of the individual. Family ties were probably involved in establishing membership in a particular *parcialidad*, as in the case of the present-day *ayllus* of the high Andes.

In fact, the similarities to recent Andean customs goes much further. Practically every social unit Netherly encountered in the documents was divided into halves, just as the people of Pacariqtambo and other villages today belong to either an "upper" or "lower" group. On the north coast, one of the two halves always outranked the other, so that its leader represented the whole community in legal affairs (though he was often accompanied by the head of the other, lesser division). Wherever there was a large population, the halves were broken down still further into quarters or even eighths, each one led by a lesser lord with particular responsibility for his own group.

What advantages did this distinctive pattern of organization offer? Netherly believes the answer is flexibility. A growing population could be subdivided indefinitely without requiring a total reorganization of the social structure. Furthermore, the numerous segments in which the people found themselves ensured a flexible response to a disaster such an El Niño flood, since the lords could easily call upon a wide variety of different combinations of manpower. In place of a cumbersome state machinery, each lord could directly mobilize his own particular subdivision of the population.

In such an unpredictable environment as the coastal desert, with its frequent floods and earthquakes, the principle of delegating authority down through a long chain of command made a good deal of sense. If a major catastrophe struck, it would affect only a particular regional authority, rather than paralyzing the entire workings of the state. In effect, the ancient Peruvians had discovered the benefits of decentralized management.

Despite its contrast to the "totalitarian" model envisaged by Kosok and others, this system was in no sense a democracy. Unlike the medieval irrigators of Valencia, the north coast farmer did not elect his lord to office. However, the legal documents make it clear that high-ranking lords frequently ruled several lower-level subdivisions. The result was a kind of nesting of relationships within the hierarchy, as each lord commanded several different levels of allegiances at once.

In other words, a powerful lord was unlikely to become a remote authority figure, distant from the affairs of all his people. More often, he would remain in direct contact with events inside a particular community or region.

Taking Turns:
The Rotation of Labor

THE CANAL NETWORKS supervised by the north coast lords varied enormously in size and scale. Some were mere ditches a few hundred feet long. At the other extreme were giant above-ground channels skillfully engineered to run for dozens of miles, delivering water to more than one valley at a time.

The layout of canals was, of course, determined by the gradient of the land, so that most networks ran parallel to the river, following the same direction as the gentle overall slope of the coastal plain down toward the sea. This created long, wedge-shaped strips of arable land in between the canals.

At the time of the Conquest, each of these long strips appears to have belonged to a particular major social grouping, or *parcialidad*. The canal itself was named after the group of people. Remarkably, the old names have persisted for centuries in many parts of the north coast. For instance, in the Chicama

A modern canal intake drawing off water from a fast-flowing stretch of the Jequetepeque River on the north coast.

Valley near Trujillo, canal names still in everyday use are identical to the titles given to *parcialidades* in sixteenth-century legal documents.

What secret lay behind the management of this enduring and efficient irrigation system? Instead of a wage or cost structure, the canals were built and maintained by a labor tax. This meant that the lords of the *parcialidades* provided food and tools for the job in return for a regular contribution of work by particular sections of the community. The lords supervised the work and made decisions about the distribution of the water. During the sixteenth century, as more Spaniards came to own land, user fees for canals were gradually introduced; however, in what was left of native land and canal holdings, the traditional pattern of communal labor persisted for centuries.

Practical aspects of maintenance, such as the annual cleaning of canals, are never envisaged as mere chores by the Andean peoples, but are seen as opportunities to conduct rituals of great significance to the well-being of the community. Indeed, much of the organizing capability of the north coast lords stemmed from the religious authority they exerted at the site of a particular maintenance job.

This was a matter of great concern as the Spanish colonial system tightened its grip. For instance, after a highland rebellion in 1565, native dignitaries were banned from riding on litters—a traditional mark of high rank among the Incas—and from horseback riding, the new privilege that had succeeded it. In 1566–67, Spanish administrators on the north coast were besieged by complaints about this ban from the lords of the *parcialidades*. Without a suitably dignified entourage, they explained, it was impossible for them to preside over the canal operations. Faced by the potential breakdown of the irrigation system, the Spanish relented and granted many licenses to individual lords to ride on horseback.

In many areas where the risk of drought was particularly severe, each lord supervised a system of taking turns to ensure that irrigation water was distributed equally. By long-established custom, the canal users farthest away from the source at the intake were allowed to irrigate first. The last to benefit were the upstream communities that were most advantageously placed in relation to the flow of water. In this way, everyone had a fair chance to receive an adequate supply.

The "taking turns" system seems to have been practiced almost universally by native Andeans. It was certainly well established in the Nazca region during early colonial times; according to legal documents studied by Gary Urton, cultivators in the Ingenio Valley, close to the northern edge of the Nazca pampa, followed a regular sequence in drawing water from their canals.

Practices of this kind were usually referred to by a Quechua word, *mit'a*. The very same word was also applied to the regular cycle of contributions that the community supplied to its lord in the form of labor. The principle of sharing was evidently crucial to Andean economics: one took turns both to contribute to and benefit from a communal resource such as a canal system. Indeed, the concept of the *mit'a* reveals typical Andean concerns: an emphasis on a high degree of order, coupled with a careful balancing out of possible conflicting interests.

Each Man Left His Mark: The Mound of the Sun

THE WORK-SHARING ASPECTS of the *mit'a* account for some of the most ambitious construction projects ever undertaken in the ancient world. One of them is represented by a colossal mud-brick mound that looms above the flat sugarcane fields of the Moche Valley on the Peruvian north coast. This mound was given the name Huaca del Sol (or Shrine of the Sun) by anti-quarians during the last century. Even at close range, the vast

Engraving of Huaca del Sol published in 1877 by the pioneer American archaeologist Ephraim Squier.

The 120-foot-high mound of Huaca del Sol was built from nearly 1½ million mud bricks during several centuries prior to 500 A.D. The largest man-made mound in South America, it evidently supported the palaces of the Moche ruling class.

dimensions and eroded condition of the mound make it difficult for the eye to accept as a man-made feature.

The strangeness of its battered appearance is accompanied by an atmosphere of utter neglect. Though the base is over 350 feet longer than that of Egypt's Great Pyramid, few tourists ever manage to find it. There are no signposts, and to reach it one must follow a disorienting dirt track that wanders for several miles through farmyards and along canal banks. In the shadow of the immense gray-brown hill there are no museums or guides, just a succession of impoverished local pot hunters who sell fragments they have grubbed up from the ancient cemetery nearby.

Difficult as it is to believe, the present remains of Huaca del Sol represent less than a third of its original size. Following a long period of looting, the Spanish diverted the nearby Moche River in 1602 so that they could use its current to flush away the entire northern and western sides of the mound. The main thrust of this plundering operation seems to have been directed at the highest, southernmost section of the cross-shaped mound; its surviving remnants rise more than 120 feet above the surrounding plain. Unlike the Egyptian pyramids, the Moche mounds did not feature subterranean crypts or secret passages. However, traces of wealthy burials have been discovered, incorporated almost incidentally in the platforms built on top of the mound. These platforms were raised in layers, one on top of the other, as Huaca del Sol was progressively enlarged. At least eight such phases of remodeling have been traced, doubtless extending over several centuries.

The purpose of each burst of building activity was probably to provide an increasingly impressive foundation for the residence of high-ranking Moche officials. Within the complex of rooms, corridors and courtyards erected on the platforms, patches of everyday refuse were often allowed to accumulate. These suggest that the activities on the summit were at least partly secular.

Though the successive platforms may well have incorporated the royal tombs of the Moche dynasty (presumably the goal of the Spanish looters), it seems that Huaca del Sol was not intended primarily as a monument to the dead. Instead, the lofty platforms supported the pinnacle of the Moche hierarchy and were an awe-inspiring symbol of their living power.

When a team of Harvard archaeologists excavated around the base of Sol in 1972, they were surprised to encounter signs of lower-class occupation. These included huts with crudely finished walls and dirt floors littered with poor-quality pot fragments. Other areas of the huge Moche site yielded quite

Facing Huaca del Sol across the main plaza at Moche was a smaller mound, Huaca del Luna, apparently reserved for more ceremonial activities. It lies at the foot of the "white hill," Cerro Blanco, which forms a striking landmark in the Moche Valley, while the ridges of the Andes rise up in the background.

different remains—for example, high-class burials accompanied by numerous fine vessels, ingots of copper, beads and pendants.

Furthermore, the other major mound at Moche, known as the Huaca del Luna (or Shrine of the Moon), seems to have had a different function from that of Huaca del Sol. Consisting of three platforms with interconnecting courts, the smaller Luna mound was undoubtedly contemporary with Sol, but was apparently the site of more sacrosanct activities. Within the structures on the three platforms, floors were kept scrupulously clean, while the walls were richly painted with multicolored murals depicting mythological scenes. No such murals adorned the rooms on top of Sol.

Although the archaeologists were able to examine only a fraction of the vast occupation area, clear evidence emerged of a wide variety of social classes and different activities at Moche. Previous assumptions that it was an "empty" ceremonial center simply reflected ignorance of what lay beneath the sun-baked surface. Instead, the site had clearly functioned as both a major settlement and as the focal point for the power of the Moche lords.

Their influence reached a peak from about A.D. 300 to 600. During this period, the Moche controlled nine separate river valleys spanning more than 200 miles of the Peruvian coast. In each valley, the appearance of Moche-style pottery and mud-brick mounds form an abrupt contrast to previous settlement remains, suggesting the imposition of a new order by conquest. (Furthermore, Moche ideology had a militaristic aspect; warriors dominate the mythological scenes painted with marvelous vigor on the surfaces of Moche pots.)

Once they had established power in these outlying valleys, Moche administrators organized the construction of architectural complexes quite similar in layout to those of their own capital, though built on a smaller scale. In fact, there was usually a range of such sites within any one particular valley, such as the Santa or the Virú. The most important mounds were always associated with a group of platforms, courtyards and compounds, clustered against a steep hillside. At the other end of the scale, more modest mounds were sometimes isolated, freestanding structures.

This wide variation in the importance of the sites probably reflected the different degrees of administrative power exerted by each lord, who doubtless resided on top of his own particular mound. The chain of command must have begun at Huaca del Sol and been passed down through the levels of each one of these regional hierarchies in turn. If this interpretation is cor-

Supernatural warriors copied from Moche pottery designs.

rect, then the kind of "decentralized management" that we know was in force along the north coast at the time of the Conquest had roots established far back in the Moche past.

In fact, evidence for a *mit'a*-like organization of labor can be detected by any visitor to Huaca del Sol. If you look carefully at the sides of the mound, the peculiarity of its construction is immediately obvious. The mud-bricks were not laid down in regular courses, but in long parallel rows or "skins," each one several adobes wide. No attempt was made to join the separate skins together. Moreover, in some sections, the skins were subdivided still further and, again, these units were never bonded together. The result is that the construction segments take on a precarious appearance, as if they were tall, freestanding chimneys. What was the purpose of this building method? It offered no particular advantage in withstanding the stresses of earth tremors, for example. A more logical explanation is that the individual segments represent the work of many different construction gangs spread over a long period of time.

Confirmation of this theory came when Mike Moseley, the leader of the Harvard archaeological team, noticed that many of the adobe bricks bore crude abstract designs. These resembled "doodles" impressed with the finger onto the surface of the brick while it was drying. Moseley was able to identify over a hundred different marks, mostly consisting of simple combinations of dots, diagonals and curved lines. The designs were not distributed at random; instead, each one corresponded exclusively to a particular construction segment.

It is highly unlikely that the marks represent the "signature" of a particular brickmaker. (One hundred artisans could scarcely have coped with manufacturing Sol's estimated total of 143 million bricks!) An alternative theory is that each mark identified the bricks supplied by a particular social group. Presumably, a team drawn from a specific landholding unit was required to manufacture bricks, transport them to Moche and then erect its particular segment of the mound. The quota of work demanded by the labor tax could have been measured conveniently by the completion of each of one of these segments in turn. In other words, the mound was built by "taking turns," just as large-scale canal networks were maintained during the sixteenth century.

Such an explanation helps account for the ambitious scale of Huaca del Sol. For the construction effort, the Moche hierarchy would have been able to call upon work gangs drawn from all nine valleys under their sphere of influence. The participation of far-flung groups in the mighty task no doubt served to cement the solidarity of Moche rule. In return, the lords must have

Moche potters crafted superb "portrait jars" of both human and supernatural beings.

+ were they looking at a code or msg..?

supervised the irrigation networks. No doubt they also presided over ceremonies that safeguarded the people against the host of malevolent supernatural beings that are frequently depicted in Moche art.

Mike Moseley points to a typical "maker's mark" on one of the millions of adobe bricks at Huaca del Sol.

Taking Turns: The Implications for Nazca

WHILE THE MOST IMPRESSIVE TRACES of the *mit'a* system are visible in the north, other parts of the Peruvian coast followed exactly similar principles of organization. Once again, numerous sixteenth-century Spanish documents testify to the rights and duties of native populations along the central coast.

For instance, one Spanish report claims that a coastal town in the valley of Chincha consisted of six thousand merchants, ten thousand fishermen and twelve thousand farmers. While the numbers may have been exaggerated, the distinction drawn between the different work categories was important, since each trade had quite separate obligations to the *mit'a*.

Many communities were inhabited solely by fishermen, who skillfully rode out into the breakers on their tiny reed boats or balsa rafts. These seafarers, owning no land themselves, frequently lodged complaints against local lords who attempted to press them into working the fields. By tradition, the fishermen's *ayllus* were exempt from the agricultural duties normally required by the *mit'a*. In return for this privilege, they supplied the lord with specific units of dried and salted fish.

Other specialists also enjoyed distinctive privileges and obligations, notably the merchants of Chincha. These men often ventured all the way up to Ecuador on balsa rafts to obtain the much-prized spondylus shells that thrived only in warm northern waters. They also traded extensively with the highlands, apparently using copper ingots as a form of currency. The merchants almost certainly belonged to special guilds that were exempt from the duties of the ordinary population.

Farther to the south, the inhabitants of the narrow coastal valleys never enjoyed the same level of prosperity and commercial activity as did the people of Chincha. Nevertheless, the familiar pattern of labor tax organization was undoubtedly present.

One of Gary Urton's most important recent discoveries was a document proving the existence of several different *ayllus* in the Nacza area during the sixteenth century. The document refers to the obligation of various *ayllus* to work in a vineyard owned by Don García de la Nasca, who resided in the Ingenio Valley beside the Nazca pampa. Some of these groups were located in other valleys, so to fulfill their obligations to Don García their members would almost certainly have had to journey across the pampa. Presumably they made their way to the Ingenio by following one of the innumerable straight-line pathways that led over the desert.

Urton's discovery has many exciting implications. It now seems highly likely that the traditions of communal labor and turn taking, still flourishing in highland villages such as Pacariqtambo, once also existed in the vastly different environment of Nazca.

This means that the lines were probably *not* created by the kind of repressive, centralized bureaucracy Kosok envisaged, or by the "chiefs" and "slaves" spoken of by Maria Reiche. Instead, a plausible alternative reconstruction of ancient Nazca society might run as follows: first, we would imagine many separate family-based groups spread out across each valley, all the farmers owning land in common. These groups (the ancient Nazca equivalents of the *ayllu*), would not all be of equal status, however. Instead, they would be arranged in a hierarchy or chain of command.

The leaders of each group would be the ultimate authorities in matters of general concern such as irrigation. When large-scale projects were planned, the leaders would help to regulate a rotating system of communal work groups (a *mit'a*-like organization). Though a particular group and its leader might exercise considerable power, its position in the hierarchy would also involve substantial obligations to the community as a whole. It might be expected to subsidize major ceremonies and provide food and tools for the groups that labored on the desert drawings.

Because the groups were probably scattered among several valleys, their members would have to travel regularly across the pampa to collaborate on joint projects; could this be one reason why so many straight-line pathways were created linking one area of the pampa to another?

If widely scattered social units were, indeed, drawn together for construction tasks, then it is easier to understand the ambitious scale of many of the triangles and trapezoids. Like the

Engraving of an oceangoing balsa, from a woodcut published in 1565.

construction of Huaca del Sol, such projects would help to reinforce the solidarity of the community and the authority of its leaders.

To push the speculation still further, it is tempting to imagine that the clearing of each triangle or trapezoid on the pampa was sponsored by one or more of the groups, just as festivals are sponsored by *ayllus* in the high Andes today. If so, then the ritual spaces created on the desert would have symbolized the interdependence of one group with another, similar to the *chutas* of Pacariqtambo. The drawings would signify cooperation more than they would exploitation.

IMPERIAL MIGHT: THE INCA CLIMAX

CHAPTER 12

Chan Chan, the Palaces
Built for the Dead

IT TOOK THE INCAS just over a century to emerge from almost total obscurity. Around A.D. 1400, they were an unsophisticated chiefdom occupying a single small mountain valley around Cuzco. By the time of the Conquest in 1532, their empire stretched for over 2,500 miles from northern Ecuador to central Chile.

Considering the highly conservative nature of the Peruvian peoples and their customs, the meteoric rise of the Inca state poses a baffling problem. The traditional character of Andean social relationships—with its emphasis on balanced, decentralized control—seems totally at odds with the qualities necessary to establish a military empire. How did Inca rulers ever manage to acquire such an intense drive toward imperial power?

In reality, the Incas were merely the last of a long series of vigorously expanding states. From about A.D. 1200 onward, for instance, the north coast kingdom of the Chimú began to exert increasing military pressure over neighboring valleys. Our knowledge of the circumstances underlying the Chimú conquests is fragmentary, based mainly on confused legends and dynastic histories recorded by sixteenth-century Spanish priests. However, it is clear that the Chimú never attempted to subjugate the highlands; at the height of their power, around 1400, their lands encompassed a long coastal strip stretching

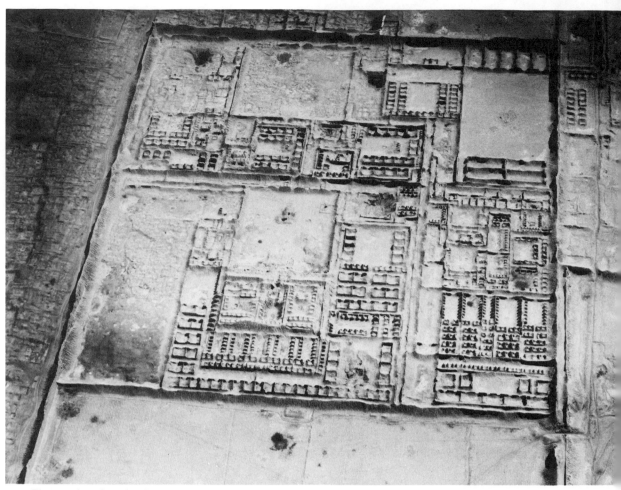

The complex of royal palaces at Chan Chan was a major center of power on the north coast from about A.D. 900 until the Chimú were defeated by the Incas in the 1460s. The rigidly organized "offices," palaces and burial mounds were screened off from ordinary dwellings by high mud-brick walls.

from southern Ecuador almost as far south as present-day Lima.

The Chimú rulers held sway over this huge territory from their capital in the Moche Valley. This was not the old site of Moche itself, but a new imperial city, Chan Chan, established close to the ocean in the outskirts of present-day Trujillo.

Had stone been as readily available to the Chimú as it was to the Incas, tourists might throng Chan Chan today as they do Cuzco or Machu Picchu. In fact, the city's miles of mud-brick walls have been severely damaged by sporadic downpours in El Niño years. The rains have caused these walls to slump into rows of unsightly ridges of soil, so that they resemble immense, neglected sand castles.

A visitor can get an inkling of the city's former grandeur by exploring a royal compound that has been partially restored and opened to the public. Once inside, the visitor is met by an intimidating labyrinth of tall, austere adobe walls and huge vacant plazas. At intervals, the eye is relieved by molded wall decorations that mostly depict lively seabirds, fish and mythical beings.

Here a Chimú king and his administrators lived out their days, protected from scrutiny by an outer wall two or three stories high. At the king's death, the compound became a vast royal tomb, a mausoleum maintained with elaborate ceremony by his junior heirs. For Chan Chan was as much a city of dead kings as it was an active seat of power.

At least three centuries of Chimú rule are represented by the nine compounds. They were built successively in two straggling rows leading from the ocean, each compound closely following the same elaborate and repetitive layout as its predecessor. The interior of a compound, nearly half a mile long by an eighth of a mile wide, was always enclosed by tall perimeter walls. There was only a single access point through the walls, a narrow entranceway located on the north side. This led to a spacious open plaza; from there onward, a maze of interweaving corridors connected hundreds of separate small rooms, some of them mere cubicles a few feet across. These passages were obviously not designed for the convenient movement of a large number of people. Instead, the dozens of rooms and corridors were almost certainly the preserve of privileged Chimú bureaucrats. Mike Moseley, the leader of a joint Peruvian-American team that excavated at Chan Chan in the early 1970s, interpreted the smallest spaces as storage facilities. In addition, he envisaged numerous rooms with U-shaped platforms as the "executive offices" of the bureaucrats. Similar thronelike U-shaped structures, Moseley pointed out, are depicted on north coast pottery. A dignitary is shown seated on each platform, presiding over other officials or captured prisoners drawn up before him.

Vandalism and erosion from occasional downpours has severely damaged the once splendid mud-brick walls of Chan Chan.

A Chimú silver drinking vessel crafted in the form of a U-shaped "office" structure, similar to those excavated at Chan Chan. A royal dignitary or bureaucrat presides over the thronelike structure (see detail, below). The bird decorations on the "office walls" are identical to the clay reliefs still visible at Chan Chan today.

While much of the space in each compound was taken over by these administrative rooms, the largest structure of all was the royal burial platform, hidden behind its own high enclosing walls. When Moseley and his team began to probe the top surface of one of these platforms, they uncovered a large T-shaped chamber that had almost certainly contained the king's body. Around this burial chamber the diggers discovered a series of rectangular pits, which had originally been filled with precious objects offered to the dead king. The contents of these pits were rich enough to keep Spanish mining companies busy well into the nineteenth century, so the archaeologists were able to find only remnants of the elaborately worked shell and wood artifacts, textiles, fine pottery and precious metals once buried there. However, they did establish that the offerings had also included human lives. In a limited sample of the pits, the diggers found remains of more than ninety young women, mostly between the ages of seventeen and twenty-four at the time of their death. In the case of the platform Moseley and his colleagues explored, an estimated 250 to 500 women accompanied their ruler to the grave.

The Chimú aristocracy clearly enjoyed immense prestige. According to the traditions recorded by sixteenth-century Spanish priests, the Chimú king believed that he and his family were descended from a special pair of stars, while the rest of the population came from a different, lesser set of stars. This belief reflected the rigid class barriers that separated the god-kings of the empire from their subjects.

The elite "sons of the stars" inside the compounds were greatly outnumbered by less fortunate artisans who were huddled outside the compounds in humble dwellings built of cane and mud walls. Few remains of any agricultural or fishing gear have been discovered inside these huts. However, abundant remnants of metalworking and weaving indicate that a great many of them functioned as craft workshops. Presumably the efforts of this specialized craft community were dedicated to filling up the king's numerous storerooms.

Though the workshops were tightly clustered together, the total area covered by the lower-class population was quite small. In fact, Moseley estimates that no more than twenty-five thousand to thirty thousand people resided in Chan Chan at its height. Had the immense compounds been constructed and maintained by a permanent, unskilled laboring class, a much larger, more sprawling layout would surely have resulted. Instead, the compounds were almost certainly built by nonresident forces following the traditional *mit'a*, or turn-taking, pattern.

Just as the structure of Huaca del Sol presents evidence of successive work gangs, so the high adobe walls of Chan Chan were evidently raised one segment at a time. Considerable variations in style and finish from one part of the wall to the next suggest that many different laboring teams were involved. Each of these roughly equal segments was divided off by a vertical marker made of a length of cane. No doubt the canes marked the units of work that were required of each construction group under the labor tax system. Probably only a comparatively small number of these outsiders ever stayed in Chan Chan at any one time.

Though the economy of the empire still functioned along traditional lines, a fundamental shift in the center of power had occurred, one that was reflected in the enormous prestige of the king and his family.

Not that class distinctions were anything new: the lords of Moche, centuries before, had obviously enjoyed a privileged status in their residences on top of the mud-brick mounds. However, the Chimú aristocracy consolidated its power into a rigid, unyielding social order. The excesses of wealth that flowed from the Chimú conquests must have gradually undercut the old structure of the landholding *ayllus*, enabling resources to be increasingly concentrated under state control. For the first time, a bureaucracy in their "executive offices" was necessary to manage the flow of goods.

Similarly, the densely packed storerooms inside the compounds represent a new phenomenon. The Moche lords had rewarded their *mit'a* laborers in relatively indirect ways—for example, by supervising canal networks and sponsoring ceremonies. Now, under the Chimú, there were tangible goods at stake, articles of high status manufactured by the artisans of Chan Chan or supplied by the tribute of conquered peoples. Once such items were in circulation, their flow controlled by the royal bureaucrats, the dependency of the subject classes deepened still further.

Above all, the imperial urge was accelerated by a cult of royal ancestor worship. If we are to believe the legends recorded by the Spanish, a period of disunity ensued on the north coast well before the founding of Chan Chan. At one time, five or more heirs to the kingdom of the Lambayeque Valley all formed their own separate lines of succession. Possibly as a result of these dynastic difficulties, the Chimú eventually adopted a system of split inheritance. This meant that the rightful heir would inherit his royal title, but the deceased king would continue to "own" all his property and revenues. The management of his estate passed to his junior heirs; they had the prestigious task of creating a mausoleum in the dead king's compound and venerating his memory.

The practical consequences of split inheritance were far-reaching. The political ambitions of younger heirs were channeled into the highly esteemed cult of ancestor worship. The newly acceded king, on the other hand, began his reign bereft of material resources, without land, revenues, or even a palace.

There were two ways for him to remedy the situation. One was to direct his *mit'a* laborers to reclaim new areas of agricultural land by means of major irrigation projects. The alternative was to use the same manpower to extend the boundaries of the empire by military force. In other words, the system of beliefs involved in split inheritance placed a strong economic incentive for conquest in the hands of every new ruler.

As a result, the fortunes of the Chimú empire grew rapidly, one ruler after another adding his own compound to the city. By the middle of the fifteenth century, however, the inevitable collision between Chimú and Inca ambitions finally came to a head. According to the traditions recorded by the Spanish, the military struggle against the Chimú was long and bloody, but eventually, around 1464, the Incas prevailed and replaced the Chimú emperor with a puppet heir.

The ninth and final compound erected at Chan Chan may have belonged to this ruler, since it appears drastically impoverished by comparison to its predecessors. With just one "executive office" and only a handful of storage facilities, its layout surely reflects the collapse of the Chimú tribute system under the impact of military defeat. Without goods to move, there could no longer be bureaucrats. In the aftermath of this breakdown, the communities of the north coast doubtless reverted to their earlier, less centralized pattern of organization.

The Rise of the Royal Cult

THE FORCES THAT LAY BEHIND the Incas' own rise to power remain controversial, partly because so many of the traditions recorded by the Spanish are untrustworthy. Heroic tales of

early Inca deeds were almost certainly invented by Inca emperors in their efforts to rewrite the past; what has survived represents Inca propaganda, not historical reality.

Despite all the distortions, the evidence suggests that a number of similar factors were at work behind the growth of both Chimú and Inca imperialism. One such factor was a state ideology strongly emphasizing the divinity of royal ancestors. Indeed, Inca religion seems to have revolved around the worship of imperial mummies. Spanish chroniclers wrote with distaste of the "statues" (the wrapped bodies of Inca kings) that were set up in the plaza at Cuzco for every major celebration. These sacred relics were also produced in the event of drought, as Father Cobo explains:

> When there was a need for water for the cultivated fields, they usually brought [Inca Roca's] body, richly dressed, with his face covered, carrying it in a procession through the fields and punas, and they were convinced that this was largely responsible for bringing rain.

Furthermore, the dead kings were often cared for as if they were still alive; the mummies were often carried around the

General view of Cuzco. Along with the Inca empire, the city grew from obscurity to preeminence in the Andean world in less than a century before the arrival of the Spanish.

temples and streets so that the dead rulers could visit one another and pay calls on the living. There was even a great feast held for the mummies in the plaza, during which they were believed to drink maize beer from gold and silver pitchers. The dead toasted one another while they were toasted in turn by their attendants.

Cobo also makes it clear that the mummy cult was the concern not only of a handful of priests but of everyone in the Inca state:

> the bodies of the kings and lords were venerated by the people as a whole, and not just by their own descendants, because they were convinced that . . . in heaven their souls played a great role in helping the people and looking after their needs.

Originally, the royal mummies were all kept in the heart of Cuzco's holiest shrine, the Coricancha, or Temple of the Sun. According to Garcilaso de la Vega, the mummies were seated on gold-plated thrones on either side of the high altar, which consisted of an image of the sun that was the size of a man, fashioned from thick, beaten gold.

Though there can be no doubt of its importance in Inca state religion, sun worship actually embraced a multitude of different aspects, notably the creator god Viracocha and the thunder god Illapa. Many other divinities with roots far back in ancient Andean beliefs, such as Mother Earth, the Moon and the Rainbow, all had their special shrines in the temple.

Despite the long traditions sanctioning these cults, it is clear that Inca rulers manipulated them to emphasize the divinity of the royal family. They gave increasing prominence to appropriate aspects of the sun god's multiple identity—particularly to

Mummified royal ancestors were an important focus of Inca religion; during key ceremonies, they were often exhibited for public veneration, as seen in Poma's woodcut from around 1600.

Detail of Inca masonry inside one of the shrines of the Coricancha, or Temple of the Sun, in Cuzco.

Inti, the sun god who had fathered the first Inca, Manco Capac. It was Inti who was thought to have sent forth Manco from the cave near Pacariqtambo to establish dominion over the world.

Inca ideology also stressed the sacred nature of corn and linked its sanctity to both the sun and the royal dynasty. In reality, the demand for state corn production grew rapidly with each new conquest, since ever-greater resources were required to feed the imperial armies. It is conceivable, then, that the increasing attention focused on the solar cult arose partly from material pressures on the Inca rulers.

History as well as religion was molded to serve the demands of the vigorously expanding state. The chief instigator was the Incas' first great warrior king, Pachakuti, whose name meant "cataclysm" (he is thought to have reigned from 1438 to 1471). Pachakuti appears to have created a largely mythical, "official" history: the petty skirmishes of his ancestors were elevated to the status of major battles. To lend credibility to his version of events, he appears to have reorganized the major building divisions within the imperial city.

In early Cuzco, there were almost certainly eight of these divisions, corresponding to the classic Andean pattern. There was an "Upper Cuzco," a "Lower Cuzco," and then further subdivisions of the population into quarters and eighths. According to anthropologist Tom Zuidema, Pachakuti probably took over the holdings of these eight traditional *ayllu* groups and reassigned them to eight legendary kings who were supposed to have preceded him. The major block of buildings belonging to each *ayllu* now became the palace of their respective ancient kings. The original pecking order of the old *ayllus* may have been preserved in the sequence of the kings as they now appeared in Pachakuti's reshuffled list of the Inca dynasty.

To give further substance to his new mythology, Pachakuti is thought to have arranged for special royal lineage groups to maintain each of the palaces in honor of a particular legendary dead king. The duties of a group included the veneration of the royal mummy and the management of his lands.

Subsequently (according to some sources), Pachakuti and later emperors built their own separate palaces, each one cared for after their deaths by their junior heirs. As at Chan Chan, the procedure of split inheritance created a succession of royal buildings within the city. It also fueled the Incas' drive for conquest, since every new ruler was forced to begin his reign from scratch, without any estates of his own.

If Zuidema's reconstruction is correct, Pachakuti's action in taking over the old *ayllu* buildings must have been an important event. Nevertheless, it was just one of many far-reaching

The traditional succession list of Inca kings (here depicted in a Spanish history book of 1738) is now thought to reflect the structure of the Inca hierarchy rather than a genuine sequence of rulers.

changes that were taking place within the fabric of Inca society. Bolstered by conquest, the royal family was attracting increasing power, undercutting the traditional importance of the communal land-owning groups.

Now the Inca economy began to drift away from its old reliance on local farming and llama herding. Instead, the state began to marshal its own substantial labor forces drawn from the taxation of conquered peoples. The new influx of imported labor was partly channeled into ambitious state construction projects, including spectacular agricultural terraces faced with stone. Local farmers were usually entitled to a portion of the corn harvest from these terraces for their own consumption. Much of their labor, however, was directed toward providing for nonagricultural sectors of the population, such as the army.

In addition, royal grants of land to privileged, private individuals increased in the last few decades before the Conquest. The status of these individuals was often enhanced still further by their removal from the *mit'a* rolls. Freed from the traditional Andean responsibilities of power, such state retainers were, in effect, Inca aristocrats. Their growing numbers meant an inexorable drift toward a rigid, authoritarian class structure.

The erosion of old community structures was further hastened by the imperial policy of establishing colonies, or *mitimaes*, consisting of substantial populations moved from other parts of the empire. Of course, the seasonal movements of llama herds and trade links with the coast had always encouraged a great deal of mobility; so, too, did the highland environment, with its extreme diversity of different growing zones. To improve the range of locally available food, a highland chief, or *curaca*, would often dispatch groups to procure lowland crops.

The Incas enlarged on this well-established practice and used it to further their imperial ends. Thus *mitimaes* were established not only for economic ends but also to impose Inca laws, religion and language upon recently conquered subjects. Sometimes the colonists included members of the royal lineage or state retainers. These dignitaries were sent off to live in native capitals so that they might set a good example and head off any possibility of revolt.

More often, the *mitimaes* consisted of peasant farmers, resettled to boost agricultural production in a specific region. For example, Garcilaso tells us that a colony from Nazca was established in the Apurimac Valley to lay out "very profitable gardens, only a short distance from Cuzco"; the Nazcans were accustomed to the intense heat of the tropical valley, which the highlanders found intolerable.

Though freed of their responsibilities to their old chief, such colonists retained the dress and ornaments of their original community. The Inca deliberately promoted ethnic diversity "to keep his dominion quiet and safe," as Father Cobo put it. Another category of *mitimaes* served this purpose even more explicitly, for it consisted of particularly troublesome or rebellious elements in a population who were physically removed to more secure or remote regions.

As a result of this policy, Cuzco became a melting pot of different nationalities; Cieza de León remembered it as a city full of strangers. They included the cult priests of conquered peoples, who were forced to remove their holiest idols to the capital. The sons of native rulers were also brought to live in the city, ostensibly to learn Inca ways, but also to serve as hostages in the event of a revolt. And, of course, there were innumerable craftsmen imported to serve the tastes of the Inca and his court, such as the community of metalworkers transplanted from Chan Chan.

Since 1978, archaeologist Ann Kendall has led Peruvian, British and American volunteers in an ambitious study of Inca settlement and subsistence at Cusicacha in the Urubumba Valley. Excavations revealed a complex of agricultural terraces and canals surrounding the town of Patallacta.

The Inca structures at Cusicacha include a shrine centered around a natural boulder, above. Kendall estimates that the field systems in the surrounding valley may have produced four times the amount of maize necessary to support the local population. The Cusicacha team has restored some 4½ miles of Inca canals to working order, right. It is hoped these will assist farmers to recover something of the agricultural prosperity of Inca times.

Inca Mathematics: The Quipu

THE HIGHLY CENTRALIZED CHARACTER of the Inca state would have been impossible to maintain without a strong bureaucracy; this, in turn, required an effective record-keeping system. The Incas never developed writing, nor did they originate their practice of compiling knotted string records, or quipus. (Examples have been found in graves dating back at least seven centuries before the Inca empire.) Nevertheless, the skill of the Inca quipu readers was legendary. Even literate Spanish observers were amazed by the efficiency with which the flow of state goods was controlled. Polo de Ondegardo commented that:

> they kept such record of everything delivered that they do not lose count of a single hen or load of firewood . . . which certainly is not a believable matter, but in this field they have great masters.

There were evidently different grades of professional quipu makers, or *quipucamoyoc*. The Inca ruler's statisticians were probably members of his royal family, while full-time retainers are likely to have kept account of state warehouses in the provinces. At the folk or community level, knotted strings were (and still are) in use to keep track of animals and crops. In early Spanish times, Indians were said to have carried quipus to church to recollect their confessions.

Since there was no single language or code underlying the quipu, each maker developed his own particular accounting methods. If the information was to survive, these private procedures had to be explained to the next generation of record keepers. Nevertheless, certain conventions were widely followed, including the concept of zero and a base-ten numbering system. Each quantity registered by the quipu maker occupied one of the many separate strings that hung from the main, central cord. They recorded the number by tying knots in clusters representing units, tens, hundreds, thousands and so on. The highest orders of numbers were placed closest to the main cord. (To give an example, the number 1708 would be expressed by a single knot, followed by a group of seven, then a space with no knots, and finally a set of eight more.)

The sum total of all the numbers present in a quipu is often recorded on a single separate string, fastened to the main cord

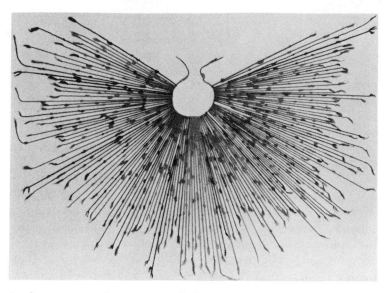

A quipucamoyoc, *or quipu-keeper, as portrayed by Poma around 1600.*

The Incas used quipus, right, *complex arrangements of knotted strings, for accounting and for recording statistical and astronomical information.*

in the opposite direction to all the others. It was these summary cords that enabled an American historian, Leland Locke, to prove the numerical, decimal character of the quipus in 1912; his breakthrough remains the single most important insight into their meaning.

Some quipus consist of recurring multiple numbers, suggesting that they refer to repetitive events such as the days in a calendar. However, all efforts to prove the astronomical identity of particular quipus have so far proved unconvincing. Attempts of this kind always involve a good deal of shuffling of the numbers, since many arbitrary choices have to be made between different combinations of knots and calendars. Even if the astronomical quipus cannot be positively identified, however, we have Spanish testimonies that Inca officials did in fact use quipus as calendar aids.

Subtle refinements allowed the quipu keepers to recall a great variety of information. By recognizing different styles of knots and variations in cord colors, they could use the quipus as memory-jogging devices. Though numbers and quantities were the type of data most commonly recorded, the Spanish reported that the quipus also helped their makers to recall ballads and legends, as well as legal and liturgical information. When Garcilaso compiled his *Royal Commentaries of the Inca,* he says that quipu officials checked on the accuracy of his text by referring to their knots:

> I was able to reassure them by rereading what I had noted down under their dictation, and they used to follow my reading, holding on to their quipus, to be certain of my exactness;

this was how I succeeded in learning many things quite as perfectly as did the Indians.

Quipus were also essential to the functioning of the Inca communications network. Messages were conveyed by runners who were posted in small huts located every 3 miles or so along the state highways. This relay system meant that news originating in Quito, for instance, might have been passed on by at least 375 different runners by the time it reached Cuzco. Under such circumstances, complex information could scarcely have been delivered by word of mouth, since it would become hopelessly garbled along the way. In reality, according to Garcilaso, quipu officials separated by long distances learned the same knot procedures, enabling them to "decode" long and detailed messages.

Arteries of the Empire

THE ROAD SYSTEM is justly celebrated as one of the Incas' most extraordinary achievements. Without such a network, it is doubtful whether they could have successfully maintained a grip over their vast territories. The roads had the practical functions of speeding the flow of information and the deployment of armies, but they also had a symbolic importance. They were visible reminders of imperial power that a conquered community could scarcely overlook, since its laborers were responsible for their construction and upkeep under the *mit'a* system.

Despite the impressiveness of the road network, few systematic surveys were attempted until an adventurous project was launched by John Hyslop, a young anthropologist at the Institute of Andean Research in New York. Between 1978 and 1981, Hyslop and his colleagues organized a series of expeditions to follow and map substantial sections of Inca roads. The sections they chose were widely scattered in Ecuador, Bolivia, northern Chile and northwest Argentina, as well as in Peru. To travel these ancient routes, they often had to explain their goals patiently to local guides, who would insist that more convenient modern paths were available. In rugged terrain, the expeditionaries made their way on light motorbikes, mules, or, most often, on foot.

Perhaps their most remarkable adventure was tracing over seventy miles of the Inca road that crosses the bleak Atacama Desert of Chile, just south of the Tropic of Capricorn. According to Garcilaso, this road had been constructed with great difficulty toward the end of the fifteenth century during the campaigns of Thupa Yupanki. This ruler had personally traveled to the edge of the desert to encourage his forces. Long after Yupanki's successful conquest of Chile, Spanish soldiers and their native bearers followed in his footsteps, many of them perishing as they made their way south. One Spanish traveler, Geronimo de Bíbar, described how the water they encountered at infrequent oases was often too salty even for their horses to

The Incas skillfully adapted their road-building techniques to a diversity of landscapes; many of their roads are still in daily use. In the highlands, right, *broad stone steps eased the footsteps of travelers up steep slopes. Below, a road along the north coast plain of the Chicama Valley. Opposite, top, a major road crosses the high-altitude landscape near the shores of Lake Titicaca, and, below, a stretch of the seventy-mile road across the Atacama desert in Chile, one of the most arduous environments on earth.*

drink. ("The drops of water on their whiskers turned to salt that looked like pearls on their mouths," Bíbar wrote.)

Hyslop found that the Inca road had been constructed with care, despite the arduous desert environment. Though it lacked typical features such as stone walls, steps and paving, and was narrower than other highland routes, much effort had still been invested in it. The ten-foot-wide path had been cleared of surface rocks and debris, while its edges were marked at frequent intervals by stone piles. The expedition also discovered numerous shelters for runners, and two or three *tampu*, or lodgings, scattered along the way.

In the early days of Spanish rule, when the native messenger system was still intact, news could travel along this desert route with astonishing speed. The runners from Cuzco sometimes

took only eight days to reach Santiago, Chile, a distance of nearly 1,700 miles.

Hyslop has mapped 14,000 miles of Inca highway throughout the Andes, and suggests that the original network may have comprised as much as 25,000 miles. There were two parallel north-south arteries, the highland road and the coast road, and these were the most impressively engineered of all. The secondary networks forged vital links between Cuzco and the provinces, bringing a vast range of resources within reach of the capital. It was said that runners from Chala on the south coast could bring fresh fish to the emperor's table in only two days.

Another section of Inca road connected the towns of Ica and Nazca; its course runs just north of the pampa and does not intrude on the area of desert drawings. Both the Inca engineers and the Nazca line builders seem to have shared a preference for straightness. Along the north coast, for example, several sections of Inca roads run for twenty-five miles or more with scarcely any visible deviation. The major coastal artery, in particular, often ignores minor geographic obstacles, passing over rocky hills rather than curving around them.

Did Inca road builders inherit their taste for straightness from the example of Nazca? Since Hyslop and his team were able to demonstrate pre-Inca origins for several roads they studied, it is conceivable that straightness was a long-established—perhaps even sacred—aspect of Andean road-building practices. On the other hand, Hyslop emphasizes that Inca roads, particularly in the highlands, *do* deviate in the face of serious obstructions such as gorges, mountains, lakes or marshes.

In the Atacama Desert, for instance, his team discovered that the road incorporates minor curves of up to 5 degrees to avoid abrupt slopes or ravines. There are also slight changes in overall direction whenever the road meets an oasis; apparently, the course of the road was planned so that it would connect separate oases as directly as possible. The surveyors may have used distant mountain peaks, or perhaps even astronomical reference points, to help establish the position of the next oasis. Hyslop is convinced that a practical concern with efficient long-distance travel influenced the majority of routes. The preference for straightness was never followed dogmatically, in defiance of rough terrain. Instead, Hyslop concludes, Inca roads "adjust to their landscape, and in some cases the best adjustment is a straight or nearly straight line."

The only undeviating pathways were those intended for spiritual or ceremonial activities rather than communication. By far the most remarkable examples of such pathways were concentrated in the Inca capital itself.

Cuzco, Mirror of the Cosmos

BEFORE THE CONQUEST, the layout of Cuzco corresponded to a precise and highly ordered vision, even though today that layout is obscured by a jumble of colonial architecture and tourist gift shops. Shortly after 1440, the great emperor Pachakuti began his reconstruction of the city by canalizing the flow of two small rivers, the Huatanay and Tullumayo. (These

Today's processions of folk dancers in Cuzco are an echo of the elaborate religious festivals of Inca times.

streams still flow through Pachakuti's conduits today, though the Inca channels are roofed by concrete slabs.)

The newly drained land embraced by the streams covered an area about 1¼ miles long by ⅓ mile wide. Within this inner core of the city, Pachakuti arranged all the city's principal buildings, many of them constructed of huge boulders laboriously hewn and artfully fitted into place. According to one Spanish estimate, there were some four thousand structures in all, arranged in gridlike wards and divided by narrow, paved streets.

The modern heart of the city, the rectangular Plaza de Armas, overlies part of a more extensive Inca plaza that belonged to the prestigious "Upper" (Hanan) half of the community. A second plaza, the focus for Hurin ("Lower," less privileged) Cuzco, lay to the east, just across the Tullumayo River. Just as in Pacariqtambo today, the organization of the capital revolved around this fundamental division into Upper and Lower Cuzco. At the time of the Conquest, everyone in the city belonged either to one of the five major *ayllu* groups of Upper Cuzco, or to one of the five groups of Lower Cuzco. Again, similar to a modern Andean village, there was a hierarchical grading among the ten *ayllus*, so that one was more influential than another. And, of

Cuzco at the time of the Conquest, showing the major Inca streets and buildings.

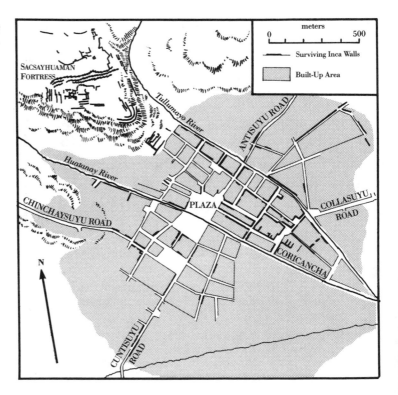

course, within an individual *ayllu* group itself, there were still further distinctions of rank, principally between commoners and those of royal lineage.

The planning of Cuzco not only reflected the internal social order of its inhabitants but was also a mirror for the entire empire that lay beyond its walls. When outsiders came to lodge in the city, they were expected to reside in an appropriate sector, corresponding to the same territory from which they had traveled. Thus, the ethnic distribution of the city became a miniature replica of the empire itself.

Besides the fundamental separation into halves, the city was further subdivided into quarters that were envisaged as extending throughout the Inca realm. Each quadrant had its own name that could refer either to its respective sector of the city or to the vast territory beyond. These names were:

> West to North: Chinchaysuyu
> North to East: Antisuyu
> West to Southeast: Cuntisuyu
> Southeast to East: Collasuyu

In fact, the imaginary boundaries between each quadrant corresponded only roughly to the cardinal points, while one of them, the division between Cuntisuyu and Collasuyu, was skewed considerably away from the south toward the southeast. Gary Urton believes that this boundary was deliberately "bent" so that it would coincide with the center of the Inca celestial universe, the midpoint of the Milky Way, as it rose above the horizon. If his theory is correct, then the basic divisions of Cuzco reflected not only human social arrangements but also the ordering of the cosmos overhead.

One of the best preserved of Cuzco's Inca roads still climbs out of the city in the direction of the Antisuyu (or roughly northeast) quadrant of the empire.

Furthermore, as we have seen, the Quechua today still think of the celestial river (the Milky Way) as connected to the flow of rivers on earth. It was probably significant, then, that the city divisions crossed one another so close to the junction of the two streams, Huatanay and Tullumayo. At this central point, where the Temple of the Sun was situated, the directions of the empire, the Milky Way and the sacred rivers were all drawn together in a single focus. Here was an orderly union between earth, sky and mankind.

Since it was believed to be the source of all cosmic forces, the Temple of the Sun was naturally regarded with awe and reverence by the inhabitants of Cuzco. (For instance, anyone approaching within about two hundred paces of the building had to remove his shoes.)

Every social group in the city was assigned its own particular relationship to this radiating source of power. The connection was made along a series of imaginary straight lines that were thought to fan out from the temple like the spokes of a wheel. Each of these forty-one lines, or *ceques*, was considered the special responsibility of a different unit of society.

As we might expect, given the Incas' love of formal order and patterning, the *ceques* were arranged in a regular sequence within each quadrant of the city. They were carefully assigned to the different grades of *ayllus* in precise rotation. Thus, the first *ceque* of Antisuyu belonged to a royal heir and his kin; the next to the junior heirs; the third to commoners; the fourth to another royal heir, and so on. Though this scheme may sound complicated, a glance at the plan (*opposite, above*) reveals the essential symmetry and simplicity of the *ceque* system.

Thanks to many years of research by Tom Zuidema, we know that the majority of the *ceques* were not actual pathways; indeed, they could not be seen at all on the ground. Neither did the course of the *ceques* physically divide up the architecture of the city. Rather, the Incas thought of them as invisible connections joining a series of holy shrines, or *huacas*, scattered along their length. Though they visualized a typical *ceque* as following a straight line, there was a certain degree of freedom in the location of its *huacas*; often they lay somewhat to the left or right of its theoretically straight course.

A good way to imagine the overall design of the *ceque* system is to compare it with the image of a quipu. If a quipu is spread out into a circle on a flat surface, a resemblance to the plan of the *ceques* is immediately clear. The cords of the quipu point outward in every direction, like the radiating lines of the *ceques*. Moreover, its knots are arranged at varying intervals along

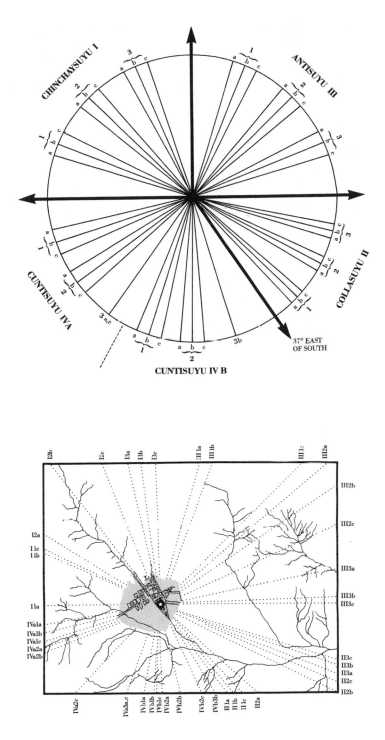

A schematic diagram of the ceque lines of Cuzco, showing how each one was assigned to a particular social group. Modern scholars have assigned numerals and letters to these groups to help clarify the Inca social pattern; many of the original Inca names and terms were recorded by early Spanish chroniclers.

The actual layout of the ceque lines across the Cuzco landscape, traced through documentary and field research by Tom Zuidema.

each cord, just like the *huacas* scattered at different points along their *ceques*.

Indeed, the quipu comparison is particularly apt since the officials in charge of each *ceque* actually did rely on knotted strings to remind themselves of their ritual duties. They had to know the exact auspicious moment in the ceremonial calendar to perform offerings and rites at each appropriate *huaca*; furthermore, they had to present an account of their activities at regular intervals to the royal administration. The proper functioning of the *ceques* and their shrines was clearly considered vital to the well-being of the state.

Much of our knowledge of the system ultimately comes from quipu records. Two Spanish chroniclers, the priest Cristóbal de Molina and the lawyer Polo de Ondegardo, both compiled useful accounts around 1570, almost certainly based on recitations of the same quipu by former Inca officials. Subsequently, the Jesuit Father Bernabé Cobo recorded a long list of more than three hundred *huacas*, noting the various idolatrous offerings presented at each shrine.

A sacred rock at Kenko in the outskirts of Cuzco, typical of the many varied huacas, *or holy natural features, worshiped by the Incas in and around the city.*

Cobo's list indicates that the number of *huacas* located along any single line could vary from three to thirteen. The shrines themselves consisted mainly of sacrosanct natural features such as stones or springs. In addition to dozens of holy hills, caves, trees and gullies, *huacas* could also be man-made objects of devotion such as fountains, bridges, and legendary tombs and battlefields. Perhaps the most impressive shrines took the form of rock outcrops hewn with immense labor into bizarre combinations of steps, caves and platforms; inside some of these sacred grottos, ancestral mummies were concealed.

Today, the inhabitants of Cuzco are familiar with about a third to a half of all the original names for the shrines recorded in Cobo's list over three hundred years ago. Though, generally speaking, the *huacas* are no longer venerated, it is still common to find offerings beside stones located at high points around the city. The offerings are usually simple tokens such as wooden crosses, colored yarn, cigarettes and little bundles of straw. This custom is, in fact, widely practiced in many parts of the Andes, notably beside high passes or at summits in the mountains. It doubtless stems from the same general kind of beliefs that were once formally organized within the *ceque* system of Cuzco.

Before the Conquest, typical offerings at the *huacas* included textiles, guinea pigs, llamas, and, more rarely, *capaccocha*, or human sacrifice. This aspect of Inca ritual naturally outraged the Spanish friars. However, according to their informants, it was carried out mainly in times of tribulation such as a famine, an epidemic or a military defeat. The coronation of a new em-

Well-preserved Inca ruins at Tambo Machay, originally a huaca *on one of the* ceque *lines of Cuzco.*

peror also called for sacrifice, sometimes of up to two hundred children.

The only regular times for such sacrifices occurred at the winter and summer solstices, the most solemn events in the Inca ceremonial calendar. During these two feasts, the administration formally reassessed the value of all the *huacas* in every town and province throughout the kingdom. Local officials from all these shrines sent gifts and young boys of about ten years of age to the capital. In addition, the priests in Cuzco chose girls of about ten to fifteen years of age from the Inca "convents" dedicated to the sun. A number of these children would then be sacrificed at various *huacas* in Cuzco. The older ones were sometimes made drunk and were then forced to walk three times around the sacred stone before they were strangled or had their hearts removed. The blood was then sprinkled on the ground or on the stone.

In some cases, boys were not killed in the capital, but were returned to their homes, accompanied by their native officials, for sacrifice. According to the chronicles, the boys were not supposed to travel along ordinary roads, but were to follow the straight line of an appropriate *ceque* out of the city. This journey directly up the steep, stony hillsides surrounding Cuzco must have been terrifying for the children, especially if they knew it was to end in death.

From the Spanish accounts, we learn that individual *ceque* lines also fulfilled many other less grisly functions. These included ritual duties connected with irrigation, the direction of the winds, and astronomy.

The Inca Observatories

BOTH MOLINA AND ONDEGARDO assert that the *ceques* were used as a kind of counting device for the Inca calendar. Though they provide no details of how this counting scheme worked, they assert that each *huaca* represented a single day of the year. From this statement, we would naturally assume that a total of about 365 *huacas* existed. The fact that there were, in reality, only 328 presented Zuidema and other scholars with an intriguing problem.

Most of the Spanish chroniclers paid scant attention to the Inca calendar; they simply noted that it consisted of twelve months and assumed that those months were similar to our own. However, the Inca had a more intricate calendar than the European one. Their months were based on more than just the simple waxing and waning of the moon's phases. Instead, they watched for a more subtle cycle, one created by the regular motion of the moon through the sky. They probably judged the moon's changing position from night to night by comparing it against the background of stars or prominent mountain peaks.

This implies that the Incas were expert observers, because they had to ignore the obvious cycle involved in the changing phases of the moon. Even though the moon would return to roughly the same spot in the sky on a regular to-and-fro basis, the particular phase of the moon would vary from one occasion to the next.

The reason for this irregularity is simple: the moon's phases follow a slightly longer rhythm than the cycle of the moon's motion. The phases, incorporated into the conventional month of 29½ days, actually last for about 2 days longer than the Inca's special lunar cycle. (This latter cycle of about 27⅓ days is known to astronomers as the sidereal month.) The importance of this cycle to the Incas is clearly reflected in the numbers involved in the *ceque* system. Thus, twelve months of 27⅓ days each results in a total of 328 days for the Inca year. It can scarcely be coincidence that this is exactly the same as the total number of *huacas* worshiped in and around Cuzco.

Because the Spanish left such vague and contradictory accounts of the Inca calendar, it is still not clear exactly how the observers matched up this "short" lunar year with other more familiar cycles, such as that of the sun. But the *ceque* lines themselves undoubtedly aided the observers, since several accounts speak of their use as astronomical sight lines.

For instance, a particular *ceque* was apparently connected with watching the setting sun at the June solstice. One of the *huacas* established along this *ceque* was dedicated to the moon. This was the waterfall of Sapi, where the Inca ruler bathed at the new moon before the June solstice, and where another offering was made at the full moon after the December solstice. Though the chroniclers do not tell us whether Inca priests watched the moon at the time of these ceremonies, it seems likely that religious duties were blended with practical calendar observations of both the sun and moon.

Where was the observing done? The Temple of the Sun is the most logical guess, since it was the place where all the *ceques* originated. Unfortunately, the written sources offer few clarifying details. According to the native-born chronicler Guaman Poma, the Incas had "observatories with windows" that enabled them to watch the rising and setting points of the sun as it moved along the horizon from one season to the next. Poma adds that the purpose of the observations was to regulate agricultural tasks such as sowing and harvesting, as well as shearing sheep, llamas and alpacas.

Several other accounts refer to a series of tall astronomical towers erected along the eastern and western horizons overlooking the city. These were evidently not observatories, but were positioned carefully to act as skyline markers when viewed from various locations in and around the city. During the early days of Spanish rule, the towers were among Cuzco's most notable landmarks; Garcilaso de la Vega claimed that some of them were over three stories tall,

The native-born chronicler Poma made this woodcut of Inca tower builders around 1600. The tower in the background is probably similar to the astronomical towers erected along the skyline of Cuzco.

> much higher than the watchtowers to be seen on the Spanish coast . . . these astronomical towers were still standing in the year 1560, and unless they have been destroyed since then, it would be possible, by watching the solstice, to find out from where the Inca confirmed it, whether from one of the towers of a Sun temple, or from elsewhere.

Garcilaso's suggestion of tracing a solstice line back to its original observation point was one of the ideas pursued some three hundred and fifty years later, when Anthony Aveni and Tom Zuidema began to collaborate on their astronomical studies of the *ceque* lines.

Their major difficulty was that the Spanish did, in fact, destroy all the towers, and with such thoroughness that not even their foundations have survived. However, Aveni and Zuidema managed to surmount this obstacle by using ingenious detective work to fix the approximate location of the towers.

First, they patiently questioned local informants about the

place names of old *huacas*, still in use today to refer to springs, stones and hills around the city. Then they matched these names against the extensive information about *huacas* supplied by Father Cobo's chronicle. A typical example of the kind of clue offered by Cobo is this entry concerning one of the *ceques* in the southwest quadrant: "Cuntisuyu—ceque 13, huaca 3: Chinchincalla is a large hill where there were two monuments at which, when the sun arrived, it was time to sow."

The two monuments were almost certainly towers similar to those described by Garcilaso and other Spanish commentators. Though, to begin with, Aveni and Zuidema had only a vague notion of which hill slope Chinchincalla might be, they were soon able to narrow the range of possibilities.

Local people recalled the names of once-sacred features of the landscape that fell on either side of *ceque* 13. In fact, it soon became clear that there was only a narrow space between this line and the two *ceques*, 12 and 14, that ran on either side of it. By using place names to pinpoint the courses of 12 and 14, Aveni and Zuidema easily spotted the hillside that the line in the middle, *ceque* 13, must once have crossed. Once they had successfully established the hill of Chinchincalla, where the towers originally stood, they could measure the sight line back to the Temple of the Sun to test it for the astronomical connection reported by Cobo.

View from Cuzco toward the western horizon, where the Incas raised four towers as calendar markers so that they could follow the sun's path in August, the time of the planting season.

Midsummer sunset viewed from a sacred rock at Lacco, northeast of Cuzco. This is said to have been a temple of the sun, where the Inca emperor retired to celebrate the June solstice.

Sure enough, the line to Chinchincalla coincided almost exactly with the direction of the December solstice as viewed from the Temple of the Sun. However, Spanish accounts were rarely perfectly correct in their description of native practices, and Cobo's entry for *ceque* 13 was no exception. In all probability, the towers were used to time the *end* of planting, rather than the beginning (as Cobo had reported), since the December solstice marked the onset of the rainy season. Despite this minor error, the essential facts reported by Cobo had been accurate.

It was certainly remarkable that Aveni and Zuidema could reconstruct an Inca sun line based on scraps of information recorded over three centuries ago. Persevering in their unique research methods, they confirmed descriptions of two other sets of astronomical towers that once stood on the western skyline overlooking Cuzco. One set of towers almost certainly marked the June solstice, while another indicated a date in August signaling the onset of plowing. (A similar August event is still celebrated by Andean communities as the opening up of "Pachamama," Mother Earth.)

However, in both these cases, the sight lines did not coincide with *ceque* lines, nor did they originate at the Temple of the Sun. Instead, these two solar events had been watched from different holy sites, one of them a sacred rock outcrop situated several miles outside the city. In other words, the Incas did not confine their astronomical observations solely within the radiating framework of the *ceque* system.

To put it simply, Aveni and Zuidema's work demonstrated that there was a highly complex and distinctive organization of Inca astronomical alignments around Cuzco. They were able to identify about a quarter of the total of forty-one *ceques* as probable astronomical sight lines. Though this was an impressive achievement, they emphasized the multitude of other social and ritual functions that the *ceques* and *huacas* are known to have served. Even the dozen or so astronomically aligned *ceques* were in no sense exclusively reserved for astronomy; the ancestral shrines scattered along the lines were dedicated to every conceivable ritual purpose from preventing earthquakes and disease to ensuring fertility and success in battle. Their connection to the calendar was just one aspect of an overall sacred framework of time and space.

The *ceque* system as a whole situated each one of Cuzco's kin groups in a precise and orderly relationship to the pinnacle of the Inca state, symbolized by the holiest shrine of all, the Temple of the Sun. This scheme not only affected the location of such groups within the city but also incorporated the passage of one calendar day after the next, and the movements of the sun, moon and Milky Way along the horizon. In fact, through myth and ritual, the kin network was extended to give meaning to most of the hills, caves, stones and springs around Cuzco, and to bring order to all the territories of the empire beyond. In this all-embracing vision, even rocks and trees, as well as the motion of the sun, lent justification to the exercise of imperial power.

Though the Inca state functioned superbly on a practical administrative level, it was clearly never conceived as a lifeless bureaucratic structure. Instead, the *ceques* must have been visualized as if they were the living veins and arteries of the realm.

What more appropriate symbol than the *ceque* could have been devised for this most centralized of all the Andean states? Within its framework, all supernatural and earthly forces converged on, and radiated from, a single point.

Not surprisingly, this emblem of Inca power was almost certainly imposed on the layout of cities other than Cuzco. Indeed, the chronicler Ondegardo claimed that the *ceque* system was used widely throughout the empire. To take one example, a distinct radial pattern seems to underlie the well-preserved ruins of an Inca administrative center known as Huánuco Pampa, in the central highlands.

An even more interesting case is a radiating pattern of roads that extends from a major settlement on the central coast, La Centinela, in the Chincha Valley. When John Hyslop explored these roads on a motorbike, he came across small roadside scatters of rocks interspersed with fragments of corncobs, fishbones, textiles and seashells. These reminded Hyslop of the *huacas* of Cuzco, where offerings of cloth and shell were often made. Since this complex of roads may well date back several centuries before the rise of the Incas, it suggests that radial pathways probably have a long history on the coast as well as in the highlands.

But the most striking comparison with the *ceques* is, of course, the network of ray centers on the Nazca pampa. As we have seen, Persis Clarkson's survey suggests that most of these centers and the lines connecting them probably date to the period following about A.D. 1000 and some of them may actually belong to Inca times. Were the beliefs incorporated in the ray centers similar to those underlying the Inca *ceques*?

If so, then the stone heaps covered with pot fragments that are so common at ray centers were perhaps the Nazca equivalent of *huacas*, shrines maintained by a particular social group at an appropriate date in the ceremonial calendar. We might imagine each ray center as the special responsibility of a different *ayllu* within the Nazca community.

If we pursue this general comparison with Cuzco further, perhaps the most important point is the multiple spiritual and social purposes we know the *ceques* to have fulfilled. An individual *ceque* line was never dedicated to any single function, such as fertility rites, ancestor worship or skywatching, but always to a combination of such practices. We can be certain that the *ceques* did indeed incorporate astronomical sight lines, but only in a minority of cases. Lacking such aids as Father Cobo's chronicle and the persistent tradition of place names around Cuzco, it will probably never be possible to identify which Nazca lines are astronomical and which are not. In any case, even if it can be proved that astronomical lines *do* exist at Nazca, their presence was almost certainly a minor aspect of a complex system of beliefs, as we know was true of Cuzco.

All the evidence seems to show that the Incas were not the first to develop the concept of radial pathways, and that the use of such pathways was not confined only to the high Andes. During their brief century of imperial power, the Inca rulers probably drew upon existing practices involving straight-line pathways and elaborated on them until the intricately organized network of Cuzco's *huacas* and *ceques* took shape. In the chaos following the Conquest, the bureaucratic chain that bound the services of even the humblest laborer to the capital was broken. Yet the image of sacred, radiating power persisted, and still does so even to the present day.

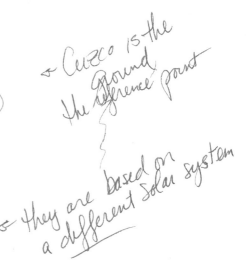

← Cuzco is the around the reference point

← they are based on a different solar system

CHAPTER 14	# IN THE REALM OF THE MOUNTAIN GODS

The Earth Shrines of Bolivia

IN 1931 THE RENOWNED FRENCH ANTHROPOLOGIST Alfred Métraux journeyed to the remote village of Chipaya, located in the treeless expanse of the Bolivian altiplano. Here, at 12,000 feet, he found the inhabitants, of native Aymara ancestry, leading an austere, impoverished existence herding sheep, pigs and llamas. Before the Spaniards came, the Aymaras had had a proud tradition of self-sufficiency and independence; for instance, they had fiercely resisted the Inca campaigns of conquest in the late fifteenth century.

Métraux discovered that many aspects of life in Chipaya closely followed an age-old Andean pattern. The community was divided into two social groups that were physically separated by a large open plaza, where the church and cemetery were situated. In the bleak landscape beyond, each family group maintained its own small, scrupulously clean chapel, a miniature version of the main village church. In front of each chapel was usually a little enclosure where the faithful met to chew coca or drink in honor of the particular divinity worshiped there.

Even smaller "oratories," or shrines, were scattered in long rows at distances of up to ten miles from the village. These shrines were cone-shaped mounds, each about the height of a person, built of turf and then whitewashed. The Aymara placed small offerings in cavities at the base of the mounds, or in east-facing niches higher up. These offerings would include little bundles of coca leaves, llama grease, tiny bottles of alcohol, or even small change.

The villagers told Métraux that the cones of earth represented the effigies of individual spirits whom they sometimes addressed by their personal names as they presented their offerings. A typical prayer went as follows:

> Little *Mal'ku*, I make you this offering. We are your sons. Don't be angry with us. I will at once make you this offering.

Métraux had difficulty in establishing precisely how the Aymara envisaged the spirits, or *Mal'ku*, to whom they spoke. *Mal'ku* seemed to combine a multitude of identities, from beneficent guardians to malevolent demons. One informant told Métraux that the *Mal'ku* were "white men" clad in white tunics and large hats; if one spoke to them, they disappeared. Others explained that *Mal'ku* could also refer to the small stuffed animals or special plants kept inside Aymara houses as protection against misfortune. In the end, Métraux concluded that *Mal'ku* often represented the vague, disembodied spiritual presence of a particular spot, rather than any specific spirit or demon.

What impressed Métraux most of all, however, were the pathways cut through the vegetation that connected one shrine to the next. There were "even roads that led in absolutely straight lines, regardless of the irregularities and slope of the ground." From one group of chapels, he was astonished to see

> five- or six-meter wide roads that led in a straight line to every point on the horizon. These great, perfectly distinct avenues did not seem to have been used for a long time. I never found the opportunity to follow them to their ends . . . [nor did] the Indians ever volunteer any information on the purpose of these chapels. The priest of Huachacalla whom I interviewed told me they served "superstitious" ends, and that he wanted to know nothing of cults and pagan practices that were secretly held there.

Métraux made no attempt to explore the mystery further. In fact, it was not until 1967 that the Bolivian lines were rediscovered, quite accidentally, by the British filmmaker Tony Morrison. Five years had passed since Morrison had first filmed the Nazca lines, and now he was directing a documentary on Andean wildlife. This required scenes of the rare pink flamingos that congregate on the high-altitude lakes of the altiplano.

Morrison described to me the astonishment he felt when he climbed the summit of a hill beside one of the lakes and found

The village of Chipaya photographed in the early 1930s by Alfred Métraux, who recorded the traditions of its Aymara inhabitants. A Chipaya priest, below, prays to an earth spirit, or Mal'ku, symbolized by the effigy in front of him.

the remains of a recently sacrificed llama, with a perfectly straight line leading away from it down the hillside. Here, in this cold, almost depopulated desert in the Andes, straight-line pathways were apparently still in use.

Ten years later, Morrison decided to investigate further, and led an expedition to the basin of the Desaguadero River, south of La Paz and Lake Titicaca. From the air, he was again surprised to see lines running continuously for over twenty miles near the slopes of Sajama, Bolivia's second-highest mountain.

When he finally began to locate similar lines on the ground, he found that they were constructed quite differently than those on the Nazca pampa. Rather than removing a layer of rock, the Aymara had uprooted the dense, waist-high *tola* bushes that constitute the main vegetation of the altiplano.

Morrison found that many lines led to small whitewashed shrines, just as Métraux had described forty years earlier. Each shrine was built of layers of small stones and mud-bricks to a

A Bolivian hilltop shrine at 12,500 feet visited by Tony Morrison in the 1970s. Straight pathways cleared through the bushes link the shrine to the village of Sajama far below.

height of about four or five feet, and was crowned by a cross. There was an east-facing niche where offerings had evidently been made, but all he could find there was little blobs of candle grease. However, Morrison did occasionally come across pottery fragments, many of them clearly modern, around the shrine and along the lines themselves.

Morrison's Aymara informants told him that only a generation back worshipers used to make their way to the shrines to fast during a fiesta held on January 2. When they reached a shrine, they would encircle it three times on their knees under the watchful eyes of the patron of the fiesta. Later, when it was time to break their fast, the women would fetch food and they would all end their meal by breaking their bowls. Then they would present the pieces of the bowls to the shrine as offerings.

Braving intense cold as they penetrated farther into the altiplano, Morrison and his companions finally reached the village of Sajama, near the slopes of the mountain. Here, at 14,000 feet, paths led in every direction, usually running from churches up to small shrines or cairns on the hilltops.

To some local people, these shrines were *calvarios*, or Stations of the Cross, and were definitely associated with Christian saints. Others, however, spoke of the *silus*, nebulous spirits who haunted the mountaintops and controlled rain, hail and frost.

Though, generally speaking, the *silus* were benevolent, they grew more powerful as one ascended the mountain. To appease each *silu* along the way, the pilgrim would leave behind offerings, often placed among the stones of a rock cairn. These cairns strongly reminded Morrison of the stone heaps he had seen on the Nazca pampa. At one of them, he discovered recently deposited coca leaves and lumps of llama grease. In addition to such individual tokens of respect, group observances were formerly conducted at specific shrines on appropriate days in the calendar. However, the direction of the paths did not appear to be influenced by astronomy, or so it appeared to Morrison in the case of one set of lines he investigated. He concluded, instead, that the directions of the lines were essentially random, depending on the particular purpose of each shrine they connected.

The radial pathways of Bolivia, with their humble mud-brick shrines, seem far removed from the *ceques* of Cuzco and the splendor of the Temple of the Sun, its walls sheathed in gold. Despite the gulf of centuries dividing them, however, it is clear that they are linked by a remarkable continuity in ceremonial beliefs. Just like the *huacas* described by Father Cobo, the Bolivian shrines are dedicated to a host of vaguely defined spiritual entities who are placated by offerings made at special days in the calendar. And, exactly like the *ceques*, the holy sites are connected by straight-line pathways, each one specially cared for by an individual kin group within the community.

Furthermore, the persistence of the *ceque* concept is obvious from the continuing use of the word in Andean languages. To refer to "a row of things" (whether it is a series of shrines, the plowed furrows of a field or simply a procession of llamas), one speaks of *ziqui* in Quechua, and *siq'i* in Aymara.

The evidence for such deep-rooted continuity of beliefs convinced Morrison that the stone heaps of Nazca must have been *huacas*, or shrines dedicated to the veneration of earth spirits. In his view, the main function of the Nazca lines was simply to connect one holy spot to another: this was the explanation of the Bolivian lines given to him by his informants in the bleak altiplano.

Although Morrison's view offers a highly plausible explanation of the ray centers and the stone heaps, it still leaves many questions unresolved. If the straight lines led to sacred places, how did they relate to the clearing of huge triangles and trapezoids? And what of the animal figures, seemingly the oldest markings on the pampa?

Another puzzling aspect is the seemingly vague character of the earth spirits reported by both Métraux and Morrison. Were the supernatural powers invoked by the Nazcans really so ill-defined? After all, the images on Nazca pots suggest that several distinctive "monster beings" were venerated for century after century. Is it possible to speculate further about the particular powers and beliefs represented by these beings?

Spirits of the Sacred Mountains

ANCIENT RITUALS are much less likely to have persisted along the south coast than in the altiplano because of the particularly devastating effects of the Spanish Conquest there. Nevertheless, as recent research by a young American anthropologist, Johan Reinhard, has shown, the fragments of traditional belief that survive there offer vital clues to the meaning of the Nazca lines.

Even in the modern town of Nazca, which has changed so much under the impact of tourism, folk healers are still active and old legends linger on. One of Maria Reiche's favorite after-dinner pastimes is to retell the many local witch stories she has heard during her forty years in the town; most of the tales she told me involved magical transformations of a sorcerer in and out of animal disguises. Unfortunately, only a few of these local folk beliefs have been properly recorded.

Nearly all of them concern Cerro Blanco, the sand dune that dominates south-facing views across the Nazca Valley. Here, on the crags overlooking the town, sand particles blown thirty miles from the coast have piled up into an immense white ridge nearly 7,000 feet above sea level.

Cerro Blanco was evidently an important focus of worship well before the Conquest. In the quaint text of the Jesuit scholar José de Acosta, published in 1590, we read of a great sand dune as the principal shrine of the *ancient* people of Nazca:

> They shewed me in Caxamalca of Nasca a little hill or great mount of sand, which was the chiefe Idoll or Huaca of the Antients. I demaunded of them what divinitie they found in it? They answered, that they did worship it for the woonder, being a very high mount of sand, in the midst of very thicke mountains of stone.

Even today, Cerro Blanco commands respect as the "Volcano of Water"; farmers in the Nazca Valley believe that it once erupted with streams of water that then turned into the underground irrigation canals. Other local stories affirm that a vast underground lake exists in the heart of the mountain, the source for all the water in the valley. Maria Reiche told me that the mountain is believed to open and close magically; anyone who dares to enter will find golden oranges growing beside the lake.

It is not surprising that the beachlike summit of Cerro Blanco is also associated with the life-giving power of the sea. According to legend, Cerro Blanco was the wife of Illa-Kata, the highest mountain of all, which overlooks Nazca to the east. Tunga, lord of the coast, insinuated himself into Illa-Kata's company by showering him with gifts of gold, jewels, rich cloaks and fine pottery. One day, while Illa-Kata slept, Tunga ran off toward the coast with Illa-Kata's wife. When Illa-Kata awoke, he roared at his wife in a clap of thunder and set off in pursuit. To disguise her, Tunga buried her under rocks and covered her with maize from his valleys. Illa-Kata passed by but did not recognize his wife. Finally he returned to the mountains, so angry that he caused earthquakes to topple the surrounding peaks. Meanwhile, Tunga was turned into the mountain that today bears his name, just before he reached the ocean. Illa-Kata's wife remained buried under a white coating of maize and is now identified as Cerro Blanco.

During his interviews with local farmers around Nazca in 1982, Gary Urton learned a number of other intriguing tales, all linking Cerro Blanco with water and fertility. In one of these (mentioned briefly in Chapter 4), the name "Nazca" is said to have arisen because the people of the valley cried out in pain during a long drought. (*Nanay* is the Quechua word for "pain" and this word eventually became "Nazca.") The legend goes on to say that the people congregated at their principal place of worship, the foot of Cerro Blanco. Finally, the god Viracocha descended from the sky to the summit of the mountain and heard his people crying out. He was so moved by their suffering that he started to weep. His tears ran down Cerro Blanco, penetrated the earth and formed the aqueducts deep in the soil.

Drought figures in another of the local tales collected by Urton. During times of extreme hardship, it is said that a man is dispatched to the ocean with a jug, which he is supposed to fill with foamy seawater from a place where the waves crash

The people of Nazca still make offerings for water to Cerro Blanco. Here anthropologist Johan Reinhard discovers fresh offerings of river stones and cotton plants on the 7,000-foot-high summit of the sand dune during a severe drought in 1983.

against the rocks. (Interestingly, the name of the god Viracocha can be translated as "foam of the sea.") The man then returns to a mountain peak above Nazca and splashes the water on the summit. If correctly carried out, this ritual will cause rain to fall in the mountains within ten to fifteen days. However, on one occasion, when water was spilled from the jug, it caused a huge destructive flood in the valley.

The tradition of supplicating Cerro Blanco in times of hardship still survives. When anthropologist Johan Reinhard climbed to the sandy summit of Cerro Blanco in 1983, he discovered little offerings of river pebbles and cotton plants freshly deposited there. This was during a severe local drought that threatened the extensive cotton plantations in the valley below.

The supernatural power of Cerro Blanco also plays a part in local healing rituals at Nazca, according to an account of one such cure said to have taken place during the 1950s. When a woman was stricken by a mysterious ailment that no one could diagnose, a powerful priest known as a *Pongo* was summoned from the town of Puquio, about sixty miles away. In a darkened room, the Pongo arranged his "table" of cult objects (doubtless similar to the *mesa* of Eduardo Calderón described in Chapter 9). He then called upon the local mountain spirits, of whom the most powerful was Cerro Blanco. Curiously, Cerro Blanco is then said to have created a problem by "speaking" only in Spanish, which the Pongo could not understand. Once an interpreter was found, Cerro Blanco began to rebuke the patient for witchcraft. One of the woman's previous victims had engaged another sorcerer to put a spell on her, and this spell had been responsible for her sickness. In a few days the woman was well again, thanks to the intervention of Cerro Blanco.

How had the Pongo been able to invoke the powers of the sacred sand mountain? His own belief was that he had learned the secrets of his calling by a six-month apprenticeship to the mountain spirits, known as *wamanis*. His training had taken place *inside* the mountains, in a strange underground city. At the end of this period, he awoke to find himself lying in a field, none the worse for his experience. However, now that he had acquired his exceptional powers, he was both respected and feared in the community of Puquio. Since one of his duties was to destroy those who had offended the *wamanis*, the Pongo himself was something of a sorcerer.

Each August the Pongo and his fellow priests used to climb a sacred mountain near Puquio to make offerings for water. There they would pray to the *wamanis*, whom they envisaged as intermediaries between man and the supreme being, known as

Inkarrí. In their minds, a clear distinction existed between their native religion and the Catholic one. This is apparent in a narrative by one of these men recorded in Puquio in the 1950s (here loosely translated from the original Quechua):

> The Wamanis exist, now and always, among us. They were created by our ancient Lord, by Inkarrí.
> The Wamani is, therefore, our second God.
> All the mountains have Wamani. In all the mountains, there is Wamani.
> The Wamani gives pastures to our animals and, to us, his veins, the Water.
> Our [Catholic] God created the clouds and rain; we receive them as His blessing. And from our fathers, the Wamanis, we receive our Water, because it pleases God and he commanded it. But everything that exists was brought into being by our ancient Inkarrí. He created the entire world.

Though all-powerful, Inkarrí was visualized as a timeless being far removed from human affairs. The *wamanis*, on the other hand, watched directly over mankind, granting fertility through the flow of rivers and streams, as well as punishing wrongdoers through the actions of their servant, the Pongo. They were often imagined as fearless lords, wealthy and generous on the one hand, but equally capable of violence and destruction on the other. The old men of Puquio believed that the *wamanis* sometimes made themselves visible in human form, although no one claimed to have seen them. Everyone agreed, however, that when summoned up in the course of a ritual, they flew to the Pongo's aid in the shape of a bird.

Similar beliefs are still widespread in almost every part of the Andes. Though the name given to the mountain spirits varies from one region to the next, the same characteristics emerge. Their personalities are always ambivalent, since they are both nourishers and punishers of mankind; they cause the herdsman's cattle to multiply, yet deride him by echoing his shouts.

In certain villages of highland Peru, the supernatural life of the surrounding peaks is visualized in great detail. Each mountaintop is identified according to a hierarchy, with offices such as mayor, deputy and judge, exactly like those of the human world. Deep underground, every mountain is said to conceal a city endowed with great riches and often populated by innocent children who have strayed in through its magical gates. In addition, the mountain lord keeps his own flocks pastured there. Foxes and pumas are thought to be his dogs and cats, while condors are his chickens. The most fearsome animal in his retinue, however, is another of his cats, the flying feline known as the Ccoa.

In traditional Andean belief, mountain peaks are often visualized as the dwelling places of supernatural beings who are both the protectors and destroyers of mankind.

The Quechua often describe the Ccoa as being somewhat larger than a domestic cat, with gray fur and black stripes on its winged body. Many farmers make daily offerings to appease its vicious temper. When the Ccoa strikes, it spits hail, urinates rain and hurls lightning or hail from its phosphorescent eyes. This behavior enables it to steal the farmers' crops at harvest time, but the fields of its servants, the sorcerers and rich people, are never touched: only the poor and the sick suffer from its malevolence. Whether the Ccoa acts on the instructions of the mountains or has a willful spirit of its own is a matter of disagreement among the Quechua.

Other Andean people share very similar beliefs about supernatural felines. The Aymara of Bolivia, for instance, consider that a sacred puma sends them hail and lightning. They visualize this creature as both a protector and destroyer; it is such a powerful and important supernatural animal to them that they believe it represents one aspect of their supreme creator god.

Besides his feline identity, the storm god is also imagined as an armed warrior, wielding lightning bolts as his weapons. Today, life-size effigies of this warrior take second place only to the Virgin in the major religious processions held in Andean towns and villages. The Quechua know him as "Santiago the Thunderer," or Saint James. It is said that the ancient thunder god became associated with Saint James, the patron saint of Spain, when the Incas heard Spanish soldiers give their famous cry of "Santiago!" just before charging into battle. In the Inca mind, the blast of muskets and the flashing of swords that followed this cry were linked to the power of thunder and lightning.

The warrior version of the storm god was worshiped long before the arrival of the Spanish. Within the Temple of the Sun in Cuzco, a golden statue of Illapa, "The Flashing One," shared the same altar as images of the sun and the creator. According to the chronicler Cobo, Illapa was made up of the stars in the sky and his garments shone with lightning. When angered, the god would hurl a stone from his sling at a celestial water jug carried by his sister. The flash of his sling was the lightning, while the cracking of the jug, which caused rain to fall, was thunder.

Although their claims are controversial, a number of scholars believe that the essential element of the storm god—a warrior hurling thunderbolts—can be traced back to some of the earliest religious images discovered in Peru. In fact, the figure of a god wielding staffs (lightning bolts?) is depicted on textiles and stone carvings that may date back as far as 1000 B.C. Perhaps the most impressive of all these "staff gods" appears somewhat later, around A.D. 300 to 700, as the centerpiece of the celebrated Gateway of the Sun at Tiahuanaco. This figure displays such typical features as a rayed headdress and twin animal-headed staffs. While some of the "staff god" beliefs must have changed over the course of thousands of years, there can be little doubt that a warrior storm god was always one of the most revered Andean deities.

The "Gateway of the Sun" at Tiahuanaco, carved from a single block of gray volcanic andesite, stands about ten feet high. Though there have been many different theories about the carving over the doorway, it probably represents one version of the traditional "storm god" of the Andes.

At any rate, this deity seems to have been important to the people of Nazca and Paracas. Although the embroidered images of the Paracas textiles are complex and richly varied, certain details recall the later beliefs in storm gods. The frequent appearance of flying creatures combining human, feline and bird characteristics is particularly suggestive. Could these creatures represent forerunners of the Quechua storm cat, the Ccoa, or the Aymara puma? The malicious expression of many of the Paracas "monsters" would certainly fit the temperament of the Ccoa. Furthermore, the trophy heads and sprouting beans they so often carry may also foreshadow the dual role of the storm cat, which both destroys its human enemies and protects its servants' crops.

As for the other identity of the storm god as a warrior with lightning staffs, this figure, too, seems to have been embroidered on the Paracas textiles. Even though he appears much more rarely than the flying creatures, several aspects of his appearance imply a connection with the warrior storm god. The double staffs or spears he carries, together with his rayed hair or headdress, resemble details of the Tiahuanaco Gateway god. Similar features such as staffs or rays also seem to be present on several of the giant drawings of humans executed on hillsides surrounding the Nazca pampa.

All this evidence suggests that one important element in Nazca

A deity wielding staffs or thunderbolts is one of the most persistent themes in ancient Peruvian art. Far left, a painted textile from the south coast that may date as far back as 800 B.C. Left, an embroidered figure from a Paracas textile, perhaps 200 B.C., resembles several humanlike designs drawn on the slopes near Palpa, below; "rays" around their heads are suggestive of the "storm god" image. Bottom, a tapestry of alpaca and cotton from the central or north coast, dating to around A.D. 800–1200.

religion was a deity associated with the control of weather and the fertility of crops. If it is reasonable to allow our speculations to be guided by present-day Andean beliefs, then the Nazcans may have visualized this storm god as both a flying cat and a human warrior. The cat was probably envisaged as the most powerful servant or representative of deities who resided in each mountain.

In Inca times, both children and animals were offered as sacrifices to the snow-peaked mountain Coropuna, still venerated even today by people of the south coast. Poma's woodcut dates to around 1600 A.D.

The Offerings Continue

PROMINENT PEAKS WERE SO IMPORTANT to the Incas that they are said to have established entire colonies to administer their shrines there. Among the most sacred were those peaks closest to the coast, since it was hoped that the mountain spirits would "call up" moisture from the ocean into the atmosphere. If the correct offerings were made, the spirits would then return the moisture to the land and eventually back to the sea through their "veins," the streams and rivers. (Like so many Andean religious ideas, this concept was based on accurate observation of the environment. In reality, the presence of the Andes plays a crucial part in the circulation of moisture as it passes up from the ocean into the atmosphere and back down again through the rivers.)

The influence of the mountains over rainfall was so vital that the shrines sometimes demanded extravagant offerings. According to the native-born chronicler Guaman Poma, the Incas once offered the lives of five hundred children to their holiest mountain, Coropuna, during a severe drought. In 1958, a similar period of hardship reportedly led to the sacrifice of a young woman on a remote mountaintop in the Bolivian altiplano not far from Tiahuanaco.

Aside from these exceptional cases, perhaps the most spectacular of all the rituals still offered to the mountains takes place each year at the time of Corpus Christi, nine weeks after Easter. Thousands of participants gather at the foot of two of the highest and holiest peaks in the Cuzco region. After ceremonial dances involving vivid costumes and masks, many of the pilgrims begin

As symbols of the life-giving power of the sea, shells have a profound importance in Andean rituals.

an arduous nighttime climb up the mountains. Eventually they reach a shrine located above the snowline on a 16,000-foot-high glacier, where they light candles and dedicate prayers to Jesus or to the lord of the mountain. Next day, each man descends to his village bearing lumps of ice that have been cut from the glacier and are believed to have healing powers.

At other times in the festival calendar, Quechua farmers undertake special rites intended to increase and protect their livestock. The priest or family head in charge of such a ceremony begins by gathering the household together at sunset. All the people remove their caps and sandals, placing them respectfully around a llama-wool blanket. In the center of this blanket, facing east, are the amulets intended to invoke fertility: coca leaves, seashells and pebbles selected because of their curious shapes, resembling animals. Then offerings of drink and food are given to the mountain lords while the leader of the ceremony addresses special prayers to them. They are particularly implored not to send their chickens, cats and dogs (condors, pumas and foxes) to eat the livestock belonging to the family. The leader then drinks wine from a seashell and casts droplets over his flock and his relatives. Finally, he flings the dregs violently in the air in all directions to satisfy the thirst of the supernaturals.

Seashells are an important element in such fertility ceremonies because they symbolize the sea and water in general. According to Cobo, the Incas considered shells a particularly appropriate offering to make at a sacred spring, because springs were "the daughters of the sea, which is mother to all waters." Fragments of shell have occasionally been found among the pottery fragments scattered over the stone heaps on the Nazca pampa, where efforts to secure water or fertility would surely have been of special concern.

The archaeologist Josue Lancho, who has lived in Nazca for many years, has studied a group of complex markings at Canta-

Plan of the Cantalloc area of the Nazca Valley by local archaeologist Josue Lancho suggests a connection between some of the ground figures and the underground canals. Length of the "Needle and Thread" at the left is almost one kilometer.

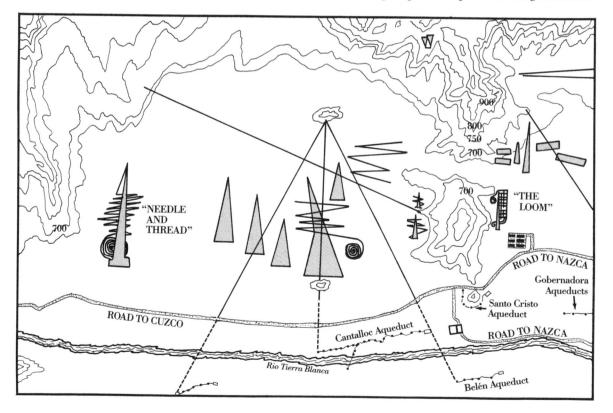

lloc, on the southern edge of the Nazca Valley, and thinks that they were partly connected to water rites. The ends of several narrow cleared triangles point toward the base of Cerro Blanco, the "Volcano of Water"; furthermore, a series of narrow lines fan out toward the valley, seemingly directed at three separate locations of underground aqueducts. If Lancho is correct, then the Cantalloc drawings appear to confirm the local legend of Cerro Blanco as the source of subterranean moisture in the Nazca Valley.

An equally interesting link between lines, water and folklore has been suggested by anthropologist Johan Reinhard, based on his recent exploration of markings in the remote deserts of northern Chile. Even though the Nazca culture never reached as far south as Chile, a spectacular cluster of drawings on a hill known as Cerro Unitas strongly recalls those at Nazca. A series of lines and broad avenues runs up the slopes of this hill, with each line ending in a cairn near the summit. Among the other markings is an immense, carefully outlined human figure, nearly 300 feet long. Reinhard argues that details of this figure

An impressive group of drawings on the slopes of Cerro Unitas in northern Chile includes lines, avenues and a partly destroyed feline figure. The huge, well-preserved humanlike figure, below, is probably connected with still-flourishing beliefs about mountain deities who control local water sources.

(notably its rayed hair or headdress) identify it as a representation of the warrior storm god. Moreover, Reinhard discovered that offerings for water are still presented to mountain gods throughout the same region. One mountain is specifically invoked "to call the water from the ocean." Local legends state that the most prominent peak visible from the markings at Cerro Unitas was the site of annual sacrifices of children; the purpose of the sacrifices was said to have been to maintain a constant water supply.

In the spring of 1985, Reinhard made an even more remarkable discovery. On a visit to a remote Bolivian village, he witnessed a ceremony involving a 2-mile-long line that led to a mountaintop. The villagers walked in a procession along the line to the summit, from which they then invoked the surrounding mountains for water. While his research is still in progress, Reinhard believes that many other Bolivian lines are still actively used in a similar way. The lines seem to function as sacred pathways to elevated spots, where prayers and offerings are directed to the mountains for water and fertility. Was this also true of the Nazca lines and ray centers?

If we speculate further, we can imagine that the triangles and trapezoids were in some way intended to "draw down" moisture from the foothills of the Andes to the east of Nazca. On the main pampa, many of the lines and clearings run roughly parallel to the Ingenio Valley, in an approximately northwest-southeast direction. Rather than indicating risings of the sun or moon, were the markings meant to point northwest toward the Andes, where the mountain lords resided? And were seashells and beautifully painted pots offered up so that the lords would send moisture and fertility down through the lines and avenues?

Extending our guesswork further back in time to the animal figures (probably the earliest markings to appear on the pampa), it is logical to suppose that they represented "messages," or votive acts, dedicated to airborne supernatural beings.

In fact, most of the animals depicted on the desert are still associated in Andean folklore either with mountain spirits or with beliefs related to fertility and water. The frequency of bird designs may be significant: we know that modern Nazca farmers interpret sightings of herons, pelicans or condors as signals of rain, while the mountain spirits usually take the shape of birds in order to "speak" to priests or sorcerers. If a hummingbird flies into a house, the Quechua believe that a mountain lord has taken possession of its body and is using the bird to demand an offering from the occupants.

Other animals depicted on the pampa play a similar role in Andean folktales; for example, dogs and foxes are also common

In April 1985, Johan Reinhard took this unique photograph of a religious procession following a line at a remote village in highland Bolivia. The line led to the hilltop in the background, from which offerings were made to local mountain deities for water.

messengers between the mountains and mankind. According to one tradition, the Incas tied dogs out in the open in the hope that their howls of hunger would persuade the gods to take pity on them and send rain.

Other creatures, such as lizards and spiders, are highly regarded in Bolivia and Peru because of their sensitivity to weather changes and rain. If a spider begins to spin a web it is a sure sign of increasing moisture, for the thread it weaves is compared to trickles or droplets of water. If it lowers itself from a web inside a house, then rain will follow, but if it begins to climb back up toward the web again, a dry spell will continue.

Such fragments of folklore suggest that the particular choice of animals drawn on the pampa was highly appropriate if their designers intended them to invoke rain. The fertility of beasts may also have been a special concern, since the outline of a few of the animal designs begins and ends in their genital areas.

Furthermore, if these animal "messages" were directed toward mountain gods, we can understand why they were executed on a giant scale. Since the gods were traditionally thought to take the shape of winged creatures such as flying felines, condors or hummingbirds, it was surely logical for the "messages" to be created so that they could best be seen from above.

With so much evidence to support the importance of beliefs in mountain gods, it is tempting to conclude that this theory represents *the* single key to the mystery of the Nazca lines. However, this would be just as misleading as supposing that mountain worship is the *only* important element in Quechua religion.

In fact, we know that the peaks are venerated along with a host of other deities related to natural features lower down in the landscape. For example, Pachamama, the Earth Mother, symbolizes the generative spirit that nourishes the fields and pastures, while the amaru, the Rainbow Serpent, is the bringer of moisture to canals, springs and streams. Water is a theme common to all these sacred forces: the mountains represent the origin of moisture, the Earth Mother the power of fertility released by it, and the Rainbow Serpent the agent that distributes it among the farmer's irrigated fields. In fact, from the highest peaks down to the deepest underground streams, the Quechua view the entire landscape as if it were alive with supernatural forces, all fundamentally related to the flow of water.

The mountains naturally command most respect because of their role as the ultimate providers of water, and also because of their remoteness from mankind: the highest mountains are often considered more powerful than the lower ones, and so on.

A Moche vessel from the north coast depicts a cluster of foxes presiding over a sacred mountain. Hallucinogenic wilka *trees, painted beneath, suggest the means by which Moche priests may have sought to communicate with the mountain deities.*

Thus, the Quechua envisage the landscape surrounding them as a hierarchy of sacred forces, graded from top to bottom.

We have seen how this concern for "upper" and "lower" is reflected in the ordering of Andean communities, where "upper" halves of the community command more importance than "lower" ones. In other words, the sacred ordering of the landscape provides order for the social world of humans, too.

Traditional Quechua beliefs are thus rooted in the sanctity of everyday surroundings. Their religious vision is literally down-to-earth and quite distinct from abstract notions such as heaven and hell that were imposed on them by Catholicism.

The Spanish friars were often bemused by the multiplicity of Inca gods, and the Indians' worship of dozens of holy rocks, springs and trees around them. However, these beliefs were often the product of acute observation of natural forces, rather than of the childlike simplicity the Spanish so often ascribed to them. (A good example is the case of the "dark cloud" animals in the Milky Way; as we saw in Chapter 6, the actions of these sky beings are precisely matched with accurate observations of animal behavior in the real world.)

Like the Quechua, and the Incas before them, it is likely that ancient Nazca people perceived a multitude of spiritual forces in their surroundings. This is suggested by the complexity of the designs painted on their pottery (in particular, the combination of realistic animals and vegetables with a variety of fantastic supernatural beings). It is doubtful whether we will ever be able to reconstruct the detailed meaning of each one of these images, any more than we can hope to explain the exact purpose of every marking on the pampa.

On the other hand, conclusions about their *general* character can certainly be drawn (see Chapter 9). For example, a belief linking death and fertility seems to have been fundamental to Nazca religion. This is apparent from the startling associations of symbols painted on the pots: severed heads are paired with sprouting plants, and vaginas with killer whale jaws. The "monster beings" were evidently agents of both destruction and pro-creation. Their ambivalent qualities seem remarkably similar to the willful personalities of Quechua mountain deities such as the Ccoa.

We can also guess that Nazca's arid environment would have encouraged religious preoccupations very similar to those of the Quechua. Since Nazca farmers still depend totally on irregular underground water sources that ultimately originate in the mountains to the east, we would surely expect beliefs relating moisture, mountains and fertility to be of critical concern. At

Mountaintop shrines marked by stone cairns, or "apachetas," are still actively worshiped in the Andes. Pilgrims usually leave offerings such as cigarettes or miniature liquor bottles among the stones.

any rate, this is exactly what is implied by most of the legends about Cerro Blanco, the sacred sand mountain.

Without oversimplifying our view of Nazca religion, then, it seems likely that mountain deities would have been the most prominent among a whole range of other venerated forces in their surroundings. Of course, some of the desert drawings may well be related to these other, lesser supernatural beings, or were perhaps created for entirely different purposes that will continue to elude us. Nevertheless, it can still be argued that the *majority* of the Nazca markings were signals or acts of piety directed to the mountain spirits of the Andes.

Much future research will be necessary before this proposition can be adequately tested. As Johan Reinhard has pointed out, one of the reasons why the Nazca lines have commanded so much attention is precisely that there are no simple answers. The variety of markings on the pampa challenges our imagination, and means there will always be room for alternative theories. It seems unlikely that the mystery will ever be fully exhausted, and it would surely be a pity if it was.

Labyrinth of the Gods

A BOUT EIGHT HUNDRED YEARS AGO, a ceremonial building resembling a labyrinth was constructed at the site of Pacatnamú on Peru's north coast. Though we might expect this extraordinary building to have generated a legend similar to that of the Cretan labyrinth of King Minos, no such legend actually survived, nor were the ruins even properly explored by archaeologists until 1983.

With a magnificent location on a promontory high above the Pacific, Pacatnamú was one of the major religious centers of the north coast in pre-Inca times.

Pacatnamú is an exceptional site for several reasons: to begin with, it enjoys one of the most captivating settings imaginable. The ruins occupy a high, narrow bluff that juts out toward the Pacific. On one side, vertical cliffs drop down to a patchwork of rice fields covering the floodplain of the local river, the Jequetepeque. On the other side, a beach of silver-gray sand sweeps past the cliffs in an immense curve. This splendid location helps to explain the special atmosphere of the site. Many visitors comment on the unusual freshness of the air and the softness of the sunlight during most of the day. These qualities perhaps contributed to the sanctity of Pacatnamú in ancient times.

As is true of most sites on the Peruvian coast, it is difficult to visualize the original appearance of the monumental architecture here. Infrequent rainstorms have reduced most of Pacatnamú's thirty-seven mud-brick pyramid mounds to undulating bumps and ridges of sand. However, once the eye becomes accustomed to picking out the shapes of these mounds, certain regularities in the layout of the site are obvious. On its northern side, each mound usually faces a large open plaza, while at the south it normally slopes down to a rectangular, walled compound.

Though a few of the larger compounds superficially resemble the palaces of Chan Chan, and may date to roughly the same period, their purpose was evidently quite different. Few of the ᴊtorage or "office" facilities so prominent at Chan Chan were present at Pacatnamú. The buildings there were not provided for the convenience of an administrative bureaucracy, but were apparently dedicated to religion.

The chronicle of Father Antonio de la Calancha, dating to 1638, informs us that a cult of moon worship was particularly important in the Jequetepeque Valley. The reputation of Pacatnamú, however, almost certainly extended far beyond the local river valley. Many aspects of the site indicate a close relationship with another shrine at Pachacamac, situated some 400 miles to the south.

The celebrated oracle of Pachacamac is known to have drawn pilgrims from every part of the Inca empire. One of Pizarro's officers, Miguel de Estete, journeyed to the shrine in 1553 and wrote of the "Devil" consulted by Pachacamac's visitors. According to his account, worshipers came from as far away as Ecuador, bringing offerings of gold, silver and cloth. Such gifts evidently meant that the shrine could function independently from the political fortunes of particular chiefs or empires. Indeed, it seems likely that both Pachacamac and Pacatnamú enjoyed a prestige somewhat similar to that of the Oracle of Apollo at Delphi. The Delphic priests managed to retain their autonomy throughout the most turbulent centuries of ancient Greek history.

What did pilgrims experience when they arrived at Pacatnamú? Until recently, only sporadic excavations had been attempted at the site, amid the usual chaos of holes dug by looters. In 1983, however, UCLA archaeologist Christopher Donnan initiated a program of investigations that he hopes to continue indefinitely, because of Pacatnamú's exceptional potential.

During his first season at the site, Donnan decided to concentrate on the largest of all the compounds. This roughly rectangular area is enclosed by the remnants of high adobe walls, running for over 500 feet on each side. As Donnan's workers began to clean off the layers of sand from the foundations of passages and rooms within the compound, the strange character of the building soon became clear.

Though the compound covers an area roughly equal to about four football fields, there was only a single entrance, just wide enough to admit one person. This suggested to Donnan that the high-walled enclosure was an exclusive precinct, reserved for an elite group or for an unusual activity.

Eventually Donnan realized that the ground plan was centered on several open courtyards and low elevated platforms. Donnan believes that rituals took place in these areas, for among other finds he uncovered the bodies of four white llamas, each ceremoniously wrapped in elaborate textiles.

Other unusual finds included numerous exquisitely woven little squares of cloth resembling decorative samplers; whatever their purpose, they were obviously not practical items of clothing. Many of these embroidered fragments had been left behind on the floors of the courtyards. Beside them were bobbins of colored yarn that had obviously been used in their manufacture. It seems likely that individuals inside wove these miniature fabrics and then abandoned their work, presumably as an offering to the gods who presided over the precinct.

They may also have engaged in ceremonial dancing and drinking. Toward the end of the digging season, Donnan found an intricately woven textile fragment, apparently depicting the activities that took place within the compound. It shows two figures sacrificing white llamas and another pair weaving with bobbins like those actually found in the courtyards. In the background, elaborately costumed dignitaries are seated on elevated platforms with drinking vessels upraised as if to celebrate a toast. Around them are other figures whose lively postures seem to indicate that they are dancing.

But the most surprising discovery of all was the ground plan

The extraordinary "labyrinth" complex at Pacatnamú, with the high perimeter wall and single narrow entrance in the foreground, below. Right and bottom left, views along the ruined mud-brick corridors. Bottom right, the narrow spiral at the center of one of the corridor systems.

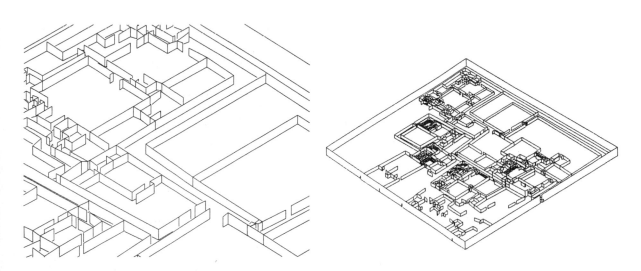

of the passages and rooms that led to the ritual areas. The complexity of the layout defies any practical explanation. For example, one of the elevated platforms is located just a few feet from the front entrance of the compound, yet to reach it, you must follow corridors running back and forth over nearly a quarter of the area of the entire enclosure.

Finally, you climb the ramp leading up to the platform and find that the passageway begins to turn into a tighter and tighter spiral. The center of the spiral is a space where only a few people can stand comfortably. Whether this was a place for solitary prayer or for consulting an oracle is not clear; however, any visitor would surely have been in an altered frame of mind by the time all the baffling passages had been negotiated.

Though his research continues and his conclusions are still tentative, Donnan told me he believes that the ground plan was, indeed, deliberately designed to disorient and overawe visitors. Its purpose, he speculates, may have been to prepare them spiritually for the ritual atmosphere of a sanctuary cut off from the everyday world.

The experiences of pilgrims who ventured into the Pacatnamú "labyrinth" invite comparisons with Nazca, and with Andean religious practices in general. Any visitor to the Nazca pampa finds that ordinary perceptions of distance or direction are easily confused by the featureless expanses of the desert. This disorienting effect would surely have been heightened if Nazca people had attempted to walk (or dance) around the outlines of the more complex zigzags, spirals or animal designs. Perhaps, as appears to have been the case at Pacatnamú, this disorientation was deliberately encouraged as a means of "letting go" of ordinary experience.

The effect might have been enhanced still further by ceremonial drinking or coca chewing. As I discovered by witnessing the fiesta at Pacariqtambo, the solemn drinking of maize beer or raw spirits is an important part of modern ritual activity. Could such practices explain the pottery fragments scattered among the stone cairns on the pampa? As mentioned earlier, the Aymara of Bolivia end a period of fasting by climbing a straight-line pathway to a hilltop shrine. Here they eventually eat and then break their bowls as an offering. Fasting, the following of a mazelike path, and intoxication by alcohol or hallucinogens may all have been practiced by the Nazca people as part of their spiritual exercises.

Another implication of the Pacatnamú site is that some aspects of ancient Peruvian religious experience were solitary and meditative in character, like the weaving of the miniature textiles. The narrow passageways and the tight spiral at the center seem to represent an utterly different concept of religious architecture from our own tradition of churches and cathedrals, designed to impress a massed congregation. Instead, the structure of the "labyrinth" seems to have been designed for individual rather than for group ceremonies, and this may also be the case with the Nazca lines.

It is highly likely, of course, that the large triangles and trapezoids were constructed by massed labor forces. On the other hand, if these cleared areas had been the scene of regular Nazca "congregations" involving hundreds of people, there would surely have been more signs of disturbance than the meager evidence observed by Persis Clarkson. Even in the protected zone near the Ingenio Valley, where both drawings and pottery fragments are concentrated most heavily, it is difficult to believe that many of the outlines could have been visited repeatedly without suffering severe damage. My own experience of walking along the whale outline (see p. 131) suggested that extreme care was necessary to avoid effacing it. This at once led me to suspect that it might be the initial act of setting out the figures that was most significant to the Nazca people, rather than any possible subsequent visits.

As for the network of ray centers, apparently the last markings to appear on the pampa, the case is even stronger that they were intended for rituals of an essentially private and solitary kind, like those reported among the Aymara by Métraux and Morrison. This is indicated by the remote locations of many ray centers, sometimes on the narrow summits of steep-sided hillocks. They may well have been places for individuals to leave offerings or engage in prayer. Once again, it is possible that the

Partly inspired by ancient monuments, conceptual artists of the 1970s sought to connect the experience of their viewers directly to the landscape. In Winifred Lutz's Hypotenuse (1977), *a portal leads one down a Nazca-like line to a platform with a shallow, inverted tetrahedron at its center. Lutz describes* Hypotenuse *as "a summer gazebo for lonely geometers and formalists."*

act of setting out a line may have been as important as its function in providing a pathway to a hilltop.

It was this private aspect of the Nazca lines that particularly attracted a number of leading sculptors such as Robert Morris and Richard Long, both of whom visited Nazca during the 1970s. They were in the forefront of a revolt against the self-contained art "object" imprisoned inside a gallery. The way in which the Nazca lines connect a solitary observer to the distant landscape strongly appealed to Morris. In his essay "Aligned with Nazca," he observes that the lines are impressive because of their "co-operation" with their setting, not because they dominate and overawe the viewer. "In spite of the distances involved in the lines of Nazca," he comments, "there is something intimate and unimposing, even offhand, about the work. The lines were constructed by a process of removal. They do not impress by indicating superhuman efforts or staggering feats of engineering. Rather it is the maker's care and economy and insight into the nature of a particular landscape that impresses."

Morris's essay usefully reminds us of the narrow expectations so often imposed by our normal experience of art; a good example is the popular assumption that somehow the lines must have been viewed from the air by their makers. This 90-degree perspective is, of course, the way we normally view pictures in a gallery.

In contrast, both the Pacatnamú "labyrinth" and the *ceques* of Cuzco indicate that ancient Peruvians developed a sense of sacred space unlike any of our own traditions of monumental art or architecture. This corresponded to the unique character of their religious experience, which emphasized the relationship of the individual to sacred forces in the landscape. It found its greatest expression of all in the Nazca markings, particularly the long lines that connected the solitary pilgrim to the distant hilltops.

When Men Turn into Jaguars

IN THE SUMMER OF 1932, George Palmer, an ex-U.S. Army pilot, made a leisurely flight from Las Vegas, Nevada, to Blythe, California. Toward the end of his excursion he was passing over desolate gravel terraces west of the lower Colorado River when he suddenly caught a glimpse of an enormous human figure. Its sticklike limbs seemed to be spread-eagled against the desert pavement. As he circled around, he spotted other human figures and a four-legged creature. Each outline appeared to be at least 100 feet or more long. Soon afterward he flew back to the site and photographed it with his box camera. He presented his snapshots of the figures to staff at the Los Angeles County Museum of Natural History, who were at once excited by the discovery. They organized an air and ground survey of the Blythe figures, the first of many subsequent investigations of California's desert drawings.

Today the Blythe sites are so popular that the ground surface is scarred in every direction with the tracks of dune buggies and motorbikes: only a series of metal and cable fences surrounding the main groups have prevented their destruction. Two such groups each consist of a gigantic human alongside a four-legged animal and a small spiral. One of the humans is encircled by a ring about 140 feet in diameter, apparently trodden into the gravel: this may have been a ceremonial dance floor. A separate group of designs includes one very straight long line connected to a circle.

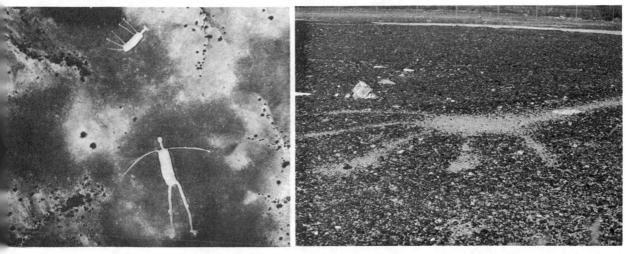

Giant ground figures at Blythe, California, of uncertain age and meaning. At right is a ground-level view of one of the figures' hands.

Like the Nazca markings, the Blythe figures were created simply by scraping aside a shallow top surface of gravel that had been oxidized to a brown-black color. This exposed the contrasting tan and gray underlying soil. Just as at Nazca, too, the main figures were outlined on such a scale that they can be appreciated only with difficulty from the ground.

Other sites also recall the Nazca markings in their labyrinthine complexity. The well-known Topock Maze, for example, occupies a location near the Colorado River similar to that of the Blythe figures, about 100 miles farther upstream. Here, eighteen acres of the river terrace are covered with ridges of rocks and gravel shaped into long parallel rows that run in various directions, sometimes straight and sometimes curved. Two huge human figures were originally incorporated in the Topock Maze, but were destroyed by railroad contractors during the 1880s. According to one theory, the site was used by the Mojave Indians for ceremonial running, intended to purge the soul of evil spirits after killing enemies in battle.

In most cases, however, the detailed meaning of the drawings is elusive, especially the identity of the giant humans. One such stick figure near Sacaton, Arizona, appears in the creation myths of the Pima. It is said to represent Hâ-âk, a sharp-toothed female being who devours children. The Pima reportedly still make offerings to this monster effigy today.

As for the Blythe figures, most archaeologists at first assumed that the four-legged creatures depicted the horses introduced by

Part of the Topock Maze, a curious pattern of parallel gravel ridges that covers about eighteen acres beside the lower Colorado River. The most plausible explanation is that it was built as a ceremonial site by predecessors of the Mojave around A.D. 1200–1500.

the Spanish. However, recent evidence (including the opinion of Mojave informants) suggests that the creatures are actually mountain lions or jaguars. These beasts were among the most important supernatural beings that Mojave healers, or shamans, traditionally attempted to contact through their dreams. Indeed, the mountain lions were so powerful that dreaming of them could cause some men to fall ill. Assuming that the identification is correct, the Blythe animals may well have been drawn to invoke the power of these sacred felines.

In the course of a long ceremonial song recorded in 1902, a Mojave shaman-doctor recited the mythological deeds of Numeta, the mountain lion, and Hatekulye, the jaguar. They were said to have created both the deer and the birds in the Colorado Valley, and to have aided neighboring tribes with their hunting skills. The doctor explained that his own ability to catch fish began when Numeta and Hatekulye appeared before him in a dream "like men." After they instructed him in fishing techniques, their hands became hairy and their fingers sprouted claws as they reverted to their feline forms.

A belief in man-animal transformations is shared by nearly all Native Americans; so, too, is the idea that sacred animals can instruct people through dreams or trances.

In the South American Amazon, shamans are thought to be able to turn themselves into jaguars at will. The jaguar disguise enables the shaman to achieve his own intentions, whether for good or ill. After a shaman dies, he turns permanently into a jaguar and so continues to exert his influence among the living. Most Colombian Indians, such as the highland Kogi, are fond of recounting tales of ancient jaguar-shamans who fought wars and established empires in the mountains. Among the Tukano

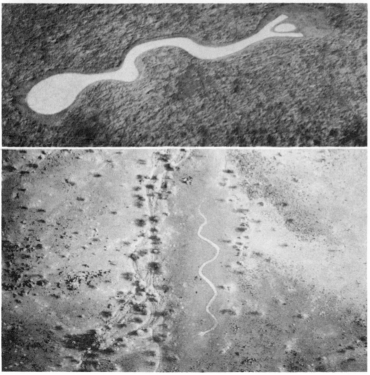

Giant serpent effigies were created by several different groups of prehistoric North Americans. The Great Serpent Mound near Locust Grove, Adams County, Ohio, excavated in 1885, was probably built by people of the Hopewell culture around 200 A.D. The coiling serpent with an egglike shape in its jaws is over 1,200 feet long. A remarkably similar 230-foot-long effigy, left, was investigated by archaeologist R. Clark Mallam in Rice County, Kansas, during 1981–82; lime was spread on the figure to make it show up from the air. Both this figure and the rattlesnake near Parker, Arizona, bottom, may have been connected with observations of the sun at the solstices.

of the rain forest, a single word can be used to refer to either jaguar or shaman, and in addition this word has associations with sexuality. To invoke the dangerous yet potent life force of the jaguar, Amazonian shamans invariably turn to plant hallucinogens. The narcotic trance is often said to "liberate" the spirit of the jaguar that is within man.

Significantly, the jaguar is visualized as a flying feline among those forest hunters who live close to the Andes. The Tacana of northern Bolivia are convinced that certain humans are transformed into flying jaguars by the Earth Mother, either at their own request or as a special punishment. Their personalities are as ambivalent as those of the Quechua storm gods: they act as guardians of all plants and animals, holding in balance both the air and the earth and the night and the day; yet they are also bringers of destructive winds and rains. When such a beast threatens the community, the Tacana attempt to drive it away by blowing snuff in its direction. Tobacco and stronger narcotics assist their shamans in contacting flying jaguars, but it is even possible to transform oneself simply by turning a somersault.

The theme of feline transformation seems to have been fundamental to the earliest known religions of the New World. As mentioned in Chapter 9, three-thousand-year-old Peruvian carvings depict part-human, part-feline creatures, sometimes associated with hallucinogenic plant designs.

But this theme was by no means confined to South America. "Were-jaguars" dominate the art of the oldest civilization of Mexico, the Olmec, celebrated for its colossal stone heads carved with stern countenances. As early as 1200 B.C., the Olmec began to build ceremonial sites, evidently dedicated to a jaguar-like god, in the rain forests of the Gulf Coast. Some of the most striking Olmec sculptures seem to capture humans in the act of their transformation into jaguars. Bird elements also appear along with the jaguar designs, perhaps because they symbolized the "flight" of the shaman under the influence of hallucinogens. Such combined bird and feline forms appear on delicately crafted jade spoons, likely to have been used for inhaling hallucinogenic snuff.

The Olmec even shaped monumental earthworks into animal images. Their first great cult center, a site known today as San Lorenzo, consisted of ceremonial mounds, lagoons and stone sculptures carefully arranged along the top of a plateau three-quarters of a mile long. On three sides, steep ravines cut deeply into the plateau, dividing it into a series of immense ridges that reach out like fingers to the north, west and south.

The first archaeologists to survey San Lorenzo naturally assumed that these ridges were a natural formation. However,

An Olmec jade carving of a "were-jaguar," suggesting the idea of transformation from the human realm to that of supernatural animal power.

when Yale archaeologist Michael Coe thoroughly investigated the site in the 1960s, he realized that the ridges were man-made. The soil had not only been dumped in artificial layers as much as 25 feet deep, but had been arranged according to a deliberate, symmetrical plan. Thus, a ridge on one side of the plateau corresponded to the mirror image of a ridge on the other. What could have been the meaning of this gigantic earth design? Coe believes that, some three thousand years ago, an Olmec ruler decided to impress both his subjects and the gods by founding San Lorenzo on top of an immense image of a bird. According to Coe's theory, the bird is flying eastward, its extended wing feathers forming ridges on the north and south sides, while its tail trails to the west. Because of its huge dimensions, the Olmec could never have perceived the bird design from the top of their sanctuary at San Lorenzo.

To the Olmec, then, we must credit one of the earliest and most impressive efforts to create an animal image that could only be appreciated from the air. It is surely significant that this idea should have arisen within a cult clearly dedicated to beliefs about animal transformation and almost certainly involved in the use of hallucinogens.

Were all such giant animal images inspired by shamanism? Probably the best-known examples outside Nazca are the mounds of the eastern United States; these man-made hillocks are scattered in the thousands from the Alleghenies to the Missouri River, and from the Great Lakes to the Gulf Coast. A century ago, many scholars regarded them as the work of a mysterious "Mound Builder" race, since they regarded American Indians as too uncivilized to have been capable of erecting them. However, archaeologists have long since demonstrated that mound building was, indeed, carried out by prehistoric Native Americans, though their activity was not confined to a single ethnic group or period of time.

One such episode of mound building is represented by the Hopewell culture, which reached a climax between 100 B.C. and A.D. 200. At that time, Hopewell influence extended far beyond its main center in the central Ohio Valley. Grave goods buried in the Ohio mounds include marine shells and sharks' teeth from Florida, mica from Virginia, chalcedony from North Dakota, and quartz crystals from Arkansas or the southern Appalachians. These widespread trading links were one aspect of a cult of the dead that also called upon massed labor forces. Besides burial mounds, the Hopewell raised huge earth banks that were often arranged in complex geometric formations. The famous group of embankments at Newark, Ohio, includes a 1500-feet-wide octagon (now a municipal golf course); altogether the

Typical ornaments of the Hopewell culture from burials at Mound City: a tobacco pipe in the shape of a frog and an eagle made of sheet copper.

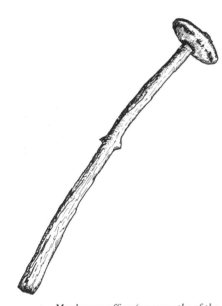

Mushroom effigy (apparently of the hallucinogenic amanita type), just over a foot long, made of wood covered with copper. It was excavated from a burial mound at Mound City, Scioto County, Ohio; it had been laid on a sheet of mica and then covered over with the cremated remains.

earthworks are estimated to have consumed as least 7 million cubic feet of soil.

The exact nature of the authority capable of commanding such resources is largely guesswork, but a number of wealthy Hopewell burials suggest a connection with shamanism. Animal skin costumes and masks have been reported from several mounds; in Illinois, one male was buried in a coat adorned with hundreds of pearls and with a headdress of antlers. The importance of animal symbolism is also suggested by earthworks such as the Great Serpent Mound near Locust Grove, Ohio, which seems to represent a writhing serpent with an egg-shaped object clasped in its jaws.

The Hopewell elite may have attempted to contact supernatural animals in the course of ceremonious tobacco smoking. Skillfully crafted stone pipes are among the most characteristic finds from the mounds (there were over two hundred of them in one Ohio mound alone). The modeled animals that decorate the pipes (usually hawks, eagles, dogs, raccoons and quails) may represent the spirits sought after by the smokers. Stronger stimulants were probably also available. At the major Hopewell site of Mound City, an object of wood and copper in the shape of a long-stemmed mushroom was found at the center of a raised burial platform. The excavator of the site suggested that this object represented the amanita or fly agaric mushroom, known for its potent hallucinogenic properties.

By about 500 A.D., the Hopewell phenomenon had declined for reasons still debated by archaeologists. However, a new tradition of building animal mounds flourished for at least another five centuries, notably in the Midwestern states of Wisconsin, Michigan and Iowa. A century ago, over fifty separate groups of these Effigy Mounds were known to exist, of which over 80 percent have subsequently been destroyed due to the negligence or willful destructiveness of landowners. Most surviving mounds are in the shapes of birds and bears, although there are usually simpler conical and linear forms close by. The grave goods were generally more modest than those in the earlier mounds, while the builders followed a mobile hunting-and-gathering existence, unlike the Hopewell, who had lived in settled agricultural communities. The Effigy Mounds may well have been the focus for ceremonies that drew scattered hunting bands together at a particular season. Perhaps these rites took the form of efforts to contact the bear and bird spirits embodied in the mounds.

The belief in communication with supernatural animals through dreams, trances or transformations is almost universal among Native Americans. To account for this wide dispersal of shamanism, most scholars now accept the idea that its roots

Animal mounds (outlined with lime) at the Chantry Hollow Mound Group in Iowa. The hunters and gatherers of the Effigy Mound culture built hundreds of similar mounds in the upper Midwest from about A.D. 650 to 1300.

stretch back over thousands of years of prehistory. Indeed, if we are to explain startling similarities between the rites of shamans in the Arctic and their counterparts in South America, we must assume that their fundamental beliefs go back very far indeed. Could they have originated with the first hunters, who crossed the Bering Strait twenty thousand or more years ago?

In fact, shamanism may well have begun among the Ice Age hunters of Siberia. Even today, Siberian rituals display many of the classic ingredients of shamanism, including beliefs in magical flights of the soul and the use of hallucinogens such as the fly agaric mushroom. Such Siberian practices may well preserve remnants of the Ice Age cults that the earliest hunters took with them to the New World. These cults, in turn, were probably ancestral to all the native religions of the Americas.

While it may seem farfetched to suggest that shamanism could date back so far, archaeological evidence tends to support the idea. One such piece of evidence comes from overhanging cliffs in southern Texas and northern Mexico, where hunting bands found shelter as early as 9000 B.C. (This was so long ago that Ice Age game such as mammoth, giant bison and wild horse still roamed the Great Basin.) Even at this remote period, the hunters indulged in the red "mescal bean"—traces of this powerful hallucinogen are consistently present in debris excavated from the ancient cliff sites. Right up to the late nineteenth century, North American shamans still prized the mescal bean for their sacred ceremonies.

At present, archaeologists are unable to trace similar evidence quite so far back in Peru. Nevertheless, the inhabitants of early coastal sites were certainly chewing coca by about 2500 B.C., as

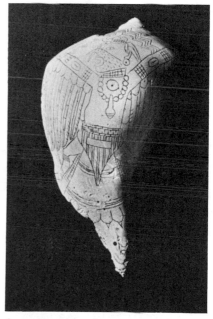

An eagle priest or dancer, engraved on a conch shell from the Spiro mound site in Oklahoma, dating to A.D. 1200–1350.

A trapezoid of boulders at the Tie Creek site near the Winnipeg River in southeastern Manitoba. Archaeological evidence suggests that some Manitoba boulder outlines may date back as far as 500 A.D., while others are probably of quite recent origin.

well as embroidering textiles with designs of mythological beasts. On the north coast, an extremely persistent tradition of healing practices is implied by Moche pottery designs dating to around A.D. 500; several vessels depict in precise detail the curing paraphernalia used by present-day healers such as Eduardo Calderón (see p. 175).

Similar traditions of healing and divination linger on in the Nazca region, even in the modern town. As we saw in the account of the priest-sorcerer, or Pongo, from the nearby town of Puquio, local healers are thought to receive their powers in dreams or trances. Like most shamans, they rely on supernatural animal helpers, usually condors or foxes, sent as messengers by the mountain gods.

As for the religion of the ancient Nazcans, there is abundant evidence of both the importance of supernatural animal powers and the use of hallucinogenic plants. The identity of the "monster beings" so prominent in Paracas and Nazca art remains elusive, yet some creatures depicted with partly human bodies may well relate to a belief in man-animal transformation.

The ability of Nazca priest-leaders to contact such supernatural beings was probably crucial to their authority. There were, after all, few natural resources in the region that could have been exploited by ambitious chiefs. The absence of storage facilities at Cahuachi reinforces the idea that the power of the

Nazca leaders was based not on hoarded wealth but on ceremonial prestige.

Of course, the cult beliefs they manipulated were probably closely connected to vital, practical concerns such as the water supply in the Nazca Valley. The planning of the underground aqueducts may well have reinforced the authority of Nazca chiefs or priests over local farmers.

Nevertheless (as argued in Chapter 10) it seems likely that the aqueducts were actually built at a late period, when highlanders were already present in the valley and Cahuachi had been deserted for centuries. Even if the aqueducts *were* built much earlier, their existence alone cannot explain why Cahuachi commanded so much influence, not only in the Nazca Valley, but throughout the south coast. The answer, surely, is that the site enjoyed a reputation similar to that of Pacatnamú; at such ceremonial centers, access to supernatural powers was almost certainly controlled by an elite priesthood. The ceremonies held by the Nazca priests doubtless drew pilgrims from a wide region.

This does not necessarily mean that there was a rigid, top-heavy hierarchy of priests, as Kosok envisaged. Based on the example of modern Andean communities, we might expect that power was divided or rotated between important family groups, whose lands and settlements were scattered across the landscape. We might further guess that the task of clearing giant triangles and trapezoids was also shared among these groups. Indeed, the responsibility of working on a particular desert drawing may have been an important way of defining one's identity within the community. If this is correct, then like the *chutas* of Pacariqtambo, the clearings would symbolize the mutual relationships and dependencies of the Nazca people.

This is not to suggest that all Nazcans lived together in perfect harmony, since the trophy heads and painted depictions of warriors imply otherwise. Under constant threat of critical water shortages, the potential for conflict must always have existed, either between family groups or between the populations of entire valleys. As the ritual battles staged in present-day Andean villages remind us, tensions run high whenever basic resources are unpredictable or are spread unevenly across the landscape.

Even so, the ambitious scale of the desert drawings suggests that creating them must have helped to diminish such tensions. The activity on the pampa drew the population together in common tasks and shared beliefs. The conviction that a Nazca priest could make direct contact with beings who controlled rain, hail and winds must have helped unify the people, even in times of severe drought.

Most of the famous white horses cut into the chalk hills of southern England are from the eighteenth century or later, but the example at Uffington, Berkshire, is thought to go back to Iron Age times (perhaps around the last few centuries B.C.), when it may have functioned as a territorial or tribal emblem.

Conclusion

Throughout this book, I have emphasized the unique character of the Andean peoples and their achievements: their tradition of rotating labor forces, for example, or their phenomenal canal-engineering skills. Even though the Nazca lines are seemingly the most original of all their works, some aspects of their meaning clearly extend beyond the Andean world. In particular, the markings reflect the common preoccupation of all Native American peoples with shamanism.

If we view the giant animal outlines in the light of shamanic practices, then they were not simply pious images offered to the gods. Rather, they were symbols of an *active* participation in the supernatural, made possible by an individual's altered state of consciousness. It is likely that the act of creating the drawings assisted the process of communicating directly with mountain spirits or their animal representatives.

Even after the decline of Cahuachi, when animal drawings, too, had probably ceased, the emphasis on personal experience of the supernatural seems to have persisted. The focus of ritual activity apparently shifted from Cahuachi to dozens of ray centers widely scattered on the open pampa. Reaching these sacred hilltops frequently involved hours of arduous walking from the nearest valley along the straight-line pathways. It is likely that such shrines were intended mainly for rites and offerings by individuals.

Indeed, if there is a common thread connecting all the Nazca earth markings, as well as those from California and the Midwest, it is surely related to the basic theme of shamanism: the solitary priest who makes personal contact with otherwordly powers.

In this general sense, the Nazca lines were not the eccentric product of an isolated people, but belong to the heritage of all Native American religions. The impulses behind the creation of the lines were ultimately linked to thousands of years of sacred traditions in the New World—indeed, to intellectual and spiritual forces that shaped the earliest civilizations of the Americas.

The ancient roots of shamanism are reflected in common elements of beliefs and paraphernalia spread widely through Asia and the Americas. A Mapuche woman shaman of Chile, above, photographed in the 1940s, beats on the classic type of drum as also displayed by a Koryak shaman of Siberia around the turn of the century.

A Special Note for Visitors to the Nazca Lines

EVEN THE BEST PHOTOGRAPHS of the Nazca lines convey little of the extraordinary spectacle they present from an aircraft. This firsthand experience of viewing the lines from the air is highly recommended to anyone planning a sightseeing tour of Peru. Indeed, Nazca has become a regular stop on the itinerary of most commercial tours operating from Lima (a seven- or eight-hour drive along Peru's major coastal artery, the Panamerican Highway).

The growing fame of the Nazca lines has also deepened the problem of preserving them. As explained in Chapter 4, the Panamerican Highway was routed directly through some of the drawings in the early 1940s. Since then, every visitor who has strayed off the road has left behind a trail of damage. Even cautious and well-meaning sightseers on foot usually discover the extreme fragility of the pampa's surface only after it is too late. One set of footprints can totally obliterate traces of the ancient lines.

My own full realization of the vulnerability of the pampa came only after I had accidentally trodden across a particularly delicate "virgin" surface. I found that my feet broke through the dark brown pebble crust as if it were thin ice. Every detail on the sole of my running shoe was imprinted on the yellow-white soil beneath. Though the wind will eventually dull these

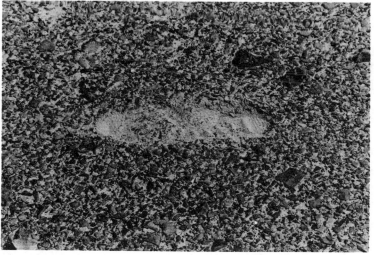

impressions to some extent by blowing dust and sand across them, it is likely that they will still be visible many years from now.

In recent years, serious conservation problems have been posed by the impact of tourism on many celebrated ancient sites, notably Stonehenge and Lascaux. There is clearly no easy solution to the task of satisfying public interest in ruins while ensuring their continuing preservation. Another related difficulty is the question of how far knowledge about a particular ruin should be broadened by archaeological investigation, since digging a site involves destroying part of the evidence.

The Nazca lines, however, raise both these issues in a particularly acute form. Even if one conscientiously attempts to walk only within an ancient line and never step outside it, this still creates damage. In fact, I observed that the tracks of even a single archaeologist, carefully walking inside a narrow line, were enough to alter its appearance entirely. Yet without some

Recent tire tracks disfigure the surface of ancient cleared areas on the Nazca pampa.

sort of on-the-spot survey work, there would never be any advance in our understanding of the lines.

In an effort to halt the destruction of the markings by casual sightseers, an area bordering the northern edge of the pampa was declared a protected zone by the Peruvian government in 1975. However, at first security was so inadequate that Maria Reiche hired three guards of her own to patrol the area on motorbikes. The salaries of these guards are still paid almost entirely through the proceeds of her book *Mystery on the Desert*, which she sells to audiences at her nightly lectures at the Tourist Hotel. Buying a copy of this modestly priced book is the best way any visitor can help to preserve the Nazca lines.

Access to the protected zone is now entirely prohibited; indeed, *anyone* straying off the Panamerican Highway risks a substantial fine and five years in jail. Besides the motorbike patrols, the pilots of the frequent tourist flights over the area will report anyone they observe trespassing on the pampa. Incidentally, all the ground-level photographs of the pampa reproduced in this book were taken under a special Peruvian government permit issued by the Institute for National Culture. I was supervised at all times by an archaeologist working under a similar permit.

The visitor *can* gain some idea of what the markings look like at low altitude, thanks to viewing facilities along the road. These include a 15-meter-high tower, built with funds from the Peruvian state oil company. The tower is open to visitors, free of charge, and overlooks several figures, including the "seaweed" and the pair of hands. A little farther to the south, visitors are also permitted to climb a low hill near the road. This hill forms a ray center, from which about fifty lines run to the horizon.

The view from both the hill and the tower may be disappointing for many, since the markings are inconspicuous even from these vantage points. The view from the air is a different story; indeed, a trip in a light aircraft is so impressive that it unquestionably offers the best way of experiencing the markings. A number of companies, notably Aerocondor, offer rides in light aircraft based at Nazca's dirt airstrip.

The future of the Nazca lines is still uncertain. The fact that they survived the flood of tourists unleashed by von Däniken's books during the 1970s and 1980s is almost totally due to the efforts of Maria Reiche. Though official negotiations are currently under way to place the pampa under UNESCO's protection, it is still open to question whether the markings will withstand further tourist pressure or the increasingly frequent acid rainfall caused by refineries along the coast. Meanwhile, the message for anyone lucky enough to be able to visit Nazca is clear: stay off the pampa and enjoy the view from the air.

Sources of Quotations

11   *As it crosses:* M. Vargas Llosa, *The Green House*, New York: Avon, 1973, pp. 25–26.

21   *The earth refused:* Inca lament, quoted in A. Kendall, *Everyday Life of the Incas*, London: Batsford, 1973, p. 205.

22   *They sometimes have to carry:* B. de Vega, quoted in J. Hemming, *The Conquest of the Incas*, London: Macmillan, 1970, p. 355.

23   *They live the most wretched:* H. de Santillán, ibid., p. 348.

25   *We cannot conceal:* F. de Armellones, ibid., p. 348.

30   *. . . to be the happiest:* B. de Las Casas, quoted in Evelyn Page, *American Genesis*, Boston: Gambit, 1973, p. 220.

30   *. . . protected modesty:* J. F. Marmontel, quoted in A. Métraux, *The History of the Incas*, New York: Schocken, 1969, p. 17.

30   *. . . succeeded more completely:* A. Morgan, *Nowhere Was Somewhere*, Chapel Hill: University of North Carolina Press, 1946, p. 21.

30   *The rulers of modern:* G. Mason, *Columbus Came Late*, New York and London: Century, 1931, p. 261.

32   *. . . they felt the labor little:* C. de León, quoted in R. Wright, *Cut Stones and Crossroads*, New York: Viking, 1984, p. 151; see H. de Ornis, tr., *The Incas of Pedro Cieza de León*, Norman: University of Oklahoma Press, 1959, p. 154.

33   *Not only in the size:* B. Cobo, tr. R. Hamilton, *History of the Inca Empire*, Austin: University of Texas Press, 1979, p. 95.

38   *Where are the foundations:* P. White, *The Past Is Human*, New York: Taplinger, 1976, p. 85.

38   *. . . built an improvised airfield:* E. von Däniken, *Return to the Stars/Gods from Outer Space*, New York: Bantam, 1970, p. 105.

38   *. . . a small vehicle:* E. von Däniken, *The Case of the Ancient Astronauts*, BBC/Nova quoted in *Early Man*, spring 1979, p. 14.

42   *I'm sure Egypt's:* J. Woodman, *Nazca: Journey to the Sun*, New York: Pocket Books, 1977, p. 23.

61   *It's just business:* M. Reiche, interview with author, 1984.

61   *. . . there came to that land:* L. de Monzon, quoted in T. Mejía Xesspe, "Aqueductos y Caminos Antiguos . . . ," in *International Congress of Americanists*, Vol. 1, Lima, 1939, p. 569.

64   *Nazca. . . must have been:* F. Engel, *Prehistoric Andean Ecology*, New York: Humanities Press, 1981, p. 17.

64   *Without the drawings:* M. Reiche, interview with author, 1984.

65   *If he hadn't died:* M. Reiche, quoted in B. Chatwin, "Riddle of the Pampa," *Daily Telegraph Colour Magazine*, London, c. 1977, p. 61.

66   *. . . terribly spoiled:* M. Reiche, Interview with author, 1984.

67   *. . . luckily my reason:* M. Reiche, quoted in V. Baird, "New Discoveries . . ." in *Lima Times*, May 11, 1984, p. 7.

70   *. . . whirling with endless questions . . . With a great thrill:* P. Kosok, "The Mysterious Markings of Nazca," in *Natural History*, Vol. 56, May 1947, p. 203.

74   *I was socially unacceptable:* M. Reiche, quoted in V. Baird, "New Discoveries," op. cit., 1984.

81   *. . . may well have been used:* P. Kosok, op. cit., 1947, page 205.

84   *. . . a tremendous control:* P. Kosok, "Astronomy, the Priesthood and the State . . . ," in *Zeitschrift für Ethnologie*, Bd. 84, 1959, p. 9.

85   *. . . these valleys:* ibid., p. 13.

88   *. . . to satisfy curiosity:* M. Reiche, interview with author, 1984.

89   *I am happy to think:* ibid.

99   *The star-sun-moon calendar theory:* G. S. Hawkins, *Beyond Stonehenge*, New York: Harper & Row, 1973, p. 117.

107   *. . . a world of nonsense:* B. Cobo, quoted in G. Urton, *At the Crossroads of the Earth and the Sky*, Austin: University of Texas Press, 1979, p. 204.

109   *. . . blacker than the night sky:* F. de Avila, quoted in G. Urton, 1981. "Animals and Astronomy in the Quechua Uni-

verse," in *Proceedings of the American Philosophical Society*, Vol. 125 (2), p. 110.

109   *They say that this Yacana:* ibid., p. 113.

115   *The primordial struggle:* J. Elias, quoted in G. Urton, unpublished Nazca field notes for 1982.

127   *Our conclusions:* G. Urton, interview with author, 1985.

129   *Pottery of all kinds:* P. Clarkson, interview with author, 1984.

130   *These foothills were most difficult:* G. S. Hawkins, *Ancient Lines in the Peruvian Desert*, Cambridge, Mass.: Smithsonian Astrophysical Observatory, 1969, p. 18.

133   *We are still busy analyzing:* A. F. Aveni, interview with author, 1985.

136   *It may seem incredible:* M. Reiche, *Mystery on the Desert*, self-published, 1949, p. 7.

167   *So many are the baths:* M. de Estete, quoted in C. M. Larrea, "El Descubrimiento y la Conquista del Perú," *Bol. de la Soc. Ecuatoriana*, Vol. I (3), p. 317.

174   *What do we look at?:* E. Calderón, in E. Calderón, R. Cowan, D. Sharon, and F. K. Sharon, *Eduardo el Curandero*, Richmond, California: North Atlantic Books, 1982, p. 41.

176   *. . . a person's mental force:* ibid., p. 36–37.

194   *although it might have been possible:* E. Lanning, *Peru Before the Incas*, Englewood Cliffs: Prentice-Hall, 1967, p. 120.

215   *When there was a need:* B. Cobo, op. cit., 1979, p. 125.

216   *. . . the bodies of the kings:* B. Cobo, *Historia del Nuevo Mundo*, ed. M. J. de la Espada, Seville, 1890–1895, p. 342–43.

218   *. . . very profitable gardens:* G. de la Vega, *Royal Commentaries of the Incas*, tr. H. V. Livermore, Austin: University of Texas Press, 1966, p. 178.

219   *. . . to keep his dominion:* B. Cobo, op. cit., 1979, p. 190.

221   *. . . they kept such record:* P. de Ondegardo, quoted in J. V. Murra, *The Economic Organization of the Inka State*, Greenwich, Conn.: JAI Press, 1980, p. 110.

222   *I was able to reassure:* G. de la Vega, op. cit., 1966, p. 333.

225   *The drops of water:* G. de Bíbar, quoted in J. Hyslop and M. Rivera, "An Expedition in the Atacama Desert," in *Archaeology*, November/December, 1984, p. 35.

226   *. . . adjust to their landscape:* J. Hyslop, *The Inka Road System*, New York: Academic Press, 1985, p. 233.

235   *. . . observatories with windows:* G. Poma, quoted in A. F. Aveni, "Horizon Astronomy in Incaic Cuzco," in R. A. Williamson, ed., *Archaeoastronomy in the Americas*, Los Altos: Ballena Press, 1981, p. 306.

235   *. . . much higher:* G. de la Vega, op. cit., 1966, p. 116–17.

236   *Cuntisuyu:* B. Cobo, quoted in A. F. Aveni, op. cit., 1981, p. 308.

241   *Little Mal'ku:* A Métraux, *"Les Indiens Uro-Čipaya de Carangas,* in *Journal de la Societé des Américanistes,* Paris, Vol. 27, p. 331.

241   . . . *even roads:* ibid., p. 340.

245   *They shewed me:* J. de Acosta, 1590, p. 308.

248   *The Wamanis exist:* J. M. Arguedas, "Puquio, una Cultura en Proceso de Cambio," in *Revista del Museo Nacional,* Lima, Vol. XXV, p. 193.

254   . . . *the daughters of the sea:* B. Cobo, quoted in A. M. Soldi, "El Agua en el Pensamiento Andino," in *Boletín de Lima,* Lima, No. 6, p. 24.

267   *In spite of the distances:* R. Morris, "Aligned with Nazca," in *Artforum,* 14, 1975, p. 39.

Bibliography

The following selection of works is not an attempt to provide an exhaustive reading list for the subjects covered in this book, but instead is a personal choice of references that the author has found particularly interesting or useful. The selection is divided into subheadings related to the content of each chapter.

RECOMMENDED READING

At present, there is no comprehensive, up-to-date book on ancient Peru available to the general reader. The following titles, however, present important background information on the many topics raised in this book, and are all highly readable.

BRUNDAGE, B.C. *Empire of the Inca*. Norman: University of Oklahoma Press, 1963. Paperback edition, 1985. (Entertaining, though somewhat uncritical and floridly written account of Inca history.)

HAWKINS, G.S. *Beyond Stonehenge*. New York: Harper & Row, and London: Hutchinson, 1973. (Popular account of 1968 Nazca survey.)

HEMMING, J. *The Conquest of the Incas*. New York: Harcourt Brace, and London: Macmillan, 1970. (Standard work, compellingly written.)

KENDALL, A. *Everyday Life of the Incas*. New York: Putnam, and London: Batsford, 1973. (Brief, well-illustrated account of the Incas.)

McINTYRE, L. *The Incredible Incas and Their Timeless Land*. Washington, D.C.: National Geographic Society, 1975. (Lavishly illustrated.)

MORRISON, T. *Pathways to the Gods*. New York: Harper & Row, and London: Paladin, 1978. (Essential reading on Nazca lines. Excellent bibliography.)

REICHE, M. *Mystery on the Desert*, 1968. (Brief, well-illustrated handbook on Nazca lines. Sold at Nazca by Maria Reiche.)

REINHARD, J. *The Nazca Lines: A New Perspective on Their Origins and Meaning*. Casilla 5147, Lima 18: Editorial Los Pinos, 1985. (Important new discussion of Nazca lines that is widely available in Lima.)

SHARON, D. *Wizard of the Four Winds: A Shaman's Story*. New York: The Free Press, 1978. (Remarkable book on Eduardo Calderón.)

VEGA, G. DE LA. *The Incas*. Translated by Maria Jolas. New York: Avon, 1971. (Unreliable historical source, but nevertheless full of interest. Paperback.)

WRIGHT, R. *Cut Stones and Crossroads*. New York and London: Viking Press, 1984. (Highly entertaining and perceptive travel narrative about Peru.)

1.1 HISTORICAL AND ARCHAEOLOGICAL BACKGROUND OF PERU

BANKS, G. *Peru Before Pizarro*. Oxford: Phaidon, 1977.

BAWDEN, G., AND CONRAD, G. W. *The Andean Heritage*. Cambridge, Mass: Peabody Museum Press, 1982.

COBO, B. *History of the Inca Empire*. Translated by R. Hamilton. Austin: University of Texas Press, 1979. (Paperback edition, 1983.)

HEMMING, J. *The Conquest of the Incas*. New York: Harcourt Brace, and London: Macmillan, 1970.

KAUFFMAN DOIG, F. *Manual de Arqueologica Peruana*. Lima: Ediciones Peisa, 1969. (Paperback edition, 1983.)

KOSOK, P. *Life, Land and Water in Ancient Peru*. New York: Long Island University Press, 1965.

LANNING, E.P. *Peru Before the Incas*. Englewood Cliffs: Prentice-Hall, 1967.

LUMBRERAS, L. G. *The Peoples and Cultures of Ancient Peru*. Washington, D.C.: Smithsonian Institution Press, 1974.

MÖRNER, M. *The Andean Past: Land, Societies and Conflicts*. New York: Columbia University Press, 1985.

MOSELEY, M.E. *Peru's Golden Treasures*. Chicago: Field Museum of Natural History, 1978.

———. "The Evolution of Andean Civilization," in *Ancient Native*

Americans. Edited by J.D. Jennings. San Francisco: W.H. Freeman, 1978, pp. 491–541.

Rowe, J.H., and Menzel, D. *Peruvian Archeology: Selected Readings.* Palo Alto: Peek Publications, 1967.

Wachtel, N. *Vision of the Vanquished.* New York: Barnes and Noble, and Hassocks, Essex: Harvester Press, 1977.

1.2 EL NIÑO AND THE PERUVIAN ENVIRONMENT

Canby, T.Y. "El Niño's Ill Wind," in *National Geographic,* 1984, Vol. 165 (2), pp. 144–183.

Feldman, R.A. "El Niño: Recent Effects in Peru," in *Field Musuem Bulletin,* 1983, Vol. 54 (8), pp. 16–18.

Nials, F.L., et al. "El Niño: The Catastrophic Flooding of Coastal Peru," in *Field Museum Bulletin,* 1979, Vol. 50 (7), pp. 4–14 and (8), pp. 4–10.

2 UNORTHODOX THEORIES ABOUT THE NAZCA LINES, TIAHUANACO AND "INCA SOCIALISM"

Baptista, M. *Tiwanaku.* Chur, Switzerland: Plata Publishing, 1975.

Davies, N. *Voyagers to the New World.* New York: Morrow, and London: Macmillan, 1979.

Heyerdahl, T. *The Kon-Tiki Expedition.* London: Allen and Unwin, and Chicago: Rand-McNally, 1950.

Kolata, A.L. "Tiwanaku: Portrait of an Andean Civilization," in *Field Museum Bulletin,* 1982, Vol. 53 (8), pp. 13–18, 23–28.

Métraux, A. *The History of the Incas.* New York: Schocken, 1969.

Murra, J.V. *The Economic Organization of the Inka State, Research in Economic Anthropology,* Supp. 1. Greenwich, Conn.: JAI Press, 1981.

Posnansky, A. *Tiahuanaco, the Cradle of American Man.* New York: J.J. Augustin, 1945.

Rossell Castro, A. *Arquelogia Sur del Peru.* Lima: Ed. Universo, 1977.

Stierlin, H. *Nazca: La Clé du Mystère.* Paris: Albin Michel, 1983.

Story, R. *The Space-Gods Revealed.* New York: Harper & Row, 1976.

———. *Guardians of the Universe?* New York: Harper & Row, 1982.

von Däniken, E. *Chariots of the Gods?* New York: Putnam, and London: Souvenir Press, 1970.

———. *Gods from Outer Space.* New York: Putnam, 1970 (Also published under the title *Return to the Stars* by Souvenir Press in London.)

Waisbard, S. *Les Pistes de Nazca.* Paris: Robert Laffont, 1977.

White, P. *The Past Is Human.* New York: Taplinger, 1974.

Woodman, J. *Nazca: Journey to the Sun.* New York: Pocket Books, and London: John Murray, 1977.

3.1 THE CHIMU FLOOD AND THE INTERVALLEY CANAL

Moseley, M.E., and Feldman, R.A. "Living with Crises: Relentless Nature Stalked Chan Chan's Fortunes," in *Early Man*, 1982, Vol. 4 (1), pp. 10–13.
Nials, F.L., et al. See reference under 1.2.
Ortloff, C.R. "Pre-Inca Hydraulics Technology on the North Coast of Peru," in *Scientific American*, forthcoming.
———, Feldman, R.A., and Moseley, M.E. "Hydraulic Engineering Aspects of the Chimu Chicama-Moche Intervalley Canal," in *American Antiquity*, 1982, Vol. 47 (3), pp. 572–595.
———. "Hydraulic Engineering and Historical Aspects of the Pre-Columbian Intravalley Canal System of the Moche Valley, Peru," in *Journal of Field Archaeology*, 1985, Vol. 12, pp. 77–98.

3.2 THE RISE OF CIVILIZATION IN PERU

Benfer, R.A. "El Proyecto Paloma . . . ," in *Zonas Aridas*, No. 2, La Molina, Lima: Universidad Nacional Agraria, 1982, pp. 33–60.
Benson, E.F., ed. *Dumbarton Oaks Conference on Chavin.* Washington, D.C.: Dumbarton Oaks, 1971.
Bryan, A.L. "South America," in *Early Man and the New World.* Edited by R. Shutler, Jr. Beverly Hills: Sage, 1983, pp. 137–146.
Donnan, C.B., ed. *Early Ceremonial Architecture in the Andes.* Washington, D.C.: Dumbarton Oaks, 1985.
Feldman, R.A. "From Maritime Chiefdom to Agricultural State in Formative Coastal Peru," in *Civilization in the Ancient Americas.* Edited by R.M. Leventhal and A.L. Kolata. University of New Mexico Press and Peabody Museum, 1983, pp. 289–311.
Moseley, M.E. *The Maritime Foundations of Andean Civilization.* Menlo Park: Cummings, 1975.
Quilter J., and Stocker, T. "Subsistence Economies and the Origins of Andean Complex Societies," in *American Anthropologist*, 1983, Vol. 85, pp. 545–562.

4 GENERAL SOURCES ON THE NAZCA LINES

Aveni, A.F., ed. *The Lines of Nazca.* Philadelphia: American Philosophical Society, forthcoming.
Hawkins, G.S. *Ancient Lines in the Peruvian Desert.* Cambridge, Mass.: Smithsonian Astrophysical Observatory, 1969.

————. *Beyond Stonehenge*. New York: Harper & Row, and London: Hutchinson, 1973.

————. "Prehistoric Desert Markings in Peru," in *National Geographic Society Research Reports, 1967 Projects*, 1974, pp. 117–144.

HERRAN, E. *Geoglifos de Nasca: Nuevos Diseños, Nuevos Enigmas*. Nazca: Eduardo Herran Producciones, 1985.

ISBELL, W. "The Prehistoric Ground Drawings of Peru," in *Scientific American*, 1978, Vol. 239, pp. 114–122.

KERN, H., and REICHE, M. *Peruanische Erdzeichen*. Munich: Kunstraum München eV, 1974.

KOSOK, P. "Astronomy, the Priesthood and the State," in *Zeitschrift für Ethnologie*, 1959, Bd. 84, pp. 5–18.

————. 1965. See listing in Section 1.1

————, and REICHE, M. "The Mysterious Markings of Nazca," in *Natural History*, 1947, vol. 56, pp. 200–207, 237–238.

————, and REICHE, M. "Ancient Drawings on the Desert of Peru," in *Archaeology*, 1949, Vol. 2, pp. 206–215.

McINTYRE, L. "Mystery of the Ancient Nazca Lines," in *National Geographic*, 1975, Vol. 147 (5), pp. 716–728.

MEJÍA XESSPE, T. "Acueductos y Caminos Antiguos de la Hoya del Rio Grande de Nasca," in *Int. Cong. of Americanists*, Lima, 1939, Vol. 1, pp. 559–569.

MORRISON, T. *Pathways to the Gods*. New York: Harper & Row, and London: Paladin, 1978.

REICHE, M. *Mystery on the Desert*. Self-published, 1949.

————. *Los Dibujos Gigantescos en el Suelo de Las Pampas de Nazca y Palpa*. Lima: Editorial Medica Peruana, 1949.

————. "Interpretación Astronómica de la Figura del Mono . . . ," in *Act. y Trab. del II Cong. Nac. del Historia del Perú*, Lima, 1958, pp. 285–286.

————. "Giant Ground Drawings on the Peruvian Desert," in *XXVIII Int. Cong. of Americanists*, 1968, Vol. L, pp. 379–384.

————. *Mystery on the Desert*. Self-published, 1968.

REINHARD, J. *The Nazca Lines: A New Perspective on Their Origins and Meaning*. Lima: Editorial Los Pinos, 1985.

RUSSELL CASTRO, A. 1977. See listing in Section 2.

WAISBARD, S. *Les Pistes de Nazca*. Paris: R. Laffont, 1977.

5 ASTRONOMICAL AND GEOMETRICAL THEORIES

AVENI, A. F. "Tropical Archaeoastronomy," in *Science*, 1981, Vol. 213 (4504), pp. 161–171.

————. ed. See listing in Section 4.

HAWKINS, G.S. See all entries in Section 4.

————. "The Need for Objectivity," in *Archaeoastronomy*, 1980, Vol. III (1), pp. 9–11.

ISBELL, W. Reviews of publications by Hawkins and Reiche, in *Archaeoastronomy*, 1979, Vol. II (4), pp. 34–40.

Kern, H., and Reiche, M. See listing in Section 4. (Note: pp. 129–130.)

Morrison, T. See listing in Section 4.

Reiche, M. 1949. See listing in Section 4.

6 ANDEAN COSMOLOGY AND ASTRONOMY

Urton, G. "Orientation in Quechua and Incaic Astronomy," in *Ethnology*, 1978, Vol. 17 (2), pp. 157–167.

———. *At the Crossroads of the Earth and the Sky*. Austin and London: University of Texas Press, 1979.

———. "Animals and Astronomy in the Quechua Universe," in *Proc. of American Phil. Soc.*, 1981, Vol. 125 (2), pp. 110–127.

———. "Astronomy and Calendrics on the Coast of Peru," in *Ethnoastronomy and Archaeoastronomy in the American Tropics*, edited by A.F. Aveni and G. Urton. *Ann. of the N.Y. Academy of Sciences*, 1982, Vol. 385, pp. 231–247.

———. "Calendrical Cycles and Their Projections in Pacariqtambo, Peru," in *Ethnoastronomy . . .*, edited by J.B. Carlson and V.D. Chamberlain. Washington, D.C.: Smithsonian Institution Press, forthcoming.

7 NEW SURVEY WORK AT NAZCA

Aveni, A. F., ed. See listing in Section 4.

Shawcross, W.E. "Mystery on the Desert—the Nazca Lines," in *Sky and Telescope*, September 1984, pp. 198–201.

8.1 PARACAS AND NAZCA TEXTILES

Bird, J.P., and Bellinger, L. *Paracas Fabrics and Nazca Needlework*. Washington, D.C.:Textile Museum, 1954.

Dwyer, J.P., and Dwyer, E.D. "The Paracas Cemeteries . . . ," in *Death and the Afterlife in Pre-Columbian America*, edited by E. P. Benson. Washington, D.C.: Dumbarton Oaks, 1975, pp. 105–128.

Hald, M. "A Contribution to the Study of the Mummy Blankets from Paracas," in *Acta Archaeologica*, 1981, Vol. 52, pp. 119–128.

Paul, A. *Paracas Textiles: Selected from the Museum's Collections, Etnologiska Studier 34*. Gothenburg: Göteborgs Etnografiska Museum, 1979.

Rowe, A.P. *A Heritage of Color*. Washington, D.C.: Textile Museum, 1973.

———, Benson, E.P., and Schaffer, A.-L., eds. *The Junius P. Bird Textile Conference*. Washington, D.C.: Textile Museum and Dumbarton Oaks, 1979.

SAWYER, A.R. "The Feline in Paracas Art," in *Cult of the Feline.* Edited by E.P. Benson. Washington, D.C.: Dumbarton Oaks, 1972, pp. 91–115.

TELLO, J.C. *Paracas. Primera Parte.* Lima: T. Scheuch, 1959.

———, and MEJÍA XESSPE, T. *Paracas, Segunda Parte.* Lima: Univ. Nac. de San Marcos, 1979.

8.2 THE IMAGERY OF NAZCA ART

ALLEN, C.J. "The Nazca Creatures: Some Problems of Iconography," in *Anthropology*, 1981, Vol. V (1), pp. 43–70.

RAMOS GOMEZ, L.J., and BOSQUED, C.B. *Ceramica Nazca*, Valladolid: Seminario Americanista, Univ. de Valladolid, 1980.

ROARK, R. P. "From Monumental to Proliferous in Nazca Pottery," in *Nawpa Pacha*, 1965, Vol. 3, pp. 1–92.

SAWYER, A. R. "Paracas and Nazca Iconography," in *Essays in Pre-Columbian Art and Archaeology*, edited by S.K. Lothrop. Cambridge, Mass.: Harvard University Press, 1961, pp. 269–298.

———. *Ancient Peruvian Ceramics.* New York: New York Graphic Society, 1966.

TOWNSEND, R.F. "Deciphering the Nazca World," in *Museum Studies*, Art Inst. of Chicago, 1985, Vol. 11 (2), pp. 117–139.

ZUIDEMA, R. T. "Meaning in Nazca Art," in *Arstryck*, 1972, pp. 35–54.

8.3 NAZCA ARCHAEOLOGY

ENGEL, F.H., ed. *Prehistoric Andean Ecology: The Deep South.* New York: Humanities Press, for the Department of Anthropology, Hunter College, City University, 1981.

HAEBERLI, J. "Twelve Nazca Panpipes: A Study," in *Ethnomusicology*, 1979, Vol 23 (1), pp. 57–74.

KROEBER, A.L. *Peruvian Archaeology in 1942.* Berkeley: Viking Fund Pubs. in Anth., No. 4, 1944.

PAULSEN, A.C. "Huaca del Loro Revisited: The Nasca-Huarpa Connection," in *Investigations of the Andean Past.* Edited by D. Sandweiss. Ithaca, New York: Department of Anthropology, Cornell University, pp. 98–121.

PETERSEN, G. *Evolución y Desaparición de las Altas Culturas Paracas-Cahuachi (Nasca).* Lima: Universidad Nacional Frederico Villareal, 1980.

ROSSELL CASTRO, A. See listing in Section 2.

ROWE, J.H. "Urban Settlements in Ancient Peru," in *Nawpa Pacha*, 1963, Vol. 1, 1–28.

STRONG, W.D. "Paracas, Nazca, and Tihuanacoid Relationships in South Coastal Peru," in *Society for American Archaeology, Memoir XIII*, 1957.

BIBLIOGRAPHY • 293

9.1 HEAD-HUNTING AND THE NAZCA TROPHY HEAD CULT

ALLEN, C.J. See listing in Section 8.2.

———. "Body and Soul in Quechua Thought," in *Journal of Latin American Lore*, 1982, Vol. 8 (2), pp. 179–196.

HARNER, M.J. *The Jívaro*. New York: Natural History Press, 1972.

KARSTEN, R. *The Head-hunters of Western Amazonas.* Helsinki: Societas Scientarium Fennica, 1935.

NEIRA, M., and COELHO, V. "Enterramientos de Cabezas de la Cultura Nasca," in *Rev. Museu Paulista*, Sao Paolo, 1972–1973, Vol. XX, pp. 109–142.

PROULX, D. A. "Headhunting in Ancient Peru," in *Archaeology*, 1971, Vol. 24 (1), pp. 16–21.

RAMOS GOMEZ, L.J., and BLASCO, M.C., *Cabezas Cortadas en la Ceramica Nazca. Cuadernos Prehispanicos*. Valladolid: Univ. of Valladolid, 1974.

RYDEN, S. "Une Tête-trophée de Nazca," in *Jnl. Soc. des Américanistes*, Paris, 1930, Vol. XXII, pp. 365–371.

9.2 RITUAL USE OF HALLUCINOGENS

CABIESES, F. manuscript. "Las Plantas Magicas del Peru Primigenio."

CALDERÓN, E., COWAN, R., SHARON, D., and SHARON, F.K., *Eduardo El Curandero*, Richmond, California: North Atlantic Books, 1982.

DOBKIN DE RIOS, M. "*Trichocereus pachanoi*—A Mescaline Cactus Used in Folk Healing in Peru," in *Economic Botany*, 1968, Vol. 22 (2), pp. 191–194.

———. "Plant Hallucinogens, Sexuality and Shamanism in the Ceramic Art of Ancient Peru," in *Journal of Psychoactive Drugs*, 1982, Vol. 14 (1–2), pp. 81–90.

———. *Hallucinogens: Cross-Cultural Perspectives*. Albuquerque: University of New Mexico Press, 1984.

———, and CARDENAS, M. "Plant Hallucinogens, Shamanism and Nazca Ceramics," in *Journal of Ethnopharmacology*, 1980, Vol. 2, pp. 233–246.

FURST, P., ed. *Flesh of the Gods*. New York: Praeger, 1972.

HARNER, M.J. *Hallucinogens and Shamanism*. New York: Oxford University Press, 1973.

SHARON, D. *Wizard of the Four Winds: A Shaman's Story*. New York: The Free Press, 1978.

———, and DONNAN, C.B. *Shamanism in Moche Iconography*, UCLA Arch. Monographs IV. Berkeley: UCLA, 1974, pp. 51–80.

———. "The Magic Cactus," in *Archaeology*, 1977, Vol. 30 (6), pp. 376–381.

10 IRRIGATION AND SOCIAL ORGANIZATION IN ANCIENT PERU

GLICK, T.F. *Irrigation and Society in Medieval Valencia.* Cambridge, Mass.: Harvard University Press, 1970.

KOSOK, P. See listings in Section 4.

MEJÍA, XESSPE, T. See listing in Section 4.

URTON, G. 1979. See listing in Section 6.

———. "Chuta: El Espacio de la Práctica Social en Pacariqtambo, Perú," in *Revista Andina*, 1984, Vol. 2 (1), pp. 7–56.

11 THE MANAGEMENT OF IRRIGATION AND LABOR

BENSON, E.P. *The Mochica.* New York: Praeger, 1972.

DONNAN, C.B. *Moche Art of Peru.* Los Angeles: Museum of Cultural History, University of California, 1978.

MOSELEY, M.E. "Prehistoric Principles of Labor Organization in the Moche Valley, Peru," in *American Antiquity*, 1975, Vol. 40, pp. 191–196.

NETHERLY, P.J. "The Management of Late Andean Irrigation Systems on the North Coast of Peru," in *American Antiquity*, 1984, Vol. 49, pp. 227–254.

ROSTWOROSKI DE DIEZ CANSECO, M. *Etnía y Sociedad.* Lima: Instit. de Estudios Peruanos, 1977.

———. "Coastal Fishermen, Merchants and Artisans in Pre-Hispanic Peru," in *The Sea in the Pre-Columbian World*, Washington, D.C.: Dumbarton Oaks, 1977, pp. 167–186.

12 THE RISE OF IMPERIAL STATES: THE CHIMÚ AND THE INCA

ASCHER, M., and ASCHER, R. *Code of the Quipu.* Ann Arbor: University of Michigan Press, 1981.

DEMAREST, A., and CONRAD, G.W. "Ideological Adaptation and the Rise of the Aztec and Inca Empires," in *Civilization in the Ancient Americas.* Edited by R.M. Leventhal and A.L. Kolata. Albuquerque: University of New Mexico Press and Cambridge, Mass.: Peabody Museum, 1983, pp. 373–400.

HYSLOP, J. *The Inka Road System.* New York and London: Academic Press, 1984.

MOSELEY, M.E. "Chan Chan: Andean Alternative of the Preindustrial City," in *Science*, 1975, Vol. 187 (4173), pp. 219–225.

———, and DAY, K.C., eds. *Chan Chan: Andean Desert City.* Albuquerque: University of New Mexico Press, 1982.

ZUIDEMA, R.T. "Reflections on Inca Historical Conceptions," in *Int. Congr. of Americanists*, Session 34, Vienna, 1962, pp. 718–721.

13 CUZCO AND THE CEQUE SYSTEM

AVENI, A.F. "Horizon Astronomy in Incaic Cuzco," in *Archaeoastronomy in the Americas*. Edited by R. A. Williamson. Ballena Press/Center for Archaeoastronomy, 1981, pp. 305–318.

ZUIDEMA, R.T. *The Ceque System of Cuzco*. Leiden: E.J. Brill, 1964.

————. "The Inca Calendar," in *Native American Astronomy*. Edited by A.F. Aveni. Austin and London: University of Texas Press, 1977, pp. 219–259.

————. "Myth and History in Ancient Peru," in *The Logic of Culture*. Edited by Ino Rossi. South Hadley, Mass.: J.F. Bergin, 1982, pp. 150–75.

14 ANDEAN RELIGIOUS BELIEFS AND CEREMONIES

ARGUEDAS, J.M. "Puquio, Una Cultura en Proceso de Cambio," in *Rev. del Museo Nac.*, Lima, 1956, Vol. 25, pp. 184–232.

BASTIEN, J.W. *Mountain of the Condor: Metaphor and Ritual in an Andean Ayllu*. New York: West Publishing, 1978.

CASAVERDE, J. "El Mundo Sobrenatural en una Communidad," in *Allpanchis*, 1970, Vol. 2, pp. 121–243.

CAYON, E. "El Hombre y Los Animales en la Cultura Quechua," in *Allpanchis*, 1971, Vol. 3, pp. 135–162.

DEMAREST, A.A. *Viracocha: The Nature and Antiquity of the Andean High God*. Monographs of the Peabody Museum, no. 6. Cambridge, Mass.: Peabody Museum, 1981.

ISBELL, B.J. *To Defend Ourselves: Ecology and Ritual in an Andean Village*. Austin and London: University of Texas Press, 1978.

MÉTRAUX, A. "Les Indiens Uro-Cipaya de Carangas," in *Jnl. de la Soc. des Américanistes*, Paris, 1935, Vol. 27, pp. 325–415.

MISHKIN, B. "The Contemporary Quechua," in *Handbook of South American Indians*, Washington, D.C.: Smithsonian Institution, 1946, Vol. 2, pp. 441–470.

REINHARD, J. See listing in Section 4.

————. "Chavin and Tiahuanaco: A New Look at Two Andean Ceremonial Centers," in *National Geographic Research Reports*, 1985, Vol. 1 (3), pp. 395–422.

SOLDI, A.M. "El Agua en el Pensamiento Andino," in *Boletín de Lima*, 1980, No. 6, pp. 21–27.

VAN KESSEL, J.J.M.M. *Holocaust al Progreso*. Amsterdam: Center for Latin American Research and Documentation, 1980.

15.1 PACATNAMÚ

KEATINGE, R.W. "The Pacatnamú Textiles," in *Archaeology*, 1978, Vol. 31 (2), pp. 30–41.

UBBELOHDE-DOERING, H. *On the Royal Highways of the Incas.* New York: Praeger, 1967.

15.2 CONTEMPORARY GROUND ART

BEARDSLEY, J. *Probing the Earth: Contemporary Land Projects.* Washington D.C.: Smithsonian Institution Press, 1977.
LIPPARD, L.R. *Overlay: Contemporary Art and the Art of Prehistory.* New York: Pantheon Books, 1983.
MORRIS, R. "Aligned with Nazca," in *Artforum*, October 14, 1975, pp. 26–39.

15.3 ANCIENT GROUND DRAWINGS OUTSIDE PERU

COE, M.D. "San Lorenzo and the Olmec Civilization," in *Dumbarton Oaks Conference on the Olmec.* Edited by E.P. Benson. Washington, D.C.: Dumbarton Oaks, 1968, pp. 41–78.
DOBKIN DE RIOS, M. "Plant Hallucinogens, Autosomatic Experiences and New World Massive Earthworks," in *Drugs, Rituals and Altered States of Consciousness.* Edited by B. du Toit. Rotterdam: Balkema, 1976, pp. 237–249.
MALLAM, R.C. *The Iowa Effigy Mounds Manifestation: An Interpretive Model.* Report No. 9, Office of State Archaeologist. Iowa City: University of Iowa, 1976.
———. "Ideology from the Earth," in *Archaeology*, 1982, Vol. 35 (4), pp. 60–62, 64.
———. *Site of the Serpent. Occ. Pubs. of Coronado-Quivira* Museum, No. 1.
MARPLES, M. *White Horses and Other Hill Figures.* Reprint of 1949 edition. Gloucester: Alan Sutton, 1981.
OLSON, G. "Scratching the Surface: A Comparison of Colorado River and Nazca Ground Art," in *ASA Journal*, 1981, Vol. 5 (1), pp. 4–19.
SETZLER, F.M. "Giant Effigies of the Southwest," in *National Geographic*, 1952, Vol. 102 (3), pp. 390–404.
VAN TILBURG, J.A., ed. *Ancient Images on Stone.* Los Angeles: Institute of Archaeology, UCLA, 1983.

15.4 INTRODUCTIONS TO SHAMANISM

CAMPBELL, J. *The Way of the Animal Powers.* San Francisco: Harper & Row, 1983.
ELIADE, M. *Shamanism: Archaic Techniques of Ecstasy.* Bollingen Series, LXXVI. New York: Pantheon Books, 1964.

PICTURE CREDITS

All the photographs in this book were taken by the author, except for those listed below. Text figures were drawn by the author based on sources also noted below.

ABBREVIATIONS: **AMNH**: American Museum of Natural History, New York; **DMR**: Documentary Media Resources, Cambridge, Mass.; **GU**: Gary Urton; **JH**: Janet Hadingham; **SAN**: Servicio Aerofotografico Nacional, Lima, Peru; **TM**: Tony Morrison, South American Pictures, London.

The author is particularly grateful to staff at the Putnam Museum, Davenport, Iowa, for permitting Janet Hadingham to photograph Nazca pots from the Museum's collection.

INTRODUCTION: 2 TM; 4 SAN; 8 TM.

CHAPTER 1: 12 Garth Bawden; 13 (*left*) Greg Smith, Gamma-Liaison Agency, (*right*) DMR; 15 TM; 16–17 after Moseley and Feldman, 1982; 18 Garth Bawden; 20–23 DMR; 24 Hans Silvester, Photo Researchers Agency.

CHAPTER 2: 26 British Library; 29 (*top*) AMNH, (*lower left and right*) DMR; 31 AMNH; 37 Marcel Homet as reproduced in Erich von Däniken's *Chariots of the Gods?*, Corgi Books, London, 1972, (*lower*) after Kern and Reiche, 1974; 39 Ann Mansbridge; 41 and 42 (*left*) Jim Woodman; 42 (*right*) after Tello, 1959.

CHAPTER 3: 45 (*top*) DMR, (*lower*) Heye Foundation, Museum of the American Indian, New York; 46 (*left*) James Kus, (*right*) after Ortloff, Feldman and Moseley, 1985; 47 after Ortloff, Moseley and Feldman, 1982; 52–53 Robert A. Benfer; 54 AMNH; 55 after Feldman, 1983; 59 Heye Foundation.

CHAPTER 4: 61 JH; 62 DMR; 63 (*right*) JH; 65 and 66 Maria Reiche collection courtesy of Dietrich Schulze; 67 TM; 70 SAN; 75 (*left and right*) Maria Reiche collection courtesy of Dietrich Schulze; 77 (*top*) William R. Shawcross, (*lower left*) after Penny and Arias, 1982; 78 (*top right*) SAN, (*middle right*) Gerald S. Hawkins, (*lower, dog vessel*) AMNH, (*bottom*) SAN; 79 (*top left*) after Kern and Reiche, 1974, (*top right and lower right*) AMNH; 81 (*left*) Persis Clarkson; 82 (*lower*) after Kern and Reiche, 1974; 83 (*lower, concentric circles*) SAN; 86 after Reiche, 1968; 89 Maria Reiche collection courtesy of Dietrich Schulze.

CHAPTER 5: 92 Persis Clarkson; 93 after Reiche, 1949; 95 Gerald S. Hawkins; 97 Gerald S. Hawkins and National Geographic Society 1967 Reports, Washington, D.C., 1974; 100 TM.

CHAPTER 6: 107 (*top*) DMR, (*lower*) GU, 108 after Urton, 1981; 112 (*lower*) and 113 GU; 116 and 119 JH.

CHAPTER 7: 121 (*lower*) SAN; 127 Gerald S. Hawkins; 128–129 Persis Clarkson; 134 after Aveni, forthcoming; 139 after Reiche in Spencer, *Bean Sprouts New Theory*, article in Peruvian Explorers Club, n.d.

CHAPTER 8: 144 (*top*) and (*left*) AMNH, (*lower right*) © 1964 Swiss-Foto S.A.; 145 (*left*) Anne Paul, (*right*) Textile Museum; 146 (*both*) AMNH; 147 Textile Museum, Washington DC; 148 (*left*) after Tello, 1959, (*right*) and (*lower*) Textile Museum; 149 (*upper*) and (*lower*) AMNH; 150 (*top*) DMR, (*lower*) TM; 152 SAN; 153 (*upper*) Cleveland Museum of Art, (*lower*) AMNH; 154 photos by JH, drawings after Sawyer in Benson et al., 1972; 156 after Strong, 1957; 157 after Haeberli, 1979; 158 JH; 159 (*right*) and 160 (*left*) W. D. Strong Museum, Columbia University; 160 (*right*) after Strong, 1957; 161 AMNH.

CHAPTER 9: 164 (*left*) DMR, (*right*) from Fritz Trupp, *The Last Indians*, Perlinger, Wörgl, Austria, 1981; 165 Milwaukee Museum; 167 JH; 168 (*upper*) DMR, (*lower*) JH; 170 (*top*) David Furman; 170–171 (*lower*) after Ramos Gomes and Bosqued, 1980; 171 (*upper*) DMR; 172 after Sharon and Donnan, 1974; 175 (*left*) and (*right*) Douglas Sharon; 176 Peabody Museum, Harvard University; 177 Debra Carroll; 178 from Federico Kauffman Doig, *Manual de Arqueologia Peruana*, Ed. Peisa, Lima, 1983; 179 (*all*) Milwaukee Museum.

CHAPTER 10: 183 (*right*) GU; 184 after Urton, forthcoming; 185 (*left*) and (*right*) GU; 186 after Urton, 1984; 188 (*lower*) GU.

CHAPTER 11: 189 JH; 190 (*lower*) GU; 193 AMNH; 194–195 Christopher Donnan courtesy of Donna McClelland; 201 (*right*) DMR; 203 AMNH; 204 after Donnan, 1978; 205 and 207 DMR.

CHAPTER 12: 210 AMNH; 212 Metropolitan Museum, New York; 216 (*top*) and 217 DMR; 219 and 220 (*all*) Cusicacha Project courtesy of Earthwatch, Belmont, Mass.; 222 (*left*) DMR, (*right*) AMNH; 224–225 John Hyslop.

CHAPTER 13: 228 after Hemming 1970; 231 (*both*) after Zuidema in Aveni, ed., 1977; 235 and 241 DMR; 242 TM; 246 Johan Reinhard; 248 Douglas Meiser; 251 (*top left*) Frederick Landmann, (*lower*) Peabody Museum, Harvard University; 252 DMR; 253 Joseph Bastien; 254 after Josue Lancho, privately printed; 255 (*both*) and 257 Johan Reinhard; 258 Peabody Museum, Harvard University.

CHAPTER 14: 265 computer diagrams by courtesy of Charles Ortloff; 267 Richard D. Liberto, Nassau County Museum of Fine Art, New York; 269 and 270 Gary Olson; 271 (*top*) Heye Foundation, (*middle*) R. Clark Mallam, (*lower*) Gary Olson; 272 after Furst in Benson, ed., 1968; 274 (*top*) and (*middle*) after Prufer, 1964, (*bottom*) after Mills, 1922; 275 (*top left and right*) R. Clark Mallam, (*below*) Heye Foundation; 276 Public Archives of Manitoba; 277 Ashmolean Museum, Oxford; 278 (*top*) Peabody Museum, Harvard University; (*bottom*) AMNH.

Index

Acosta, José de, 245
agriculture:
  constellations related to, 112–14
  and distribution of communally
    owned lands, 187
  and loss of cultivated land, 18
  Nazca lines as astronomical
    calendar for, 5–7, 86–87, 102–
    105, 118–19
  in Nazca Valley, 63–64, 115–17
  origins of, in Peru, 52, 56–58
  skywatching and, 84, 85, 87, 112–
    14, 235, 236, 237
  water resources and, 62–63, 115–
    16, 117
  see also irrigation
Albert, Prince, 168–69
"Aligned with Nazca" (Morris), 267
altars, for festival of Saint Peter, 181
amaru (Rainbow Serpent), 110, 258
Amazon, as Garden of Eden, 27–28
ancestor worship:
  in Chimú empire, 213–14
  in Inca empire, 215–16
anchovy industry, 15–16
ancient Peru, *see* Nazcans, ancient;
  Peru, ancient
Andes:
  geological activity in, 16–17, 50, 57
animal figures (Nazca lines), 54, 75–
  81, 244

Andean folktales and, 256–58
as badges or totems, 83
as ceremonial pathways, 80
constellations related to, 86–87,
  102–4, 106, 118–19
continuous outlines of, 76–80
dating of, 131–33
discovery of, 69, 75–76
"fading" of, 73–74
folk healers and, 8
geometry of, 87, 138–39
location of, 80, 131
magical flight and, 177
Nazca pottery and, 131–33, 155
ray centers related to, 133
solar lines related to, 80, 104
spiral patterns and, 82
animals:
  on ancient Peruvian textiles, 54,
    145
  ceremonial mounds in shapes of,
    271, 274
  dark cloud, 108–11, 112, 117
  supernatural, 8, 58, 248–49, 250–
    52, 270–72
  transformations of men into, 270–
    72, 273, 276
Antares, 104
Apollo, Oracle of, at Delphi, 262–63
Apurimac Valley, Nazcans' colony
  in, 218

aqueducts:
  in La Cumbre canal, 47–49
  in medieval Mediterranean and
    Near East, 191, 195–96
  in Nazca Valley, 189–92, 254–55,
    277
architecture:
  ceremonial mounds, 54–56, 57,
    193, 195, 201–6, 271, 273–74
  circular temples, 160–61, 191–92
Armellones, Fernando de, 25
arutam (ancestor ghost soul), 165–66
Aspero, ceremonial mound at, 55–56,
  57
astronomer-priests, 84–85, 87, 88
astronomical theory, 5–7, 84–119
  agricultural cycles and, 5–7, 118–
    19
  animal figures related to
    constellations in, 86–87, 102–4,
    106, 118–19
  atmospheric conditions and, 92
  Aveni and Urton's conclusions on,
    133–34
  dating issue and, 133
  Hawkins' refutation of, 95–101, 105
  Kosok's formulation of, 70–71, 84–
    85, 90, 94, 102
  Morrison's approach to, 101–2
  Reiche's espousal of, 5, 71, 80, 85–
    95, 96, 102–5, 133

on Inca cosmology, 106–7
on Inca mummy cult, 215–16
on shell symbolism, 254
coca, 171, 275–76
Coe, Michael, 273
Coelho, Vera, 169
computers, astronomical alignments
and, 96, 97–99
constellations:
agriculture and, 112–14
animal figures related to, 86–87,
102–4, 106, 118–19
dark cloud, 108–11, 112, 117
Quechua skywatching and, 106, 111–
14
Coricancha (Temple of the Sun), 216,
230, 235, 236, 237, 238, 249
corn, in Inca ideology, 217
Coropuna, 252
creation myths, 34–36, 269
Cristóbal de Molina, 232, 234
Cruz Velakuy, festival, 114
Cusicacha, Inca sites at, 219–20
Cuzco, 215–19, 227–39
astronomical alignments and
towers around, 234–38
ayllus in, 228–29, 230
ceque system in, 230–39
layout of, 227–39
Milky Way and, 229–30
mummy cult in, 215–16, 217
Temple of the Sun in, 216, 230,
235, 236, 237, 238, 249
uprising in (1553), 21

datura, 172, 174
dark cloud animals, 108–11, 112, 117
Quechua myths and, 110–11
death:
fertility associated with, 166, 167,
168, 170, 259
killer whale as symbol of, 168
De Bry, Theodore, 28
December solstice, 117, 118
deer, hallucinogens associated with,
172
deities and spirits:
Bolivian earth spirits, 240–44
Earth Mother (Pachamama), 167,
258, 272
in Inca ideology, 216–17
Mal'ku, 241
mountain, 9, 247–48, 256, 258
storm god, 249–52, 256
supernatural animals, 8, 248–49,
250–52, 270–72
Viracocha, 34–36, 62, 216, 246, 247
Delphi, Oracle of Apollo at, 262–63

Desceliers, Pierre, 27
desert varnish, 73
design techniques, see drawing and
design techniques
despotism:
irrigation linked to, 68, 192–96
of Kosok's astronomer-priests, 84–
85
directions, see orientation
disease, Spanish Conquest and, 19,
24–25
domesticated plants, origins of, 58
Donnan, Christopher, 261–63
drawing and design techniques
(Nazca lines), 135–40
droughts:
El Niño events and, 14
highland influence and, 162

Earth Mother (Pachamama), 167,
258, 272
earthquakes, 16
Earthwatch, 123, 135–36, 137,
139
Ecuador, 149, 164
Eduardo the Healer, 174
Effigy Mounds, 274, 275
Egypt, ancient, 192, 195
calendar of, 103
pyramids of, 48, 139–40, 202
El Dorado, 22
Elias, Juan, 115–16
El Niño, 11–16, 44–45, 51, 57, 73
causes of, 13–14
El Paraiso, building complexes at,
55, 56
Engel, Fréderic, 56, 64
Engels, Friedrich, 192
England, white horse figures in, 277
espingo (hallucinogen), 172
Essays (Montaigne), 28
Estete, Miguel de, 167, 262
extraterrestrials, Nazca lines and, 36–
40, 43

falcons, in Nazca art, 176–77, 178
fasting, 266
Feldman, Robert, 55
felines, supernatural, 58, 248–49
storm god as, 249, 250–52
transformations of, 270–72
Fempellec, 45
fertility:
Andean folklore and, 253–60
Cerro Blanco linked to, 246
death associated with, 166, 167,
168, 170, 259
in Jívaro beliefs, 166

Nazca art and, 152, 154, 168
Nazca lines and, 125–26, 254–59
Paracas "monster beings" and, 148
fishermen, duties of, 206
fish figures (Nazca lines), 76, 138
flower figure (Nazca lines), 76, 102
Flying Saucers from the Moon
(Wilkins), 36
fog oases (lomas), 52
folktales, 143
animal figures and, 256–58
Cerro Blanco in, 245–48, 260
dark cloud animals and, 109–11
fortifications, Nazca sites and, 155–56
fox, in Andean folklore, 109, 256, 258
for or dog figure (Nazca lines), 78
frigate bird, 76, 79
"furrow tracers," 138

García de la Nasca, 207
Garcilaso de la Vega, 216, 218, 222–
23, 224, 235, 236
Garden of Eden, in South America,
27–28
Gateway of the Sun, Tiahuanaco, 250
geological activity:
earthquakes, 16
uplift in Andes, 16–17, 50, 57
geometric figures (Nazca lines), 80–83
see also cleared areas; rectangles;
trapezoids; triangles
geometry of Nazca figures, 135–40
giant bird (Nazca lines), 78, 80, 86, 102
"giant" theory, 33–34
gods, see deities and spirits
gold mining, 163
Great Bear (Big Dipper), 86–87
Great Pyramid (Egypt), 48, 139–40,
202
Great Rectangle (Nazca lines), 76, 80,
93, 99, 100, 101–2
construction of, 139
Pleiades and, 101–2, 104
pottery finds at, 129
Great Serpent Mound (Ohio), 271,
274
Great Temple (Cahuachi), 151, 156
Green House, The (Vargas Llosa), 11
guano, 15, 16

Hâ-âk, 269
Haeberli, Jorge, 157
hallucinogens, 7–8, 171–78, 266, 272,
273, 274, 275–76
depicted on Nazca pottery, 171,
172, 173, 176–77
healers' use of, 171, 173, 174, 176,
178

Nazca lines (*continued*)
  hands figure in, 5, 76, 281
  Hawkins' survey of, 96–101
  human figures in, 5, 76, 250–51
  hummingbird figures in, 74, 79,
    138, 177, 256
  as "Inca roads," 37
  Kosok's interpretation of, 70–71,
    83–85, 90, 94, 102
  length units in, 138–39
  lizard figures in, 76
  llama figures in, 76, 80
  magical flight and, 176–78
  manpower needed for construction
    of, 139–40
  monkey figure in, 76, 78, 80, 86–87
  as pathways, 8–9, 69, 80, 125, 127,
    207
  pottery finds along, 129–33
  preservation of, 279–81
  ray centers in, *see* ray centers
  rectangles in, *see* rectangles
  Reiche's interpretation of, 71, 80,
    85–95, 96, 102–5
  rugged terrain and, 123–25
  sculptors influenced by, 267–68
  solitary rituals likely at, 124, 266–
    67
  solstice lines and, 70, 71, 80, 86, 90–
    95, 98–99, 102
  spider figure in, 75–76, 77, 86, 102–
    4, 106, 138, 139
  statistics and, 93–101, 133–34
  stone features and, 81, 83, 84, 99–
    100, 125–26, 127, 128, 135–36,
    143, 239, 244
  straightness of, 127, 136, 138, 226
  trapezoids and, *see* trapezoids
  underground moisture and, 118–
    19, 126, 254–56
  in water and fertility rites, 254–56
Nazcans, ancient, 141–62
  aqueducts constructed by, 189–92,
    254–55, 277
  Cahuachi as "capital" of, 141–42,
    150–58, 159
  hallucinogens of, 171, 172, 173
  highland influences on, 160–62,
    192
  imagery of, 151–55, 158–59, 161–62
  mummified human heads of, 167–
    70
  music of, 156–57
  pottery of, *see* Nazca pottery
  religious traditions of, 156–58, 159,
    167–78, 276–77
  style of Paracas vs., 151–52, 154
  textiles of, 150–52, 153, 154

theories about empire of, 155–58
  see also Peru, ancient
Nazca pampa, climate and geology,
    72–73, 92
Nazca Plate, 16–17
Nazca pottery, 152–53, 154–55, 158–
    59, 161–62, 167–68, 259
  Classic style, 129–32, 155
  Early style, 151–55
  feline images on, 154
  fertility and sexual themes on, 168
  hallucinogens depicted on, 171,
    172, 173, 176–77
  highland influences on, 161, 162
  Late style, 158–59, 161–62
  "monster beings" on, 154, 159, 162,
    167–68, 177–78, 244
  trophy heads on, 152, 154, 155, 159,
    167
  warriors on, 170–1
Nazca River, 63
Nazca Valley:
  agriculture in, 63–64, 115–17
  aqueducts in, 189–92, 254–55, 277
  climate of, 62, 92
  water resources in, 62–63
"Nazca Yard," 138–39
Necropolis, Paracas, 145, 149
Needle and Thread figure (Nazca
    lines), 82, 254
Neira, Maximo, 169
Netherly, Patricia, 197–98
Newark (Ohio), earthworks at, 273–
    74
"Noble Savage" notion, 28–30
Nott, Julian, 41, 43
Nova, 37, 38
Numeta, Mojave deity, 270

ocean currents, El Niño events and,
    13–14
Olmec, 272–73
oracles:
  of Apollo at Delphi, 262–63
  of Pachacamac, 262–63
"oriental despotism" theory, 192–93
orientation:
  of Andean villages, 117–18
  of Cuzco, 229–30
Orion:
  pelican associated with, 106, 117
  as Plow, 112
  spider figure related to, 86, 102–4,
    106
Ortloff, Charles, 49–50, 265
out-of-body experiences, 176–78
  birds associated with, 176–77, 178,
    272

shamanism and, 270–72
  see also hallucinogens

Pacariqtambo (Tambo), 112–14, 117,
    180–88, 198
  astronomy in, 112–14
  chutas in, 180–81, 185, 186–87, 208
  farming in, 112–14, 187
  festivals in, 114, 180–88
Pacatnamú, 261–66, 268, 277
Pachacamac, oracle of, 262–63
Pachakuti, 217–18, 227–28
Pachamama (Earth Mother), 167,
    216, 258, 272
Pacheco, 161, 162
Pacific, El Niño events and, 13–14
Palmer, George, 268
Paloma, excavations at, 51, 52–54
Pampa Grande, ceremonial mound
    at, 193, 195–96
Panamerican Highway, 12, 64, 76, 279
panpipes, 149, 156–57
Paracas, prehistoric cemetery, 39,
    143–51
  discovery of burials at, 143, 145
  theories about, 149
  Trident of, 38–40
Paracas textiles, 40, 143, 145–51
  function of, 147–49
  head motifs in, 146, 167
  large-scale plain-weave fabrics, 150
  "monster beings" in, 145, 146, 148,
    149, 154, 159, 167–68, 177–78,
    250
  motif groupings in, 149–50
  storm god in, 250, 251
  style, compared to Nazca art, 151–
    52, 154
Paradise in the New World (Pinelo),
    28
parcialidades (social units), 199–200
Past Is Human, The (White), 38
pathways:
  ceremonial, in Bolivia, 241–44, 256
  ceremonial, of Incas, *see* ceques
  Nazca lines as, 8–9, 69, 80, 125,
    127, 207
Pathways to the Gods (Morrison),
    101–2
pelican, Orion associated with, 106,
    117
Peru:
  earthquakes in, 16
  El Niño weather phenomena in, 11–
    16, 44–45, 51, 57, 73
  geological activity in, 16–17, 50, 57
Peru, ancient, 33–59
  balloon flight in, 42–43

Chimú empire in, 45–50, 209–14, 215
contact between South or Central America and, 58
creation myths and, 34–36
despotism theory and, 192–96
early civilization in, 51–59
El Niño in, 44–45
extraterrestrial theory and, 36–40, 43
food exchanges in, 51–52
"giant" theory and, 33–34
hunter-gatherers in, 52, 58
irrigation in, 45–50, 189–201, 277
origins of agriculture in, 52, 56–58
seafood consumption in, 52–54, 57, 58
skywatching in, *see* skywatching
social order in, 83–85, 192–208, *see also* labor organization
surveying in, 49–50
textiles in, 42, 54
see also Nazcans, ancient
Peruvian Air Force, 97
Peruvian Geophysical Institute, 97
Peter, Saint, festival of, 180–83, 188
photogrammetry, 97
Pima, 269
Pinelo, León, 28
Pisco Valley, 149
Piura, 11–12
Pizarro, Francisco, 19–21, 28
plant motifs, 76, 102
on Nazca pottery, 42, 154–55, 168
on Paracas textiles, 148, 168
plants, domestication of, 58
Plaza de Armas (Cuzco), 228
Pleiades, 93
Great Rectangle and, 101–2, 104
as Storehouse, 112, 117
Plow (Quechua constellation), 112
Polo de Ondegardo, 111, 232, 234, 238
Poma, Guaman, 216, 222, 234, 252
Posnansky, Arthur, 34
posts, at La Estaquería, 159–60
Potosí mines, 23
pottery:
of Moche, 175–76, 204, 205, 258, 276
along Nazca lines, 129–33
see also Nazca pottery
pre-Columbian period, *see* Inca empire; Nazcans, ancient; Peru, ancient
pregnancy, depictions of, 168

priests, theory of astronomer-, 84–85, 87, 88
pyramids, Egyptian, 48, 139–40, 202

Quechua:
dark cloud animals and, 108–11, 112
direction scheme of, 117–18
festivals of, *see* Pacariqtambo
religious traditions of, 245–48, 252–54, 258–60
skywatching traditions of, 106, 107–14, 117–19
social order of, 184–88, 192–208
quipus, 221–23
ceques compared to, 230–32
Quispe Herrera, Baltazar, 180, 181, 185, 186–87

radial pathways, *see ceques*
radiating centers (Nazca lines), *see* ray centers
rain:
predicting of, 117
stars associated with, 109–10, 117
Rainbow (Inca deity), 216
Rainbow Serpent (*amaru*), 110, 258
ray centers (Nazca lines):
absolute straightness of lines in, 123, 127
animal figures related to, 133
astronomical theory and, 133–34
Aveni and Urton's study of, 121–27, 133–34
ceques compared to, 239
characteristic features of, 123–26
as continuous grid or network, 127
dating of, 130, 133
pathway theory of, 125, 127, 207
pottery finds along, 129–33
private and solitary rituals likely at, 124, 266–68, 278
rugged terrain and, 123–25
trapezoids or cleared figures near, 125–26
rectangles (Nazca lines), 76, 80–82
animal figures related to, 80–81
as ceremonial enclosures, 81
exit points from, 81–82
Great, 76, 80, 93, 99, 100, 101–2, 104, 129, 139
stone piles in, 81
as symbolic fields, 125–26
see also cleared areas; trapezoids
Regulus, 104
Reiche, Maria, 37, 60–61, 64–67, 71–82, 83, 85–95, 207, 245, 281
aerial photographs by, 75

animal figures related to constellations by, 86–87, 118–19
astronomer-priests in theories of, 85, 87, 88
astronomical theory of, 5, 71, 80, 85–95, 96, 102–5, 133
background of, 65–67
criticisms of, 88–95
on drawing and design techniques, 136–39
funding for studies of, 74
geometry of animal figures studied by, 87, 138–39
living conditions of, 61, 74
Nazca first visited by, 71
pottery finds of, 129
ray centers charted by, 121–22
skywatching traditions and, 106
solstice lines and, 71, 80, 86, 90–95
Reiche, Renate, 60, 65–66, 74
Reinhard, Johan, 244, 246, 247, 255–56, 260
religious traditions, 7–10, 240–60
of ancient Nazcans, 156–58, 159, 167–78, 276–77
astronomer-priests and, 84–85, 87, 88
ceremonial mounds and, 54–56, 57, 193, 195, 201–6, 271, 273–74
Cerro Blanco in, 245–48, 255
hallucinogens in, 7–8, 171–78, 266, 272, 273, 274, 275–76
healers and, 8, 171, 173, 174–78, 245, 247, 270, 276
human sacrifice in, 232–33, 252, 256
in Inca empire, 215–17, 232–33, 252, 254, 259, 262
intoxication in, 183, 266
of Jívaro, 165–66, 167, 168
landscape and night sky symbolized in, 10
mummified human heads in, 7, 56, 159, 167–70
of Native Americans, 273–75
pathway rituals and, 8–9, 241–44
preservation of, 107, 244–45
of Quechua, 245–48, 250–54, 258–60
shamanism and, 270–75, 278
solitary and meditative experiences in, 266–68
Trident of Paracas and, 39–40
see also deities and spirits
Return to the Stars (von Däniken), 38
Río Grande de Nazca, 62–63
ritualized battles, 167